Critical Junctures in Mobile Capital

During the recent financial crisis, the conflict between sovereign states and banks over who controls the creation of money was thrown into sharp relief. This collection investigates the relationship between states and banks, arguing that conflicts between the two over control of money produces critical junctures. Drawing on Max Weber's concept of 'mobile capital', the book examines the mobility of capital networks in contexts of funding warfare, global bubbles and dangerous instability disengaged from social-economic activity. It proposes that mobile capital is the primary class conflict of capitalism, and furthermore, argues that the perennial, hierarchical struggles between nation-states and global banks is intrinsic to capitalism. Featuring authors writing from an impressively diverse range of academic backgrounds (including sociology, geography, economics and politics), *Critical Junctures in Mobile Capital* presents a variety of analyses using current or past examples from different countries, federations, and of differing forms of mobile capital.

JOCELYN PIXLEY is Honorary Professor at Macquarie University, Sydney, Australia, and Professorial Research Fellow with the Global Policy Institute. An economic sociologist, her fieldwork involves interviewing top officials in financial centres. She is the author of *Emotions in Finance*, now in its second edition (2012), and she edited a volume on the same theme entitled *New Perspectives on Emotions in Finance* (2012). With Geoff Harcourt, she edited the volume *Financial Crises and the Nature of Capitalist Money* (2013).

HELENA FLAM is Emeritus Professor of Sociology at the University of Leipzig, Germany. Previous to this appointment, she assisted in setting up the Swedish Collegium for Advanced Study and was a fellow at Max Planck Institute for Social Research in Cologne. She has written and organized conferences on transnational social movements, transitional justice and transnational financial institutions.

Critical Junctures in Mobile Capital

Edited by

JOCELYN PIXLEY
Macquarie University

HELENA FLAM
Leipzig University

CAMBRIDGE
UNIVERSITY PRESS

CAMBRIDGE
UNIVERSITY PRESS

University Printing House, Cambridge CB2 8BS, United Kingdom

One Liberty Plaza, 20th Floor, New York, NY 10006, USA

477 Williamstown Road, Port Melbourne, VIC 3207, Australia

314–321, 3rd Floor, Plot 3, Splendor Forum, Jasola District Centre,
New Delhi – 110025, India

79 Anson Road, #06–04/06, Singapore 079906

Cambridge University Press is part of the University of Cambridge.

It furthers the University's mission by disseminating knowledge in the pursuit of
education, learning, and research at the highest international levels of excellence.

www.cambridge.org
Information on this title: www.cambridge.org/9781107189515
DOI: 10.1017/9781316995327

© Cambridge University Press 2018

First published 2018

Printed in the United Kingdom by Clays, St Ives plc

A catalogue record for this publication is available from the British Library.

ISBN 978-1-107-18951-5 Hardback

Cambridge University Press has no responsibility for the persistence or accuracy
of URLs for external or third-party internet websites referred to in this publication
and does not guarantee that any content on such websites is, or will remain,
accurate or appropriate.

Cover illustration: 'Survey', 2007, originally shown in the ISCP, New York, USA.
© Louisa Dawson (louisadawson.com).

To Maria Renata Márkus

Contents

vii

Figures

Tables

Contributors

Massimo Amato is Associate Professor of Economic History and History of Economic Thought at Bocconi University, Milan, Italy. His main interest is on money *as an institution*, and his approach to the phenomenon is at the same time philosophical, economical and historical. His consideration for theory leads him to engage in concrete projects of monetary reform, in particular in the field of complementary currencies. Among his books are *The End of Finance* (2012), *Saving the Market from Capitalism* (2014), both with L. Fantacci, and *L'énigme de la monnaie* (2015).

Iwan Azis is Professor at Charles H. Dyson School of Applied Economics and Management at Cornell University, Ithaca, New York, USA, since 1992 and Professor of Economics at the University of Indonesia since 1977. His major interest is on the link between macrofinancial development and social issues, and he has done consulting work for various international organizations and universities. He was in charge of Asia's regional integration and cooperation at the Asian Development Bank. His recent book, co-authored with Hyun Song Shin of the Bank for International Settlements (BIS), is *Managing Elevated Risk* (2015). He was awarded 'Distinguished Scholar in Regional Science, Financial Economics, and Economic Modeling' in July 2006.

Dick Bryan is Professor of Political Economy at the University of Sydney, Australia, where he researches the expanding frontiers of financial derivatives, and the incorporation of households into global financial processes. An ongoing theme is the breaking down of national barriers to trade, investment and finance and the associated breaking down of national systems of economic calculation.

Luca Fantacci teaches economic history at Bocconi University, Milan, Italy. His research focuses on the history of financial systems and economic thought. He is the coeditor of *Money and Calculation* (2010) and the author, together with Massimo Amato, of *The End of Finance* (2011) and *Saving the Market from Capitalism* (2014).

Helena Flam did her Fil.Kand. in Lund, Sweden and her PhD at Columbia University in New York City, USA. She has done research on organizations, institutional discrimination, emotions and social movements. She currently directs a project on 'critical lawyers' in Germany and is on the executive board of a funding program entitled, 'Eastern Europe – Global Area?'. Her most recent coedited volume is entitled *Methods of Exploring Emotions*. She is the initiator and the current president of the Thematic Group 08 on Society and Emotions of the International Sociological Association. On April Fools' Day 2017, she mutated into Emerita.

Lucio Gobbi studied economics, finance and social sciences at Bocconi University, Milan, Italy. His research interests include international economics, finance and the application of network analysis to the study of financial markets. He is currently working on a PhD thesis at the University of Trento, Italy, on clearing mechanisms in real and financial markets.

Helmut Kuzmics studied economics and sociology in Graz and Vienna. He was Professor of Sociology at the University of Graz, Austria, until his retirement in May 2013. He is co-author of *Authority, State and National Character: The Civilizing Process in Austria and England, 1700–1900* (with R. Axtmann, 2007) and *Emotionen, Habitus und Erster Weltkrieg Soziologische Studien zum militärischen Untergang der Habsburgermonarchie* (with Sabine Haring, 2013), and co-editor of *Theorizing Emotions. Sociological Explorations and Applications* (with D. Hopkins, J. Kleres and H. Flam, 2009). His research interests include historical and comparative sociology, and the sociology of emotions.

Renate Mayntz is Emeritus Director of the Max Planck Institute for the Study of Societies (MPIfG) in Cologne, Germany. She is editor of *Crisis and Control: Institutional Change in Financial Market Regulation* (2012) and *Die Reformierbarkeit der Demokratie: Innovationen und Blockaden* (with Wolfgang Streeck, 2003). She has also authored the articles 'Markt oder Staat? Kooperationsprobleme in der Europäischen Union' (2014) and 'Die Finanzmarktkrise im Licht einer Theorie funktioneller Differenzierung' (2014). In addition, she has a paper on 'Financial Market Regulation in the Shadow of the Sovereign Debt Crisis' (2013).

Andreas Nölke is Professor of Political Science with a focus on International Relations and International Political Economy at Goethe University in Frankfurt, Germany. He is also associated with the Centre for the Study of Globalisation and Regionalisation (CSGR), University of Warwick. Before joining Goethe University, he taught at the universities of Konstanz, Leipzig, Amsterdam and Utrecht. His articles have appeared in journals such as *World Politics, Review of International Political Economy, Business and Politics, International Politics, Journal of International Relations and Development, Competition and Change, Critical Perspectives on International Business, European Journal of International Relations* and the *Journal of Common Market Studies.*

Jocelyn Pixley is Honorary Professor in Sociology at Macquarie University, Sydney, Australia. An economic sociologist, she has published six books as well as journal articles in the *BJS, T&S, Contemporary Sociology, Journal of Socio-Economics* and *AJES*. Her publications include *Emotions in Finance: Booms, Busts and Uncertainty*, second Edition (2012; first edn, 2004; Cambridge University Press), and an edited *New Perspectives on Emotions in Finance* (2012). She co-edited *Financial Crises and the Nature of Capitalist Money* (with Geoff Harcourt, 2013). She is currently writing on money's role in economic activity and on central banks for Cambridge University Press. Her empirical work mostly comprises interviews with international financiers, central bankers and financial journalists.

Michael Rafferty is Australian Research Council Future Fellow in the School of Business at the University of Sydney. His research focuses on finance, risk and everyday life, especially expressed via the changing role of private pension schemes; and also on international portfolio investment flows.

Laura Sartori is Associate Professor of Sociology at the Department of Political and Social Sciences at the University of Bologna, Italy.

She holds a PhD in sociology and social research from the University of Trento, Italy. She works on several topics in economic sociology, social innovation and the social and political implications of information and communication technology (ICT). Current projects are about complementary currencies and the sociology of money, sociology of disasters and social innovation, and the social and political implications of Internet of Things. She recently published 'From Complementary Currency to Institution: A Micro-Macro Study of the Sardex Mutual Credit System' (with P. Dini, 2016) and 'Social Innovation and Natural Disasters: The Case of the Casa Italia Plan' (with F. Pagliacci and M. Russo, 2017).

Herman Mark Schwartz is Professor in the Politics Department of the University of Virginia, Charlottesville, USA. He authored or coedited seven books, and has authored over sixty articles and chapters on development, welfare states and global capital flows.

Sam Whimster is Professorial Research Fellow at the Global Policy Institute, London, UK, and before that Fellow at the Käte Hamburger College for Advanced Studies at the University of Bonn, Germany. He is also editor of Max Weber Studies and brought out *Max Weber: Collected Methodological Writings* with Hans Henrik Bruun (2012). Among his articles are 'Morality and Capitalism in Sociological Perspective', *Social Europe Journal,* 2009, and 'Weber in the World of Empire', in *Max Weber in der Welt* (2014). His books include *Understanding Weber* (2007), *Reforming the City* (2009) and *Global Finance and Urban Living* (with Leslie Budd, 1992). Currently he is concerned with re-evaluating social economics as a central focus of Weber's final version of *Economy and Society (Wirtschaft und Gesellschaft)*.

Shaun Wilson is Associate Professor in the Department of Sociology at Macquarie University, Sydney, Australia. Shaun works on projects related to political sociology, the sociology of work and the sociology of labour movements, and he teaches courses on social policy, social inequality and social movements in the Department. At present, he is writing on the shifting politics of the minimum wage in the Anglo-democracies and attitudes to immigration and asylum seekers in Australia. In his spare time, Shaun loves birdwatching in Australia and in faraway lands.

David Woodruff is Associate Professor of Comparative Politics at the London School of Economics and Political Science, UK. He is the author of *Money Unmade: Barter and the Fate of Russian Capitalism* (1999) and a number of articles on Russian and Soviet political economy. His prior work also includes 'Governing by Panic: The Politics of the Eurozone Crisis' (2016).

Acknowledgements

Books are brimming with debts to those who enjoy their gifts and collaboration from past generations, and in the present. These debts are unlike those to creditors, which comprise mobile capital, its self-justifications and hoarding instead of creating money committed to decent, global full employment. In contrast, the debts herein are acknowledgements to the many analysts of capitalist money. There are no lists of those who are amply cited in the chapters in this volume, in gratitude for writers and scholars with whom they agree or disagree. Nor are there precise details of debts to the authors who contributed to the collection and their enormous help. This was in writing their chapters and, as important, in assisting in many ways to further the book's design and composition. The book is dedicated to Maria Márkus (1936–2017) of the Budapest School who created a community of scholars. It was a privilege to work with her at university; she supervised her many, devoted PhD students (myself in the 1980s) to aim to have something worthwhile to say. In editing to my theme and contributing, too, I hope to reach for that; Maria knew our book had left the shore to the sea of others' judgement.

Thanks are to the anonymous referees and particularly to the insights of Phil Good, Cambridge University Press's Commissioning Editor, who did urge that Cambridge University Press take a bet on the book's success. This is the hope, because more debate and (polite) disputations are sorely needed. Adam Hooper organized Cambridge University Press's production of the book with great patience. Informally, thanks are to Harry Field and Sam Dawson who gave it such thoughtful critical reading and to all the other friends for their solidarity.

Introduction

JOCELYN PIXLEY

One of the strange and bitter pills of contemporary life is the activities of the big banks and financial markets, and their dubious sanctifications over many years. Strange because few want to think about the role money plays in the world. This indifference suggests potential fears about money – it's easier to imagine money and its institutions are rock-solid, not flimsy social creations, promises and sources of threat. Governments are prone to this escape route – into fantasy. This book analyses such aspects of money – of mobile capital's multiple relations with states and populations, and with hegemons and denizens.

Far better understood than money are the world's two great threats: nuclear war and climate change. They bring destruction either of instant death or gradual ruin to the end of this world. The social forces arrayed against efforts to prevent irreparable destruction from climate change are far more hysterical than the grim knowledge and disapproval of mutually assured destruction – MAD – of nuclear war. Political leaders who raise nuclear arms races truly shock: agreement is wide but counter action limited. States resist.

There is less consensus with climate change but equally no fantasy. Culprits in the climate denial movement are chiefly economic, the fossil fuel industries, since supporting politicians only gain unpopularity. Think of the Chinese command economy running out of water and clean air; leaders must act. Likewise, the Pentagon sees 'security' dangers. Capitalism is threatened more by climate change than its restraint and, even if profits from wind-solar powered clothes driers are pitiful, more firms accept renewable energy. States can benefit from centralized energy supplies for population or diplomatic control, and this is as short-sighted as governments refusing to lay down nuclear weapons.

Mobile capital is a social force that profits from funding and encouraging both these threats and often other socially useless activities, although it is rarely seen as a 'force' (and one reliant on states) until

1

a financial crisis. Why is this? Our collective book is not about nuclear or climate destruction *except* for the complicit, pecuniary relations that capitalist financial sectors have with war finance and climate change. I mention them not to scare (further), but to give perspective. Money is much more ambiguous and intangible. Who are the culprits in financial disturbances, when pollution deniers are so easy to identify? There's a cacophony of *narratives and moralism*, some of which poses as science. Theories of money are not the science that safeguards surgical operations, or the science of climate change. Because money is social, a complex relation of debtors, creditors and states, there can be no natural science, as about (say) the effects of nuclear warfare. Money is maddeningly unpredictable, reliant on debt servicing into the future. From where, is the next question.

Far from money being a rock-solid *thing*, if undoubtedly handy to use, that comforting fantasy is constantly disrupted. For three decades before the 1914–18 war, money seemed peaceful and socially useful. Not for the majority non-voters or colonized but for ruling class Europeans who, as if by nature *adjusted* the denizens downward to rebalance the gold standard. Gold never prevented money from becoming unstable, and the centre always lifted the gold standard to suit itself – notably under London City panics – although large gold discoveries did mitigate business trends towards 'chronic depression' (Morgan 1943; Veblen 1904: 235). And, after the World War 1 that created unheard-of full employment, it was savagely stopped by 1920, disturbances became extreme and, far from financial 'diplomacy', during the 1920s–30s a vicious race to the bottom set in. The City of London kept the UK domestic economy stagnant for the period. There was considerable resolution after World War 2. But since the critical 1970s, financial sectors became increasingly socially useless and sponsor political neo-liberalism to return to pre-democracy.

However, this sketch has *crucial elements, usually hidden*: States spend money into existence, and taxpayers are their coerced debtors to service the National Debt. Taxes are only needed to keep money trustworthy, not to *pay directly* for state spending on war and peace. Banks also create money by depositing loans – to governments, to businesses and households. Another *logical* point, then, in an introduction to the secrets recounted in this Volume, is that all money is debt. However not all debt is money – my IOU (on a scrap of paper) for goods or services cannot be presented to pay a supermarket bill, as it is not transferable. There are, then, types of private 'near money'. Adults need paid jobs, money to pay taxes, bank debts and, above all purchasing power for household survival. Banks *require* but do not invariably create economic activity for their advances to be serviced.

This Volume is a work of macro-economic sociology, political science and macroeconomics that explores capitalist-state money creation. Everyone loves to hate banks and, while that is not wrong, there's more to the problems of money creation than just banking's role. Max Weber (1981: 337) remarked that capitalism depended on mobile capital's ability to play off nation states. If there were to be a global 'empire', he warned, capitalism might not survive. The birth of capitalist money 400 years ago was a 'memorable alliance' between nation states and merchant-money classes, Weber said (1978:353). The deal was one where states would 'rule' and merchants would 'make money'. The sovereign state is motivated to secure war finance and peace finance, and after various experiments with monarchs to fund their wars, a deal was clinched in London. From the English Civil War's regicide, a mob of merchants took parliamentary power from aristocrats and made a loan deal in 1694 with an imported king from the money-smart Amsterdam. William of Orange created their Bank of England to perfect the trick, repellent as it was. This Bank lent gold and silver to the Crown which granted it a charter to 'securitize' its state debt (backed by imposing on the Crown tax collection), to make advances of *the same amount* (in notes) to the private sector.

That doubled the 'money' that becomes acceptable at the tax office, for wars and the bourgeois class. Geoff Ingham explains this money is the symbiotic capitalist-state money we all use. Repellent or not, moralism is out of place. To this day, the (capitalist) state protects banks and makes markets for mobile capital possible.

Not everyone in the Volume agrees *precisely* with Weber on how 'mobile' it is, but all explore capital's disconnections from today's electorates, economies and the public sphere. Both money manufacturers – capitalist banks with their finance sectors, and capitalist states with their spending treasuries – are equally substantial and often malign forces. We didn't need the 2016 election in America to tell us about the return of the malign state, elected by, yet ignoring highly disaffected populations. We have worried far longer about problems of the global market fantasy. Entire constitutions have been written to prevent malign threats, hence 'checks and balances', separation of powers and tempering approaches to corporate and state excesses. The social democratic states were the most moderating and peaceable.

These central relations between states and mobile capital need healthy public airing since they are barely discussed. Short-term, alarming conjectures or worse, *predictions* about election results or money market crises are hourly headlines, but rarely about money creation as a 'memorable alliance' of ruling elites. That is, unless one takes the New York Stock Exchange peaks in 2017 as saying something meaningful about US Congress and the White House, which they don't. In fact, financial market results give no analysis of current affairs whatsoever, since traders are mimetic, they just copy each other and rely on the entire market in which they trade to remain *liquid*. Market results are only informative when liquidity stops, that is, when no one wants to buy junk bonds or whatever, and everyone is frantic to sell, dump, run for the exit door.[1]

The dramatic parts are easy to portray, compared to the political management of banks and sovereign debts between networks of economic-political actors, mostly in impersonal, official capacities. These economic-political relations are more important than naked interest conspiracies and personal economic advantage from deploying state powers (increasing though they are). No one doubts plots and subterfuge occur, yet open alliances can also involve manipulation of, and disconnection from, people's needs.

Debates about the mobility of capital are rare in mainstream agendas, public opinion polls, you name it. How is this linked to the global role of the US dollar? Money creation itself is never mentioned unless to blame governments for spending (creating) 'too much' money (seldom 'too little'). Least useful is indignation against *either* states *or* banks. Neither is so attractive, both can be destructive or socially useful, and our novel aim is to stress critical thinking about their symbiotic alliances. Moralism is especially ill-informed. There are very few sainted savers or creditors to whom deep moral obligations are said to be owed (that Claus Offe 2015 argued). Banks only use a fraction of savers' deposits, to advance loans out of nothing. Loans may be sold aggressively, loans going nowhere for long term good, and therefore less likely to generate

---

[1] Clothes drier profits are peg sales. These paragraphs draw on Weber 1978; 1981; Ingham 2004; Orléan 2014; Pixley 2013.

profits and wages on which loan-advances can be serviced. Creditors advance 'money' they do not have, for (likely) future profit and by definition, do not exist without their debtors – states, businesses and households – from whom they profit. Similarly, states in surplus do not exist without deficit states, so high-minded superiority is out of place. Political-social relations are unpredictable, threats can shift.

Mobile Capital

In world-historical comparisons, mobile capital, Weber insisted in his *General Economic History* (1981: 337), was the capital of a new European merchant class through which modern capitalism arose from alliances between this class and nation states. This juncture was a joint dependency that secured unheard-of levels of financing of the state (mostly for wars, colonies), for economic development, and the flourishing of this class. Mobile capital exists within a national context although it could 'play off nation-states' and profit from financing their conflicts, or lose. Thus, it also exists in a global context, which is probably the most common understanding of the term.

Questions on analogies to centuries ago – on how mobile today or tied to each nation state – are considered in the Volume's chapters. Of much import is the position of the hegemonic state, the United States. Its military stockpile is the largest ever yet few look at whether arms funding relies on mobile capital. Warfare is directly considered in Chapter 4 and the United States's world currency status in Chapter 6. Other chapters consider lack of capital controls, impacts on regions, and on labour relations of mobile and less-mobile capital. Before that, let me introduce the shifting 'value' of money and sources of its perpetual instability.

The heated 1970s and 80s conflicts were over money's value. More democratic states from the grim 1930s had attempted to tame capitalist-state money somewhat, but by the 1980s, that reversed. State policies and mobile capital transformed rapidly. Poverty and inequality took off (again). Anti-democratic popularizers gave inordinate praise for 'unstoppable' capitalist money. The *New York Times* journalist Thomas Friedman offered a hymn to a world-wide financial 'golden straitjacket' (1999) and American philosopher Francis Fukuyama proposed an equally scandalous idea of the 'end of history'. In contrast John Eatwell, whose analysis of the 1970s origins of global unemployment from this (then) celebrated 'straitjacket' has not lost its validity, argued against this hymn. But he and others stressed that any simple return to past policies was difficult:

The money markets and foreign exchange markets become dominated by simple slogans - larger fiscal deficits lead to higher interest rates, public expenditure bad, private expenditure good – even when these slogans are persistently *refuted by events. To these simplistic rules of the game there is added a demand for governments to publish their own financial targets. (Eatwell 1993)*

Legitimation problems were glaring already; some governments welcomed these moves, reduced top taxes rates, stifled unions and excised social democratic projects. Whereas from 1940 to 1980, the top 1 per cent of OECD income shares were *somewhat* modest as so many benefited from wage growth and jobs, that reversed after 1980. The 1 per cent share doubled in the United States and United Kingdom.[2] Eatwell showed that 'hot money' flows (90 per cent in 1994) far exceeded global trade and long-term investment (10 per cent): the *opposite* to the pre-1970s more careful mobile capital. Heterodox economists and a handful of sociologists who understood money all along, explained Nixon's 1971 US dollar float, and end of fixed exchanges with the compelling analyses.[3] Their informed caution was dismissed to the hymn of unfettered financial markets and the banks behind them: until they had to run to their hated 'nanny-states' and the US Fed. Most governments had little choice in 2008, but many gave *unconditional* bailouts.

Thorstein Veblen's analysis of the robber-baron world of late nineteenth century United States stands as a warning against facile analogies and determinist *laws*. Historical analyses of earlier phases of capitalism put in question any 'outburst' over money's value, such as the 1970s, that could be called unique. Thus, the volume's title is

[2] Economic Policy Institute 2012, Chart 'Share of income' 1913–2009; Crotty 2012: 89 on austerity; Crotty shows the United States lowest quintile had –0.3 per cent income 'growth' 1979–2009. See Pixley Chapter 9.
[3] Heterodox monetary macroeconomists include Eatwell, John Smithin on his 1980s 'revenge of the rentiers'; Randall Wray on 'modern money theory'; Randall Collins 198 and Geoff Ingham led sociology, and Schumpeterian scholars, from Minsky to Sweezy. Some were sidelined upstairs: Eatwell, Giddens and Meghnad Desai to the U'K House of Lords. The labour theory of value as Bryan and Rafferty's Chapter 5 use it is also constructive.

mindful that earlier apocalyptic troubles were under very different contexts. So, in 1900 United States the lack of democratic engagement was marked, and the US state was still to grow. Veblen analysed a new phase of capitalism of that era and, drawing on the European 'historical school', he contested classical and neo-classical economics about their depiction of 'the life history of objective values' and their 'laws'. The point was that laws of 'supply and demand' were abstracted from the life history of the social relations among humankind of a given era. These 'laws' are somewhat like the 'straitjacket' and often convenient to the powerful social forces of the day. For example, utilitarian and classical theory's 'failure to discriminate between capital as investment and capital as industrial appliances' that Veblen attacked, has been repeated tirelessly in many different circumstances.[4]

Veblen's 1904 *Theory of Business Enterprise* analyses the US enterprise's methods, principles and motives for 'pecuniary gain' of the era, and the enterprise's bearing on 'the modern cultural situation' in 1900 America. Instead of the harmonious timelessness of orthodox laws, free of human unpredictability, Veblen's capitalism had a bullying persona of a new 'financier-businessman' who creates huge instability purely from 'his' conjectures about 'the metaphysical stability of the money unit'. Although money's value is fought over and so cannot be orthodoxy's 'objective value', it is this 1900 US businessman who was at the seat of depressions and exaltations (1904: vi; 20; 238). Everything that is counted is 'run in terms of the value unit', and a *reduction* of earnings, as so 'rated' in those terms . . .

. . .is felt as an impoverishment . . . even if it carries no hardship in the way of a reduced command over the material means of production, of life, or of comfort. . . . A business man's rating . . . rests on the pecuniary magnitude . . . not on the mechanical serviceability of his establishment or output. An enhancement is a source of gratification and self-respect . . . Veblen (1904: 232–3)

Instead of laws of declining rates of profits (and so on), Veblen pointed to a teensy fall in the value unit as a shock to the robber baron's status *versus* his competitors, and not to his conspicuous consumption

---

[4] The historical school included Weber and Schumpeter. Veblen 1899: 421, and if with Marx, he was against him on 'laws' e.g. declining rate of profit, p. 234. Contributors make sharp distinctions, and against similar assumptions of QE, we see later.

(Veblen 1904: 234; [1899] 1953). It is sociologically familiar as class; stigma; invidious distinctions; the power of squeaky wheels, yet the *shock* about the shifts in the 1970s' value unit was not comparable in every other way. The US Administration was huge by then, central banks allegedly interfered, unionists had rights and democratic participation was much enhanced since Veblen's day (US voting rights only truly extended in 1970). Present data shows long-term investment through bank money is much reduced, and mobile capital and the un-owned corporation has replaced the robber-baron financier-business 'man', his 'trusts' and brutality to unionists. Impersonal institutions can mask their methods.

Yet this variable fluctuation of the value of the money unit in wage inflation (say), is the nightmare of the financial world although the absentee businessman is now a stock owner. Not one cares a jot about the old nineteenth century creative, cooperative venture itself. Money's instability is why Bryan and Rafferty use the 'anchor' metaphor for financial traders' efforts to seek a constancy that cannot exist, given money's deflation and many kinds of inflation. As their Chapter 5 supports, what was *assumed* in Veblen's 1900 was not so by 1970; deflation could not be so blandly if cruelly imposed as before WW2. A 'natural rate' of unemployment was not law but expressed owners' power. Unions notably in Britain and the United States, appallingly treated for some centuries, had the temerity to raise wage claims in the 1970s, out of a modicum of fair shares between labour-capital of the full employment (FE) era. Suddenly the financier cast *wage inflation* into a sole scandal, that neglected the 1973 oil inflation, asset inflation, nuclear and Vietnam War inflation (Chapter 4).

An excellent work of James Forder (2014) argues that *laws* to destroy FE like the still extant 'Phillips curve' was *myth*. Milton Friedman accused post war authorities of being inflationary (ignoring multiple inflations) 'in order' to maintain full employment, castigating a Phillips curve, unproven, *unused*, disliked and rejected by Bill Phillips! In fact, authorities fought all inflations up to 1970. Nixon's dollar float brought asset inflation, Wall Street's total dominance, and the Fed's inflation for CREEP expanded the price-wage spiral. The Fed switched to attack wages from 1974, and full employment ended by 1980. With the apparent certainty of cutting wages and destroying 'unpredictable' union activity, bank-money inflation took off to new heights. But in today's deflation of money's value, authorities are desperate to *raise* wage-price inflation *up* to the low postwar, 2 per cent levels, but still use a Phillips curve against jobs. Central banks plea for wage rises, arguing the bargaining power of unions has evaporated to economic detriment.

Veblen said Captains of Industry influenced the markets, their competitors and investors, via 'interstitial disturbances' in the chance for profits, to knock out rivals, and form trust companies (conglomerates). In consequence, the 'management of industrial affairs through pecuniary transactions, therefore, has been to dissociate the interests of those men who exercise this discretion from the interests of the community'. They have 'an interest in making the disturbances large and frequent', no matter widespread hardship, since they are like bull or bear speculators disrupting enterprises regardless of efficiency (Veblen 1904: 28–30). These owner-managers were often financiers, and thus Wall Street entered the robber-baron networks and rivalries (J. P. Morgan notably) until Wall Street had a huge crash in 1907. Afterwards, income taxes were imposed (via referendum) but, also in 1913, Congress designed the Federal Reserve to promote Wall Street and the US dollar, which dominated after financing WW1.[5]

This disruptive capitalist 'investment' Veblen recounted is now in corporate finance sectors. In contributing to criticisms of today's financial mess, many chapters herein insist that the decisive failure of banks to lend for new business ideas, to maintain decent enterprises and therefore (taxable) jobs, is the old, forgotten (Schumpeter or Keynes) problem of mobile capital. Instead of fulfilling the reasons for banks' privileged state licences to manufacture money and to 'pick winners', lending increasingly went to predatory and no-hoper schemes and bets on price changes (in financialization, in currencies, derivatives and securities). Only states can reverse depression, but chose austerity to increase the value of debt to the money-creators, banks, to fund US war finance (see Chapter 4) and thus extend stagnation to depressions.

---

[5] Greider 1987 US Fed; it should also be noted that US robber-barons had unionists murdered in the 1890s; union taming succeeded, also US WW1 financed the Allies. And, whereas Veblen's idols were craft workers and 'workmanship', Schumpeter (1934; 1954) idolized the 'entrepreneur', given permission by bankers to develop the new 'combinations' in 'creative destruction', or capitalism's dynamism. However, he agreed that Veblen was a top economist, although he criticised him for saying 'efficiency' was not the goal of pecuniary interests, or capitalism per se.

Before moving on, let me say that Veblen (1904: 237), and Schumpeter cannot avoid 'national' views, about the US robber-barons seeking 'secure gratification' in the 'nominal capitalization which they have set their hearts on', or about Germany or Austria whose banks fostered capitalist-industrial dynamism, to Schumpeter (1934). The same applies herein, yet trends are similar and the United States is still the hegemon to the world for good and ill. The City of London excelled in ignoring Britain's industrial firms (Ingham 1984) so that by 1900 industry declined against Europe, Japan and America.

Ever since 2007–08, a larger picture is emerging against facile histories. Few politicians confess that only a quarter of bank lending is to productive business now, but a half of that business lending is for Commercial Property speculation. Worse, most deny facts that public debt *declined* despite the world wars and GFC bank bailout costs (which raised deficits). From 1975–80, private debt took off (Schularick 2014; Turner 2013). States refuse to spend to meet needs either; the reverse in arms races. The situation is bleak even to mainstream standards. But where 1990s articles warned 'Don't Mess with Moody's', in that a poor credit rating could destroy a country better than nuclear bombs, todays' warn against *messing* with Wall Street. Heterodox macroeconomists and sociologists (and distressed populations) are sidelined by what financial sectors and governments want: extreme libertarianism in economics and postmodernism.

Banking Today

Libertarians are personified in bank executives, *de jure* managers of edifices that rely on governments (taxpayers), and on central banks when they make advances, the contracted debts of which may not ever be serviced. US banks – apparently at a *safe* distance – lent sub-prime mortgages to people highly unlikely to be able to service any loans. That remains our large question as to why governments in the post-GFC continuing fall-out remain unwilling to control banking (Mayntz in Chapter 1). The payments system, for which banks were licenced to maintain, nearly collapsed. That 'rock-solid' everyday use of bank money disappeared, were it not for governments creating more money. It 'expands and contracts' as economists say, rarely mentioning the political reasons why bank money above all, does the same.

The idea of a banking 'mentality' is somewhat limited, though ably boosted with Veblen (1904: 42–4) on how 'scruples' are 'sentimental' constraints from which the 'uncreative' Captains-Financiers are exempt. One British bank CEO was so affronted at criticisms after the 2008 virtual nationalization, that he sued *The Guardian* for describing him as a 'banker'. A comment on the movie 'Margin Call' suggested it was about the 'big payoffs going to people who, in critically important ways, don't have a clue what they are doing'.[6] This persona is evident in an interview with Jamie Dimon, the CEO of J. P. Morgan, following its 2012 public scandal of 'the London Whale', a Morgan operator. Dimon was *enduring* criticisms of 'low standards', as reporter Jessica Pressler said:

Dimon pulls [his critic] up, then said: 'I want you to know the London Whale issue is dead,' he says. 'The Whale has been harpooned. Desiccated. Cremated.' But it didn't die and 'the media that had lionized Dimon began to chafe at some of his condescending comments. 'You don't even make any money,' he told one group of reporters.'

[To Pressler] 'Dimon can come across like an overgrown frat boy. 'Don't sell a product to anyone you wouldn't sell your motha,' he likes to warn employees... For Dimon, who had boasted ... of the bank's risk management and 'fortress balance sheet,' the blunder [the Whale] was particularly, specifically embarrassing. ... [yet to Dimon]: 'Most bankers are decent, honorable people. We're wrapped up in all this crap right now. We made a mistake. We're sorry.' ... But, when I ask if this episode has made him regret being such an outspoken defender of the banking industry, he looks at me point blank. 'I'm an outspoken defender of the truth ... This is not the Soviet Union. This is the United States of America. That's what I remember. Guess what,' he says, almost shouting now. 'It's a *free. F –cking. Country.*'[7]

Was Goldman Sachs's CEO making a joke of the GFC when he said the firm was 'doing god's work'? Veblen's world was 'dominated' by a 'crackpot realism of utopian capitalists and monomaniacs' playing 'the chief fanatics in their delusional world.' The sole aim is to 'realize gains', so *impersonal* that care for the 'aggregate of consumers' and bank clients is dispensable. Distance gives 'an easier conscience'.[8]

---

[6] Quiggin, J. 'Boring is Good' in *Inside Story* - http://inside.org.au 8 March 2012, on the movie Margin Call

[7] Pressler, Jessica 2012 (it sounds like she had a ghastly time).

[8] C. Wright Mills, Introduction to the *Theory of the Leisure Class* ([1899] 1953): vii, xii. Veblen 1904: 50–3 on conscience.

Veblen's contrasts were with modest 'craftsmen' and engineers.
They re-emerged. In 2008, risk managers often physicists, at a large
German bank said sackings resulted from warning their CEO against
'sub-prime'. Since then, what has changed? One *FT* columnist pleaded,
futilely, in 2012:

The Barclays firestorm has also featured calls to change banking's 'culture'.
When policy debates are dominated by the c-word, you know we are out of
practical ideas. . . . But the structure of modern finance – vast institutions that
borrow cheaply because taxpayers are on the hook to save them – is an
abomination that must stop.[9]

Policy-makers still urge a change to banking's 'culture', when banking's
line management sends orders, larded with aggressive self-entitlement
and overestimated self-esteem. J. P. Morgan started with the robber-
barons, then WW1 finance – it was king of Wall Street's global
infiltration.

'States Are Weak' Is a Weak Argument

No economist should dare to rail at any lack of political 'will', because
willpower has never been lacking. 1980s political leaders shouted the
virtues of the market and, while centralizing and amassing their states'
policing power, at the same time hectored about 'governments being
the problem'. These slogans won the praise of finance sectors which
regularly hounded social democratic governments from office (capital
strikes). Some labour governments joined the pro-market club. But
states have separate motives from markets, regardless the political
visions (or lack thereof) of those dependent on electoral support. For
one, they need war and peace finance.

Therefore, a lot more is at stake, given what seemed *easier* was to
pass off state duties to markets, while extending the warmongering
police state; perhaps (re) privatizing segments such as mercenaries,
prisons and arms production. Passing off former state duties to the
market is always a short-term proposition because electorates will still
blame governments. Due to capitalism's private nature, we cannot vote
out clueless, foul-mouthed bankers. The problem with capitalist-state

[9] I promised anonymity to the Chairman, who wanted to *promote* the bank's risk
managers, unlike most banks; Mallaby, S. 2012 FT

money is much more deeply rooted. Governments when inside this entirely closed world of finance-states, are by no means *the problem*. No, the only problems are democratically elected, socially responsive governments with professional public servants and a vigorous public sphere to tell truth to power. Not only that, but governments exist in a world of states that rarely seek consensus but compete.

If one were to retreat into the present completely, we might conclude that a technocratic management of economies and people via the state's arms-length distance is defunct: I am not so sure. The current crop of 'strongmen and strongwomen' – political fixers – may be short-lived since worrying trends so far mentioned continue. Immediate worries are the intemperate and uncivil recipes of demagogues could land the world into more alarming disasters and exacerbate recessions. Anything as simplistic as taking a few mendacious elections to be an epochal change, fails to take the longer view.

Warnings long ago stressed the negative consequences to be expected from internationalizing banking rules in policies *designed* to narrow the role of democratic states. In effect this stopped governments from stimulating new projects or circumscribing the direction of financial activity towards lasting, beneficial projects. No: states would rule through independent or out-sourced entities, convenient to politicians, though demands to slash wages for rentier-capital profit required more policing. Warnings were overwhelmed by a rapid move to all things global, above all of money. Washington-Wall Street saw a halcyon era from the 1980s, a 'Great Moderation' (to former US Fed Chair Ben Bernanke even in 2013). From our point of view, that 'Great Moderation' is better recast as the 'Great Excess' ignored as financial crises multiplied.

Technological determinism remains popular. A theorist of money who taught Helmut Kuzmics said the monetarist idea to steer the supply of money merely by guaranteeing a steady flow from central banks, was like trying to control air-temperature by rubbing the thermometer, Kuzmics recollects. Not only, but little is said on war-peace states, or problems of liquidity (save our honorable exceptions). When buy-sells of near money stops, a trader is rational to exit. The market's hidden hand is shown as copycat, the fallacy of composition erupts in terrible collective results. It is also funny that so many countries longed for a 'Wall Street' centre, but states are not so sure now.

14 Jocelyn Pixley

Combining Analysis of Mobile Capital and States

One contributor said to me as 2016 ended that it was time 'we took the gloves off'. Let me parry to start, before we move to the weighty chapters. One retrospectively amusing incident was the re-ignition of the Tobin Tax idea, often called a financial transaction tax. Back on 8 November 2009 at a meeting of G20 finance ministers at St. Andrews (Scotland), then UK Prime Minister, Gordon Brown proposed a tax on financial transactions. Here a Robin Hood element came back (as Tobin 1996 complained) that is totally incorrect. Although long rejected by the US Administration and financial sectors, Brown gained endorsement of this tax by President Sarkozy and Chancellor Merkel (Parker 2010). Their idea was that it would force banks to pay for state costs of bank bailouts and stimulus packages, it would curb 'excesses' in financial trading; and perhaps fund global development and energy alternatives. It sounds like magic.

It was: a Tobin tax doesn't work with the *direct* intention of 'increasing the contribution made by the financial sector to broader social objectives', as UK Treasury put it airily (HM Treasury 2009). The idea was proposed in 1972 by US economist James Tobin who argued for a small tax on 'all spot conversions of one currency into another, proportional to the size of the transaction' (Tobin 1978: 155), as a financial disincentive aiming to induce, *through the market,* slower financial movements. Tobin said it would mitigate the problem of 'excessive inter-currency mobility of private financial capital' (1978: 153).

In fact, up to the GFC, currency transactions (alone), per the Bank for International Settlements (BIS) estimates in 2007 (*before the crisis*), comprised some US $3,200 billion in daily turnover in foreign exchange markets.[10] Of that, Forex trade by 'non-financials' was about 17 per cent, and hedging-speculation comprised more than 80 per cent (Garnaut 2009: 68–71). Overall, the total turnover in the main spot and derivatives markets rose from 22 times world GDP in 1995, to nearly 70 times in 2007 (Darvas & Weizsacker 2010: 3–4). Today, nothing is happening against High Frequency Trading (HFT)

[10] In BIS 2007, back in 1998, Forex daily turnover was US$1,490 billion. On Tobin-type tax revenue, Barber & Packer 2009 cited France's foreign minister, Bernard Kouchner, estimating €20 billion to €30 billion a year could be raised by a levy of only 0.005 per cent. That is wrong if the tax worked.

either, a technically legal form of insider trading by which computers are programmed with the knowledge of buy/sells fractions of seconds before. This is 'front running' against pensions funds and stocks of listed firms. A Tobin tax would immediately stop this 'race to zero' as Andrew Haldane, Bank of England calls HFT (2011), when he showed that General Electric stocks dropped to zero for 0.005 seconds during a 'flash crash' in US stocks on May 6, 2010.

Only in the sense that, were transaction costs to be raised against playing this destructive game, and its dangers thus minimized, could we see an indirect, broader 'social objective'. If the tax *worked* to discourage this negative activity, its tax revenues ideally should reduce to near zero. My view is that politicians were keen to show they were doing *anything*, at a time when the public was disgusted with governments and banks. But that promise of magical new revenue from Tobin's idea was a sham (as is most populism); it treated electorates as idiots, offered mere snake oil, when it was obvious that corporate taxes on J. P. Morgan through to Royal Bank of Scotland (the largest bailout the world has ever seen) were already minimal. US and UK authorities hadn't the nerve to nationalize the banks they largely owned after 2008.

And what were the financial sectors' responses? This is the instructive part where one could die laughing. The arguments deployed by Timothy Geithner (then US Treasury Secretary, also foul-mouthed, former head of the privately-owned NY District Fed, on which Dimon still is a board member for J. P. Morgan), Dominique Strauss-Kahn (then IMF managing director) *et al*, against Brown's idea were presented as technical. So, too, the financial sector's opposition also claimed to be a 'technical' rebuttal of Tobin's 'technical' idea. Political-technical opposition that a tax is not feasible – i.e. not *possible*, is different from opposition claiming to be 'technical' but with serious differences in economic theories and, ultimately, social theories, democratic relationships and systemic relations, on *desirable* reforms. Obviously, it was a mass exercise in collective lobbying, but it was funnier than that.

The first objection it is not feasible 'technically' as taxes would be difficult to collect is untrue. The United Kingdom's lucrative stamp duty on the value of spot share transactions is cheap to collect; so too many others, like Australia's tax on share trading (Darvas & Weizsacker 2010: 7). The BIS supervises the computer infrastructure at the interbank level. Tobin radicals argued years ago that existing technology could easily be put to 'democratic ends' (Patomaki 2001: 146–7; Wahl & Wardlow 2001). It is disingenuous of banks to oppose a transaction tax on such grounds, because they charge customers for conversions of currencies, *ad nauseam*. The second argument, by Geithner, Dimon, *et al*, is that banks would pass the costs of *any* controls (e.g. a proposed ban on charges for 'pre-payments' of mortgages) or transaction taxes, onto customers (and the rest of society) – and similarly that the United Kingdom's 50 per cent (one-off) tax on executive remuneration 'could be easily circumvented' (Parker & Murphy 2010). Plain threats of the unscrupulous.

A third objection is that *any tax* wouldn't work unless all countries joined, on grounds of relocation off-shore. Tobin supported a system of international uniformity enforced by the IMF, but saw (sociologically):

I realize that . . . I am seriously opposed by a powerful tide. . . I cannot expect bankers and others who would pay the tax, or suffer any reduction it might cause in the transactions from which they profit, to approve. They, of course, have considerable influence on central bankers and on international monetary and financial officials' (Tobin 1996: 498).

A technical counter-argument is that most currency transactions start and end in five or six currencies. In 2007, UK Forex transactions, for example, were US dollar and euro primarily, then yen and pound sterling and, to a lesser extent, the Swiss franc, Australian dollar and Swedish krona (BoE 2007). Over 97 per cent of EU spot and derivative transactions take place in the United Kingdom and Germany (Darvas & Weizsacker 2010: 9). Orthodoxy's defence of the benign nature of financial markets won *even when*, as Paul Volcker said to US bankers there is no scrap of evidence to show *any benefits* from financial inventions of the past 20 years except ATMs (Luce & Braithwaite 2010).

What of the tax's *desirability* according to different theories of proponents and opponents? This question places the legitimacy of states in difficulty since, in democracies, agreements must be sought among major conflicting social groups.

Wealth creation raises the *most sensitive question* – the social purposes of money and the exclusive obligations of banking (to Adair Turner: 2010). Tobin had a Keynesian view to justify his tax idea; Joseph Schumpeter also influenced him. Perhaps banks need reminding that they are the 'engine of capitalism' (Schumpeter 1954: 318; 278), and not innocent 'intermediaries' between lenders (sainted 'savers') and borrowers of orthodox theory. The special purpose of banks is to *take the dangers* of funding new social development, which creates future wealth. But, under competitive pressures to 'disintermediation', the dynamism of credit-money creation was precariously put to trading financial products in the capital (wholesale) markets on high levels of leverage. That resulted only in a 'small proportion' of UK credit going to financing investment and trade (Turner 2010: 17). Shadow banks also created and sold financial products (promises). Banks' failure to maintain the payments system led to the first run on a bank in the United Kingdom since 1866, Northern Rock in 2007 and its further US horror after Lehman's 2008 bankruptcy.

As a few see, banks' money-creating powers are 'special'. Unlike the arduous production of goods and services, money is manufactured in mere acts of lending and borrowing. Credit-money is created 'without limit', as banks can do collectively, and is dangerous because 'the quantity of new purchasing power ... is supported and limited ... by *future* goods at *present* prices' (Schumpeter 1934: 115, his emphases). Credit bank-money is 'freely produced', but *too much* can create inflation (and then deflation) in the absence of *limits* – preferably imposed by the authorities to make money scarce (Ingham 2008: 75) and not by post-fact limits that US mortgage holders were unable or refused to meet mortgage payments.

Lending for new combinations in *potentially* profitable developments for other parts of the economy is 'self-amortizing: it creates a debt, but also the value-added to repay principal and interest. By contrast, loans to create or buy financial assets and instruments are not' (Bezemer 2009: 9). Credit booms in exclusively *financial innovations* are zero-sum games reliant on *general economic activity* to support debt-based consumerism, which eventually cannot produce revenue sufficient to pay interest payments. Products packaged on jobless mortgagees expressed the bankruptcy of propaganda about bank innovations. Bank claims to title deeds met US court definitions of corruption with 'Foreclosuregate' in late 2010.

Tobin opponents insist wholesale money markets must not be touched; there are no dubious products but simply an innocent stream of *neutral liquid lubricants* to the 'real' economy. Licensed banks' purposes of creating money to fund wealth-creating future development or *whatever* are merely a function of the spreads, the narrower the more efficient. But if low transaction costs played a role in the explosion of trading activity, that rise 'significantly outperformed the pace of expansion in economic activity' from 2000–07. Therefore, banks' allocation of capital and risk to the production process cannot have been as 'efficient' as market defenders claim (Darvas & Weizsacker 2010: 5–6). In other words, more transaction activity was generating less economic activity in the (weakened) non-financial sector.

However, the really amusing part is that unlike most economic sectors, *the finance sector is essentially exempt from value added taxation.* The funny (or macabre) thing is the difficulties in measuring the 'value added' in financial products (Darvas & Weizsacker 2010: 8). The realist side, signified in the phrase 'financial services *industry* ' is a perception by the *industry* that, like others, they are creating and selling value-added service products. The same occurs when workers add 'value' to unworked or otherwise unsaleable raw goods. This raises two problems: If financial products do not create value, do they allocate capital and risk efficiently and so perform 'benefits for the real economy' (Turner 2010: 1) that taxes whether VAT or Tobin would 'distort'? And, secondly, if they do *create value services,* why are they not taxed at comparable rates to others? This takes the discussion away from the Tobin tax or the levels at which states normally tax economic processes, to another, Veblen-type analysis of what constitutes value, money creation and not *innocent* allocation.[11]

The question is, which transactions are *running a book* on socially undesirable transactions and contribute to systemic risk? Veblen (1904: 35–41) said financier-businessmen's aim was not 'efficiency' instead, 'systematic ineptitude', disruption, 'waste' and opposition to consolidation, say of the US railroads. All we can say is they got built (poor 'workmanship' though) and were at least indirectly serviceable

---

[11] The reason for historic social compromises in *democracies* is due to vital purposes of money, intrinsic to capitalist economies, and need for state legitimacy when saving creditors at grievous costs to debtor-firms or *vice versa* (Ingham 2008; plus, 'varieties of capitalism', in money and in some security for workers, savers-debtors). Value is not magically found in market clearing mechanisms of 'equilibrium' notions, but rather, as Max Weber insisted, via brutal social conflicts of creditors-debtors and labour-capital in shifting combinations and outcomes: see Polanyi and Veblen, less Schumpeter. See too, many chapters herein.

for everyone's needs.[12] This by-product is ever more dissociated with todays' mobile capital. We can never predict which speculation will later prove destabilizing, but that suggests a precautionary strategy, particularly when a high volume of trading, by private superannuation or pension funds for example, tends to lose overall. Governments could call the bluff in this way. If the financial sector wants to avoid taxes, it should prove that it does not 'add value' with the inference that it is socially useless. A Tobin tax that does not drive out the legitimate, slow *social purposes* of banks might well be thought preferable to a value-added tax.

Of course, there are other ways to control finance sectors. Few know that the Canadian Parliament regularly scrutinizes bank licences. How compelling! In transaction tax arguments, the banks *et al* insist they do not add value. But governments acquiesce to socially useless banking, so destructive that state deficits increased on bailouts more than usual. Another misconception is to argue states formerly taxed and 'now' they borrow at interest, which increases the income of 'what the well-to-do can afford to lend to the state' (Offe, 2015:21). But capitalist states always borrowed and just used taxes to reassure *creditors*, in alliances with capital in 17th century Europe onwards.

The Other Concept: Critical Junctures

Our title 'Critical Junctures of Mobile Capital' is unusual. These terms are the framework of our twin questions. Let me turn from 'mobile capital' to the idea of global 'critical junctures'. The Volume proposes that we face social problems about which no predictions can be made and, as I said, we refuse to retreat into the present. That occurs endlessly – petit-bourgeois intellectuals making long-term predictions on short-term or sudden surprises. A President Trump could press the nuclear codes, but he may just go away; not all electorates are voting for demagogues (at the time of writing).

Many financial and economic crises have occurred during the last 30–40 years, and alarming accounts dampen thought: cautious analysis is more persuasive. Will any critical event be taken as an opportunity to reflect on financial and economic crises? The joke is economists have predicted 20 of the past five crises. Grim examples are plentiful.

[12] Two rail lines built to collide; two ran parallel nearly from Atlantic to Pacific.

English rulers starved about a million Irish people to death in the potato famine: *laws* of supply and demand to keep. Stalin did not remove ('disappear') the Kulaks as petit bourgeois, but for creating rural price inflation. We ask what might be 'critical' or historically *new*, democracy being the main one. Will those reflecting on causes of crises propose productive ways of responding *or be heard*? So far, governments have tried varied interventions to salvage some security or stability out of the mess of the biggest crisis ever of 2008, although only the Australian government responded in 2008 with a massive, successful stimulus albeit with (somewhat) well-controlled banks. Most tried the disaster, long well-known, of austerity with moralism, Australia too since 2013.

There is a lot to be said for arguments about the global influence of 'neoliberalism' and yet, ideas only explain so much. They are not sufficient to explain the (costly) debasement of electoral politics, dubious privatizations nor why governments *remain* so active against electors' wishes. Some ask why the 'criminal and plutocratic insurgents' of money laundering and money or, more mildly, why a huge 'informal' mobile capital sector became predators on the liberal welfare state, environment, economy and society.[13] Contributors sketch long term tendencies that contributed to the current situation and discuss how mobile capital operates on *reactive* strategies of enormous scale and influence. Populations are divided in many ways but rarely when money was not believable as in 2008. Since then, mobility of near money like derivatives have only intensified. High frequency trading is programmed to cheat. Key leaders of the world's elites who mention that this dubious liquidity might represent a danger, let alone a 'critical juncture' of serious change for the worse, are few.

If there is some 'critical juncture' in the distortions of mobile capital, we should compare it with Eric Helleiner's pointed argument (2010) about why 'Bretton Woods' in 1944 was unique. This is useful for our approach to money, since he says the world is currently in a situation more like a long 'interregnum'. Even that might be too extreme, however, the GFC is not met in a simple stimulus-response

---

[13] The first quote is by a deputy Chancellor of the University of California, Berkeley in the *The American Interest*, June 2014; the second by Keith Hart, the Polanyi expert on embeddedness: personal communication.

Pavlovian way – that baseless prediction for institutional change. There is no sudden Global Financial Reform. But in the 1920s–30s, protection, stagnation, competitive devaluation and later WW2 *stopped mobile capital* (trading with the enemy laws), and financiers were not invited to Bretton Woods. Roosevelt had previously curbed the *political* control of Wall Street, and war had halted its economic networks.[14] The Bretton Woods institutions were a globally hopeful result, a 'juncture', giving rise to many improvements that lasted for 30 years. One little-discussed factor was the postwar revival of new and old mobile capital networks (more impersonal, as several chapters herein attest, with the US dollar hegemon). Another the nuclear arms race.

After the 'critical' 1980s, the global financial sector gradually became 'too big to fail or even save' although it still seems to rely on state issued currencies as the most 'liquid', acceptable money (and/or last resort High Powered Money, HPM, notably the US dollar). This fragility could imply changing power relations, for good or ill. Shifting social identities, and different economic and policy/political networks may ally in unusual interplays between tradable and non-tradable assets, some being financial instruments (money, portfolios, mortgage assets, etc.), as contributors point out. These uneven developments move in territorial-temporal formations and can converge or take opposite directions, perhaps to peaceful cohabitation (we only hope).

The Volume's position is that capitalist money still holds a promise: not only of economic stagnation, crises of hot money, warfare, but also democratic promise of *project capital*: money is one of the world's greatest social inventions and experiment. Early actors of mobile capital (a tiny but rising network) aimed to temper, and benefit from, the Sovereign's war activities through *exclusive* bourgeois parliamentary alliances.

Whatever may be unfolding, the darkest is maintaining a mésalliance between war states and bourgeois money merchants. Since we cannot know, at least we can say there's something fishy, as my philosophy lecturer used to say. To Ingham (2004), a central element lies in the perennial struggles for control over money production between states

[14] Ingham's compelling argument is that war *broke* the mobile networks. Grandfather of G. W. Bush, Prescott Bush, had a Wall Street firm suspected of trading with the enemy.

and banks, which is usually only 'won' by states in total war. There is a lot to be said for this idea, particularly when even the august, secretive Bank of England (McLeay et al 2014) published some pamphlets on the creation of money by private banks and by states. That is, the Volume's key concerns are acceded inside one of money's heartlands. Yet the continuing obfuscation and concealment of the battle for control remain far above the heads of brain-dead bankers and politicians.

We are amazed that the Asian Financial Crisis (AFC) of 1997 and the Russian near default of 1998 were totally neglected in OECD countries' policies, save for bailing out their own artful dodgers. Norms of money creation – for capitalist *and* state financing – in a symbiotic alliance of the state and mobile capital are mutating ever since neo-liberal policy changes, mostly urged by Wall Street *ad nauseam* under concrete threats. The present crisis (since 2007); and the total uncertainties around any ludicrously called post-crisis, mean that the world leaps from one ghastly event to another, in a purely reactive way. The more decent leaders have barely a moment to reflect or to read anything. It sounds undignified to plead for caution ('wets' to Thatcher) when surrounded by intemperate 'know-nothings'. That refers to a nineteenth century US right-wing political party.

Democracy

The Volume cannot hold out much hope, but give reasoned discussions and look for small openings to sunny avenues lined with trees, and not the foul-mouthed and mendacious highway speedsters who rage, way above these very same political and financial leaders' heads who drive recklessly in the fast lanes.

Enough of metaphors, the financial world is awash in water metaphors: Liquidity is always 'good'; but a stream runs into a swamp (of conspiracies); a river of money sloshes around the world. Or the whole Atlantic Ocean comprises money and not plastic waste. We don't need these stand-ins that mask concrete social relations – even 'money laundering' suggests human action.

From the hints I've given so far, the argument is that the tense alliances that began 400 or more years ago, created the world's first *relatively* secure money creation, the logic of which has not changed. This is silenced. The state is the guarantor of bank IOU creation through the national debt and taxes. State-bank money unlocked capitalist and nation state development albeit with disruptions since money is not a *thing* but an IOU. This is a 'Chartalist' and credit conception.[15] All money is debt, but not all debt is money. Some IOUs are not acceptable or trusted. One question asked in this Volume is whether states are neither able nor willing to change collectively, or are **able but not willing to do so**. It looks like governments shut their eyes and thought processes to war and hot money tactics.

The battle for control is waged in asocial ways and is far from democratic, even at the best of times. In Geoff Mann's words, 'money is a space of exception'. Mobile capital does not victimize states, since states have their own competitive battles; the US over holding the privileged hegemonic currency or others having some financial clout. However foolish, there's always *schadenfreude* in seeing one's competitor collapse into default and massive disaffection. Empire was not a mere permission from a mobile capital that always requires state debt (HPM); other states in the nineteenth century took different routes albeit under the (sterling) hegemon. It sounds a bit like the 1990s Washington-Wall Street consensus.

Social democracies have the worst of it, ever since the twinges of democracy appeared only 150 years ago. Since the 1970s, they have again been subject to vicious attack, although they politely exclude revolution. As do the contributors herein, as far as I can judge from knowing them well. We are certainly fed up with the special pleading and whining of states and financial sectors, which forever mistake as enemies their nearest and most modest threats – a few capital controls? A plea for democratic processes or even the rule of law? Caution? Peace? Taxpaying? Social justice that brings monetary stability in a better bargain? The scary acronym FIRE is ever more apposite – Finance, Insurance and Real Estate. States are colluding – as usual, with FIRE as the sole, pitiful economic activity (say in United Kingdom or Switzerland). These guys want to torch the place rather than lose. Do we have to be run by a bunch of arsonists?

---

[15] Like these scholars, Geoff Ingham, André Orléan and others e.g. Geoff Mann, I look to Schumpeter; Keynes; Minsky; also, lesser-used work of Thorstein Veblen (the disruptive 'financier-businessman'), on an era that met with a response in Teddy Roosevelt's Anti-Trust laws, but he promoted imperial United States too. My philosophy lecturer was the late Gyorgy Markus.

About the Chapters

The unifying themes and debates look at the large questions: How *national* is mobile capital? Banks need clients – trusting or gullible. Or is this capital *globally deceptive,* save for bailouts? Who asks where war finance comes from these days? The term *mobile* makes a useful distinction to *fixed* capital that serves needs for economic activity, but mobile capital can be long-lasting, and service sector trading is now global in call centres to university administrations' on-line tricks to remove local creativity and cultural needs. What are the *junctures,* from which vantage points – or which historical occasions proved 'critical' for good or ill, and what are just *mutton dressed as lamb?* Can anyone identify a special nature about the past 40 years or is that 200 years *too early* to look back? Perhaps some changes in money relations merely express similar patterns, such as 400 years of 'manias, panics and crashes' – Charles Kindleberger always warned sensibly – and states desires for war funding.

We are not forced to retreat into the present with slapdash commentary about a 'new normal'. Rather, we take Norbert Elias's rule (1987) to heart: there are social, cultural and physical needs and desires of humankind, and their possibilities can never be perfected. They can be improved though. Some arrangements seem bleak, others idyllic, but no one can project the present onto fragmentary records of the past. James Scott of *Weapons of the Weak* fame said anthropologists wrongly assumed 'untouched' isolated social structures of those peoples *discovered* recently. Many though, were huddling away from slave catchers of the first ancient globalization era. We have no pristine earlier records but anachronistic Eurocentric myths (Marx or Smith). Only around 1500 AD were peasant and aboriginal resistance to nation states recorded; foot dragging, guerrilla or go-slow tactics. We cannot understand *resistances* to and by social forces of mobile capital without modesty; the nature of promises, our topic, has varied meanings and reasons, whether as money that we use or as notations of promising, among some or many. Promises are made for specific futures with uncertain outcomes that the book aims to examine.

Contributors bring their gifts and expertise, with specific theoretical viewpoints and world views. In common is their generosity and openness to others' ideas, unlike the many know-alls who run the place.[16] No contributor believes that 'In the beginning' there were markets: it is the crudest projection onto mythical pasts to avoid the word 'capitalism'. Money relations between (war) states and mobile capital are hidden in obscurities; uncivil world views with much public shouting about state debts rule out people's modest desires. Deep silence drops over licenced banks which create and destroy money in the act of advancing or withdrawing guarantees; that silence is pernicious. Questions on the purposes of money creation must be asked: the contributors' brief.

The sequential ordering of chapters starts with problems of contemporary mobile capital, the aims of money's promises. It moves on to variations, historical and analytic approaches to the title theme that don't eulogize the 'latest', or spot a critical 'juncture' from yesterday, the outcome of which none of us can predict. Indeed, predictions are part of the problem, since they are not possible. Our interest is in relations that now enormous financial sectors have set up, and whether new developments are further divorced from economies or resemble old disruptive patterns in capitalism. Nation states are the other side of the coin, as it were, in creating money. Overall, the book's position sees money as a social relation, so we examine its character and the conflictual to peaceful balances of money's relations, heavily loaded or slightly evenly distributed.

Since the reasoned claims of democracy are *new*, my impression is of the chapters' mindfulness of how little that electoral processes have tempered imbalances or mésalliances; whether, to the pessimistic, money can ever be democratized. Certainly, the postwar achievements show far fewer inflations–recessions than now. This indicates the situation was, and could be, different and authors keep this in mind.

Chapter 1 lays the groundwork in the nuances of economic governance. Renate Mayntz starts with nation state interventions in economies, in global trade and legal rules for banking, securities and insurance. After the short Bretton Woods stability under the US dollar exchange rate, financial sectors opened again to outside competition. State encouragement is a critical factor, however, since Mayntz shows precisely the de-regulation and *re-regulation* to '*openness to*

---

[16] Elias, 1987; Kindleberger 1989; Scott's review 2013, gives perspective. Homo sapiens is around for 200,000 years, groups forming stateless societies (not markets): nation states were brutally *effective* a tiny time ago.

global markets' within national domestic policy changes. Everyone had to be competitive. As well, the US and UK finance hubs started the process of demanding 'openness' to financial flows; a demand writ large in the IMF's treatment. My question is to what extent this was embraced for political electoral advantages or if there was little choice, even for established economies and states. Detail on international standards and institutions in her chapter is truly depressing because most are merely 'recommendations'. Since the GFC, not even 20 nations of the world can suggest any agreed controls. Renate Mayntz explores this conundrum of global financial structures with her telling concept of *'economic patriotism'*.

Yet there was a major attempt to rise above 'patriotism'. In Chapter 2, Iwan Azis describes the heavy-handed influence of the IMF on Southeast Asian countries to open their economies to hot money, and its culmination *not in the first instance* in the GFC, but with the massive crash in the Southeast Asian financial crisis of 1997. This is remarkably little noted elsewhere, but the AFC shocked the Asia-Pacific region, notably the sight of Michel Camdessus of the IMF standing, arms folded, over a seated President Suharto being forced to concede to harsh IMF austerities. Azis shows first that arrangements were made among these countries to coordinate resistance to capital flows, but second, these faltered as the GFC took its toll in expanding domestic inequality. Nevertheless, South Korea's capital controls give Azis a hope that separate nation states can act against hot money.

The United States patronizingly ignored the relevance of the AFC, but the GFC confirmed Mayntz's point of the depths to which Wall Street (etc.) had gone. Europe was heavily involved too, since work to combine into the European Monetary Union (EMU) grievously ignored the impact of Wall Street and the City on the major banks, mainly French and German, in Chapter 3. The Euro involved a longer effort at *union* than SE Asia, whereas it was not until the 1997 AFC that SE Asian countries formulated any collective defence to Wall Street and the United States (aka IMF). The EU had non-economic antecedents, less ASEAN, but the EMU came at an inauspicious time, after finance sectors demanded the end to *financial repression*, lower economic activity (stagnation), and authorities obliged *everywhere*. Fiscal policy was ugly, if downgraded. Pixley suggests the EMU project was too ambitious, and neglected mobile capital to laud free markets during a seeming absence of crisis. But, through comparing the lengthy (fitful) development of finally full monetary federations in the United States, Canada and Australia, and the Dis-United Kingdom, distinctions are possible. Critics of the Euro either refuse to look at their own messes (United Kingdom, United States), or criticise their European Union (Streeck, Offe) via neglecting external messes like the United Kingdom, or capital mobility.

Chapter 3's argument is mono states or federated unions are equally vicious *or* moderately egalitarian, and conflicts over money's *value* creates divisions not ameliorated by fiscal policies alone, but wider collective demands. Social democracy is a distinguishing mark of Europe. Canada has the loosest 'confederation' that could be a EU model if say, Europe's workers' movements could combine on specific wage strategies (not offered in ultra-patriotic parties) and the EU Parliament agreed on fair, unified financial and bank controls. The Bank of England is probably unlikely ever to have a remit for full employment, but that's no reason why the ECB could not follow Australia's or (with reservations) the United States's dual central bank remits.

The starkest and most of all ignored reservation about the United States is in the next Chapter 4 on 'mobile capital as the ultimate form of war finance', primarily in America's enormous arsenal. Fantacci and Gobbi are more taken with Keynes's position (than say Weber's conflict one) on the mutual dependency of creditors and debtors, which is also stressed in the EU debate and later. Instead of Keynes's hopes for 'financial disarmament' in a bancor, that stressed *benefits* for creditor countries' obligations to buy from deficit countries, as 4 explains, the United States opted for war finance (Weber's brutal cynicism indicates). To Fantacci and Gobbi, a critical juncture at Bretton Woods solidified in the Cold War into *freeing* capital markets by the 1980s. Mobile capital enabled the US military hegemon *never* to repay the costs of its persistent belligerence.

To my mind, a frightening aspect is that democratic settlements emerged in WW2 partly because the carnage of WW1 resulted *post-war* in cruelty to surviving troops and entire populations after 1920. By WW2 the few democratic countries had to concede to people's demands. However, warring states developed armaments that dispensed with troops (partially) to instead destroy civilians via fire-bombing or nuclear bombs. There are no democratic constraints on a President to deploy MAD (as I said).

Barring that end of everything, we must press on to a league of problems and hopes, that draw in working populations (in Chapter 5), the US hegemonic dollar (Chapter 6), as well as Emerging Markets like China's responses to mobile capital (Nölke, Chapter 7). The 400-year-old fixed financial networks in Venice are a counterpoint to today's mésalliances (Chapter 8), whereas the wide gap between the '1 per cent' and the rest, is posed in Chapter 9 as a direct consequence of 1980s free capital markets. This was seen in earlier eras such as Veblen's day, with a changed character. The lack of effective grass-roots opposition to the GFC, (Chapter 10), may well relate back to warring states' 'ultimate form of war finance' (Chapter 4) or the *longee duree* of financiers' habitus (Chapter 11). Whether workers (Chapter 12) must become as 'mobile' as capital ('Get on your bike' said a 1980s Tory), or must move under climate change (the Pentagon!) these are used for divisiveness or war threats.

With Bryan and Rafferty's Chapter 5, then, another tangent from Weber's analysis is enormously useful. Workers, aka 'households' as they say, lost control of the postwar social norms pertaining to the value of labour as subsistence in a national *social* economy. Forced or sucked into global debt relations especially, since we saw in Chapter 4 workers had to endure austerity for nuclear war finance *somehow*. Chapter 5 suggests 'the emergent social relations of labour' are not necessarily those of workers as victims, because attempts of mobile capital to capture value or at least find some *anchor* for fleeting calculations since the 1970s, has been via workers framed as house-holds with tradable, securitized mortgages. Perhaps, given the GFC, mobile capital 'sabotaged its own unit of measure': this is a (social) Marxian *not* Ricardian conception. Bryan and Rafferty argue debtors' resistance to treating a home as a mere house to be flipped – banks' attempt at overturning the social and moral norms of a home for subsistence like wages before, with contracts on MBS and ABS for health, electricity *et al* – gives possibilities for (new) union strategies. Households barely coping, precariously, have refused to default; more-over, they 'absorb risks for capital markets'. States step in to prop up these unequal relations *and* to 'crush' organized labour, but these social relations can be challenged by labour.

In Chapter 6, Herman Schwartz examines the hegemonic US dollar, also not from a Weberian point of view as, he argues, mobile capital does not lack 'nationality', or is not totally mobile. His key point is that 'inside money' typically overshoots its bank-money production; this raises centuries-old global difficulties for the currency hegemon, the creator of 'outside money', and for all countries. Banks go anywhere to evade local rules, to inevitable crashes and succour by their governments. But the IRC (international reserve currency) lacks the *global legitimacy* of say Keynes's bancor (Chapter 4). Schwartz compares theoretical differences to Bryan and Rafferty's Marxian chapter (his more Schumpeter-Sweezy), as does Pixley to both in Chapter 9 with Veblen, and Kuzmics in Chapter 12 with Norbert Elias. To me their approaches are on quite different problems, workers, shaky derivative creation: the other on the IRC and why the Euro can't be a US-dollar competitor (Chapter 3). Schwartz calls for a global composition of the US FOMC (a forbidden *empire* topic, he knows).

Andreas Nölke in Chapter 7 looks at resistance to mobile capital in large Emerging Markets of China and India, not before recounting the expansion of financialization in the OECD and its dangers from the 1980s. To emerging markets, the 'fickle' nature of mobile capital undermines these countries' development aims (as Azis's Chapter 2) and companies' aims. Variations in protective strategies range from little in Central and Eastern European economies, to significant 'state-permeation' of markets in China, India, Brazil and South Africa (at times). Of note, those with huge domestic markets (India and China) barely need mobile capital, so have by far the highest restrictions and comprehensive capital controls; also, foreign ownership is slight as in *Japan* (cf. heavy in United Kingdom, more so Slovakia). Public ownership or involvement is highest in China and India too, and internal funds and (mainly state-owned) bank credit (not equity) finance *new* investment. Whether this points to conflicts or (say) the IMF's recent acceptance of these strategies, new emphases are national sovereignty (over mobile labour and trade). Nölke says it's too early to tell.

After Nölke's insights on bulwarks to inflows-outflows in the largest rising economies, we step back in time to fourteenth century Venice. There we find according to Chapter 8, a contrasting conception of 'mobile capital' with the 'immobility in the Lagoon' of Venice – that to Sam Whimster gave no basis for subsequent rational capitalism. Sure, merchant networks traded as far as Britain or Syria, but he shows Venetian banks (tables on the Rialto) had to fund city-state debt. Everyone bowed to Venice's imperial needs for warfare. Its total control of bank networks and taxpayers, laid out in Chapter 8, left no legacy that, I add, other scholars suggest from Keynes's line that *financiers choose* between trading to beat financial competition or instead garner profits on long returns for economic activity: the by-products being jobs, purchasing power, dignity and survival. Instead, to Whimster's sources, Amsterdam and London invented a new money in league with their states, not Venice. And fair enough, in the Doges' Palace is a lock-up cubicle, from which culprits were taken across the Bridge of Sighs. In Bologna, an ugly fate from the Via Dei Terribilia awaited miscreant merchants, unlike the London Whigs after 1694, lording it in Parliament.

Chapter 9 shows social impacts, six centuries later, of the rise in mobile capital that resemble the grossly unequal era of the 1900s–1930s. Even after their responsibility for the GFC, financial sectors profited further amid chronic recession and stagnation. Data emphasizes the 1970s (again) as the turning point *(juncture?)* in the sector's disdain for investment and switch to dealing in financial assets as *more* profitable. Disruptive and reactive competition among rivals were enhanced with authorities' Quantitative Easing; with their failure to control the explosion of asset deals (under their very eyes). But 1970s search for 'stable prices' – money's value as 'objective' – was *always* fictitious, because it was the balance of power relations that was changed. In freeing finance from *repression*, workers had to be (further) repressed, also social democracy and the mixed economy; results continuing are neither efficient nor socially useful, Pixley argues. Distress and disaffection are inchoate and directed in negative as much as positive directions, given the chasm dividing absentee holders of liquidity (saleable assets) from political, social and economic relations, riven and torn as they are.

Helena Flam in Chapter 10 uses most interesting pamphlets of Occupy Wall Street, ATTAC and the Jubilee movement to show that the activists trying to control financialisation were not as ill-informed as many assume. They have experts by the mile, and notably Jubilee had great success over writing off underdeveloped countries' debts. Explanations for Jubilee, or for failures of OWS and ATTAC, I suggest, are explored in the following shorter chapters and earlier ones. The problems are fear of money among rich democracies; short-term survival tactics, or nausea at the structures of personality running the show. At best, surrogate currencies (we see) are an effective means to keep economic activity going under deflation.

Mark Blyth in *Austerity* also puts a case that diverse conservatives took up 'Astro-Turfing' and deploy immense funds. These fake grass-roots cover high income-wealth quintiles, and look *under* the astro-turf, to angry small business associations which defend Wall Street, low wages and austerity (counterproductively), or to anti-migration or attacks on alternative energy.

The Volume does not end on a conclusion (that is, not more Pixley), instead the potential for further debates is opened with a few shorter chapters. In Chapter 11, Helmut Kuzmics takes the long-term perspective on our questions. In seeing states as 'survival units' emerging from pre-history, Kuzmics is hesitant to date the origins of present crises and global dislocations, but cites the 1970s as a place to start. States lost control over money, and the scale of money creation expanded greatly. If mostly unintentional, a 'functional de-democratization' occurred via *removing* wage earners' bargaining power. Struggles between states (war finance) also furthered financial markets (see Chapter 4). Yet this present stage is built on earlier ones. Kuzmics reminds us states provided internal peace not only external wars; systems of money and credit raised fears of (uncertain) economic loss. Norbert Elias's concept of 'social (or national) habitus' he suggests, helps explain how money is handled in different state-formations: (western) maritime or continental, or China's ancient 'pacifying codes': respectively, shareholder-value, welfare-state or diligent wealth-acquisition cultures. Variations exist, as well, recent events can impact on habitus. In Germany, *precaution* is today prevalent, after traumas of the 1922 hyperinflation and decivilizing of dictatorship. In contrast, the Soviet bloc collapse gave a temporary 'mono-polar system' that *expanded the asset inflation* of the US economic model abroad.

With workers the focus, Shaun Wilson Chapter 12 draws attention to parallel processes of labour mobility to mobile capital (also from the 1970s), such that about 150 million people (a large 'country') are global migrant workers. He examines the concept of 'superdiversity' in the labour markets of rich democracies, with its positive welcoming but exploitative underside. Although many *non-migrants* are also exploited, evidence shows super-exploitation for migrant workers. Wilson considers the worst forms of exploitation – less a functional logic of capital – suggest employers opportunistically use a range of sources to enforce further social inequalities. Inequalities mount up from ancient discriminations: I agree that assimilation super-imposed on women, migrants or minorities was always double-sided as the in-group did not accept cultural diversity but nor did it enjoy the out-group becoming the *same*. That undermined in-group exclusivity, argued Elias or Veblen. Wilson suggests some Marxian analyses, but with liberal concepts of injustice, help to explain the common mechanisms such as deportation threats; or benefits and vulnerabilities of transnational migrant networks. Thus, as mobile capital increases the transitory nature of economic activity, with financial crises impacts of sudden dislocation, the deregulation of labour markets combines with superdiversity of workers as Wilson says, to 'alter the terms' for profit-seeking employers to exploit migrant and refugee workers to the max.

A potential logic of pure capital is given a thorough treatment in Massimo Amato's debate about Bitcoin (Chapter 13). Here too, Marxian and classic (Keynesian) liberal analyses are deployed in another (ugly) opposite. Amato offers an eye-opener on Bitcoin's anarchic libertarian notion of a *pure capital* untouched by any economic activity whatever. In this utopia (dystopia) are no invigorating tensions between creditors and debtors, as Chapters 4 and 5 recount negatively (warfare) and hopefully (household subsistence). Instead there is a permanent deflation aimed via keeping Bitcoin scarce – like the old gold standard that perennially favoured so-called creditors. The algorithm 'running' the show gives *liberation* from third parties that try to control money creation. Bitcoin aims to refuse debt as the source of money issue, to make it a fixed commodity. But the temptation to hoard Bitcoin makes it volatile, unbalanced and dangerous. Third parties enable 'a chain of signifiers' that the algorithm abolishes – to Hayek's notion of money as 'absolute property'. Bitcoin is fully *disembedded* from lively social relations; it is a 'heavy' and anti-social currency, not the money as light as a mere intermediary.

In contrast however, we do see hope for 'light intermediaries' that are modest and preventative. Surrogate currencies recounted in the next two chapters also enlarge all the debates. These currencies compare most successfully against extremes of mobile capital (Bitcoin one) since, David Woodruff explains (Chapter 14), resistance from below to arbitrary economic destructiveness is perennial. Deflation is the disaster to be avoided (cf. welcomed in the scarce Bitcoin), mostly difficult to achieve as we saw – given central banks' and austerity's increase in inequality. Woodruff's case is how local Argentinian authorities temporarily imposed a *bonos* as a surrogate local currency to pay their workers when the pesos was under a dollar-peg in the hot money crisis of 1997–1998. It kept council and local activities going, prevented wage theft (that Wilson also notes) and Councils accepted it as the legal means to pay local taxes. Moreover, Argentina's economy recovered rapidly once the state regained legal monetary sovereignty over the pesos (in Knapp's sense). Compromises 'third party' were made between creditors and debtors fairly, with this temporary (substitute) bonos that kept economic life alive.

Sardex also has similar positive effects if differently (Chapter 15). From the ECB's original aim to club the economy over the entire Eurozone, (Chapter 3), we see the vitality of money's 'light' role in the *complementary legal* currency of Sardex (also the Swiss WIR). A dearth of 'heavy' money or *dear money* spells economic death. Laura Sartori shows Sardinia's *local* less impersonal Exchange Network, just for business to business, is a collective resistance to deflation. Non-convertible to the Euro (the *unit of account*), Sardex (nominally €1 each) is a medium of exchange (with no interest on negative balances), only spent and earned via the balanced Network. As she says, Weber's dramatic rendering of the struggle between creditors and debtors puts paid to orthodoxy's objectification of money. Examples of alternatives show the fruitful, generative if fragile aspects of the money as a mutual promise (of trust), with a third party that at best, inspires and defends people and their livelihoods. When the third party (for the serious unit of account) is taken over by mobile capital, as Amato suggests (Chapter 13), it is not 'impartial' and, to Sartori, money's fictitious commodification merely masks money's social struggles. Yet the 'third' principle can be and has been changed. Sardex is not about purely economic benefits (or less, utopian hopes) but widens social values, unmasks the 'struggle' and broadens local community needs and desires.

I began pointing to misunderstandings and fears of money that have crippled electorates' knowledgeable entry to political debates, particularly when money nearly disappeared after 2007. Yet, even if our ideas were fortified via the knowledge that all money is debt, there are conflicting battles for control of money's production; war finance and pure capital at each extreme. In democracies, such conflicts garner grassroots and astro-turf social movements for numerous sides: The largest public sphere, legislatures, are fought over for crackpot or autocratic obsessions, for defenders of existing wealth distribution, to the modest legislators for social amelioration. Thus, not all small business creates surrogate currencies to continue economic activities and thus jobs. Some support social movements and parties that aim to cut wages further, often via attacking 'out-groups', but end with business activities declining; this is the fallacy of composition long well-known. Others want to slash government debt (so the top gain) and most states oblige only to maintain war finance.

In effect, moves to hide political decisions about winners and losers behind technocratic rules for central banks and other authorities, would beat inflation, destroy debtors, after an interim of 30–40 years when money was required to do decent work. The 1970s was a *critical juncture*: austerity drives economies further downwards, traders for mobile capital hasten the process, and further privatization tries to win over the credit raters of state deficits. These thin reeds, known to sell any credit rating for a buck, are no substitute for a trustworthy authority that adjudicates between creditors and debtors. States turned the task over to Moody's or S&P, but any adjudicator even Moody's knows there is a limit to bankrupting economies and all that entails.

In the face of promises to a further bleak future, this book then opens debates over what might be above all positive possibilities. Our values are openly stated, mostly through posing contrasting and creative options against the dour to tyrannical *money businesses* of states and mobile capital. These possibilities are not the savage ones of the current situation and, of course, are hugely popular among electorates. Certainly, in disabling informed voices, the fact free and masking slogans of political-economic faux *theories* and *mentalities* dominate, but these are trifles compared with the consequences of business as usual that serves no public interests whatever.

References

Bank of England 2007. 'BIS triennial survey of foreign exchange and over-the-counter derivatives markets in April 2007 – UK data – results summary' (www.bankofengland.co.uk/statistics)

Barber, T. & G. Packer 2009. 'European leaders push case for Tobin tax', *FT* December 12–13: 4

Bezemer, D. 2009. 'Lending must support the real economy', *Financial Times 5* November 2009: 9

BIS 2007. 'Triennial central bank survey or foreign exchange and derivatives, 2007' (Bis.org)

Collins, R. 1986. *Weberian Sociological Theory*. Cambridge University Press

Crotty, J. 2012. 'The great austerity war', *Cambridge Journal of Economics* 36: 79–104

Darvas, Z. & J. Weizsacker 2010. 'Financial-transaction tax: small is beautiful', *Breugel Policy Contribution Issue* 2010/02 (www.bruegel.org)

Eatwell, J. 1993. 'The global money trap?' *The American Prospect* Winter. Prospect.org

Elias, N. 1987. 'The retreat of sociology into the present', *Theory, Culture & Society* 4: 223–47

Forder, J. 2014. *Macroeconomics and the Phillips Curve Myth*. Oxford University Press

Friedman, T. 1999. *The Lexus and the Olive Tree* London: HarperCollins

Garnaut, R. 2009. *The Great Crash of 2008*. Melbourne University Press.

Greider, W. 1987. *Secrets of the Temple*. NYC: Simon & Schuster

Haldane, A. 2011 'The race to zero' Speech to IEA Congress, Beijing. 8 July at www.bankofengland.co.uk/publications/speeches

Harcourt, G. C. 1994. 'Taming speculators and putting the world on course to prosperity: a 'modest proposal'', *Economic and Political Weekly* 29 (38), September 17: 2490–2492

Helleiner, E. 2010. 'A Bretton Woods moment?', *International Affairs* 86 (3): 619–636

HM Treasury 2009. 'Risk, reward and responsibility: the financial sector and society' December; f#461CA9. pdf accessed hm-treasury.gov.uk on 6 January 2010

Ingham, G. 1984. *Capitalism Divided?* Houndmills: Macmillan
2004. *The Nature of Money*. Cambridge: Polity
2008. *Capitalism*. Cambridge: Polity

Kindleberger, C. P. 1989. *Manias, Panics, and Crashes: A History of Financial Crises*, 2nd Edn. London: Macmillan

Luce, E. & Braithwaite, T. 2010. '"Volcker rule" takes bankers by surprise' *FT*, January 21, 2010

Mallaby, S. 2012. 'Woodrow Wilson knew how to beard behemoths' *FT* July 5

McLeay, M., Radia, A. & Thomas, R. 2014. 'Money creation in the modern economy', *Bank of England Quarterly Bulletin* Q1: 4–27

Morgan, V. 1943. *The Theory and Practice of Central Banking 1797–1913*. Cambridge University Press

Nitzan, J. (1998). 'Differential accumulation: towards a new political economy of capital' *Review of International Political Economy* 5(2): 169–216

Offe C. 2015. *Europe Entrapped.* Cambridge: Polity

Panić, M. 2007. 'Does Europe need neoliberal reforms?' *Cambridge Journal of Economics* 31: 145–169

Parker, G. & Murphy M. 2010. 'UK fails to alter bank bonus culture' *FT* 6 January 6: 6

Parker, G. 2010. 'Brown leads push for deal on global bank levy' *FT* 11 March: 2

Patomaki, H. 2001. *Democratising Globalisation: The Leverage of the Tobin Tax* (Zed Books, London)

Pixley, J. F. 2013. 'Geoffrey Ingham's theory, money's conflicts and social change' in Pixley, J. F. & Harcourt, G. C. (eds.): *Financial Crises and the Nature of Capitalist Money.* London: Palgrave Macmillan: 273–299

  unpublished 2010. 'Tobin tax revisited' Society for Heterodox Economics paper UNSW, Sydney

Pressler, J. 2012. '122 minutes with Jamie Dimon' New York Magazine August 12. http://nymag.com/news/intelligencer/encounter/jamie-dimon-2012-8/

Quiggin, J. 2012. 'Boring is Good': film review of *Margin Call* in *Inside Story* - http://inside.org.au 8 March

Schularick, M. 2014. 'Public and Private Debt: 'The Historical Record (1870–2010)', *German Economic Review* 15 (1): 191–207

Schumpeter, J. A. 1934 [1911]. *The Theory of Economic Development New Brunswick*, NJ: Transaction Publishers

  1954. *History of Economic Analysis.* NYC: Oxford University Press

Scott, J. 2013. 'Crops, towns, governments' *London Review of Books* 35 (22)

Smithin, J. N. 1996. *Macroeconomic Policy and the Future of Capitalism: The Revenge of the Rentiers and the Threat to Prosperity.* Cheltenham: Edward Elgar

Tobin, J. 1978. 'A proposal for international monetary reform', *Cowles Foundation Paper 495*, from *Eastern Economic Journal*, July/October 1978: 153–9

  1996. 'A currency transactions tax, why and how' *Open Economies Review* 7: 493–499

Turner, A. 2010. 'What do banks do, what should they do and what public policies are needed to ensure best results for the real economy?' Lecture at CASS Business School, 17 March 2010. www.fsa.gov.uk/pubs/speeches/at_17mar10.pdf

  2013. 'Debt, money and Mephistopheles: How do we get out of this mess?' *Cass Business School*, 6 February 2013: 1–46. Available at: www.fsa.gov.uk/library/communication/speeches/(2013)/0206-at

Veblen, T. 1899 'The Preconceptions of Economic Science: II' *The Quarterly Journal of Economics*, 13, (4) July: 396–426

1904. *The Theory of Business Enterprise.* New York: Charles Scribner & Sons

1953 [1899]. *The Theory of the Leisure Class.* New York: Mentor

Wahl, P. & Wardlow P. 2001 'Currency Transaction Tax – a Concept with a Future' *WEED Working Paper*, World Economy Ecology and Development Association (weedbonn.org)

Weber, M. 1978. *Economy and Society*, eds. G. Roth & C. Wittich, Berkeley CA: University of California Press

1981 [1927]. *General Economic History*, Trans. F. H. Knight. New Brunswick, NJ: Transaction Books

1 | *Sovereign Nations and the Governance of International Finance*

RENATE MAYNTZ

The public regulation of financial markets developed together with the modern nation state. For centuries, the main object of political intervention into the economy had been neither finance nor production, but trade. When states finally claimed the task to govern the financial system, the main objects of regulation were banks, trans-border capital movements, credit giving, and interest. But it took until the twentieth century for modern states to establish centralized and formalized regulatory systems, including a legal framework covering all key areas of the banking industry: banks, exchanges, securities, and insurance. (Goodhart 2007) Three distinct sectors developed, ruled by separate legal acts, and there were special supervisors for banking, securities, and insurance.

Relatively strict financial regulation characterized the period between the two world wars. Exchange rates and even interest to be paid were fixed by governments. Toward the end of World War II, the Bretton Woods institutions – the International Monetary Fund (IMF), World Bank, and GATT (later WTO) – were established, their main purpose being the stabilization of the international economy and the removal of trade barriers. The so-called Washington Consensus was the basis of the "embedded liberalism" (Ruggie 1982) that characterized the 1950s and 1960s. Nothing much changed with respect to financial regulation until the 1970s. There was much talk about free trade, but in fact most governments tried to shield their domestic financial markets from competition. The financial industry continued to be regulated nationally. Governments used banks for purposes of fiscal policy, and in many countries also for industrial policy.

Between 1950 and the end of the century, three interdependent developments took place, concerning the economy, the financial system, and financial governance (Mayes and Wood 2007). As for the economy, trade and industrial production in the Western World started increasingly to transcend national boundaries. Transnational

38

corporations developed alongside national ones, and foreign direct investment increased. Following the expansion and internationalization of markets and the rise of transnational corporations, financial markets also expanded and became internationalized. In the past, financial markets – transactions and capital flows – have only intermittently been contained within national borders, but they have never been as transnational in scope as towards the end of the twentieth century, even if they remained fragmented into the First, Second, and Third Worlds. Both developments in the economy and in finance have been greatly facilitated by developments in information and communication technologies.

Starting in the late 1970s, the internal structure of the financial system also underwent important changes. The size of banks grew, and their activities were increasingly diversified, turning them into multifunctional financial institutions. The boundaries between the three sectors of banking, securities, and insurance eroded. Banks engaged increasingly in proprietary trading, and created complex financial instruments (e.g., collateralized debt obligations, CDO; credit default swaps, CDS), pursuing the "originate-and-distribute" strategy instead of the classical strategy "originate-and-hold." At the same time, there were changes in the field of investors, where the weight of big corporate investors (pension funds, investment funds) came to dominate the dispersed mass of small investors. With these changes, the role of rating agencies became ever more important.

In response to these changes, there were two apparently contradictory developments in financial governance: Financial markets were both deregulated and reregulated. Liberalization in general had already been part of the "Washington Consensus," but this concerned at first mainly trade. Following the breakdown of the Bretton Woods system in the 1970s, Western states started to deregulate capital markets. There were no longer fixed exchange rates, no restrictions on credit and loans, and no barriers to capital movement. The United States and, later on, Great Britain, pushed the process of deregulation, but the European Union soon followed suit. The two oil crises and massive unemployment in the 1970s motivated further liberalization of capital markets, the purpose still being to remove barriers to international trade. Deregulation opened domestic financial markets to foreign competition. This reinforced the already-noted development of a financial system transcending national borders.

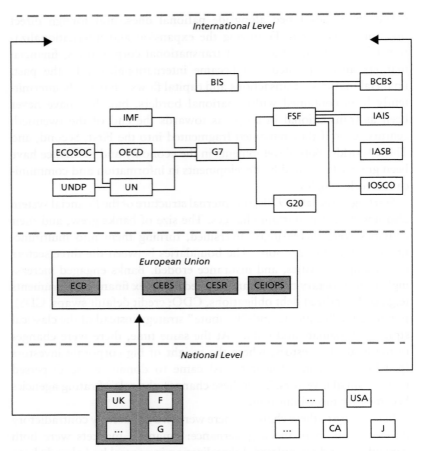

Figure 1.1 Regulatory Structure of Financial Market Governance before the Crisis, 2000.

Parallel and in response to the development of a complex, international financial system, there were changes in financial governance at all political levels (Busch 2009; Davies and Green 2008), as Figure 1.1 shows. In some countries, the separate supervisory authorities for banks, securities, and insurance were merged to form an integrated financial supervisor, such as the German Bundesanstalt für Finanzdienstleistungen (BaFin), and the British Financial Services Authority (FSA). Starting in the 1970s, and spurred among other things by the crisis triggered by the bankruptcy of the German Herstatt bank and later by the Asian crisis, international bodies with standardization and coordination functions started to be established (Lütz 2009). Up to that point there was only one important international body dealing with issues of financial stability, the Bank for International Settlement (BIS) founded in 1930, originally for the settlement of German reparation payments. The Committee for Payment and Settlement Systems (CPSS) and the Financial Stability Institute (FSI) are spin-offs from the BIS. The IMF, a treaty-based international organization, was generally supportive of capital account liberalization; it surveyed the state of member country economies and tied any lending to severe fiscal and economic policy conditions, but had no specific mandate with respect to financial stability and regulation. Regulating the globalizing financial system became the task of international standardization organizations. The first standardization organization founded after World War II was the International Accounting Standards Committee (IASB) established in 1973, followed in 1974 by the Basel Committee for Banking Supervision (BCBS). The BCBS was to define capital requirements for banks, and rules for the cooperation of national supervisors. In 1983, the International Organization of Securities Commissions (IOSCO) was established, to try and harmonize the rules for dealing with securities. After banking and securities, the insurance sector, too, became the object of international standardization: in 1996, the International Association of Insurance Supervisors (IAIS) was established. The international standard setters were to be loosely coordinated by the Joint Forum. Already in 1990, the G7 established the Financial Stability Forum (FSF) that was to deal with issues of global financial stability. In 1999, the finance ministers of the G7, who were increasingly concerned with questions of financial stability, set up the G20, a forum where the finance ministers and central bank governors of the twenty largest market economies meet to safeguard the stability of the international financial system.

Different from the Bretton Woods institutions, these financial governance institutions had not been conferred decision-making competences by their member states; the rules and norms they developed had only the character of recommendations and were not supported by sanctions. As a consequence, such international standards as did exist before 2007–2008 were frequently disregarded by their addressees, or adopted formally but not complied with. At the regional level of the European Union, newly established Committees of European Banking

Supervisors, of European Securities Regulators, and of European Insurance and Occupational Pensions Supervisors had a similarly limited mandate, focusing on coordination.

At the turn of the century (Figure 1.1), these were the major international institutions concerned with regulating and coordinating the global financial system. Financial market governance consisted of a loosely knit, functionally fragmented set of mainly, but not exclusively, public bodies of varying geographical scope and with partly overlapping mandates. The IMF was the only classical supranational organization involved, disposing of a large bureaucratic staff; the G20 and standard-setters like the BCBS had a restricted membership and were initially dominated by the developed Western countries. Most importantly, the rules developed and the decisions made by most of these bodies were not the work of an expert bureaucracy, but of the delegates from *national* finance ministries, central banks, and supervisory agencies. These delegates normally acted not as technocratic problem solvers but as "economic nationalists." States therefore remained clearly the dominant actors, both in the formulation and subsequently in the ratification and implementation of international rules and standards. As Aaron Major (2012) has pointed out, up to the 1980s, financial market regulation had been depoliticized and was mainly a matter of technocratic expertise. National sovereignty was hardly impaired by this form of governance.

When the financial crisis of 2007–2008 erupted, it was widely attributed to regulatory deficits. Agencies at all political levels started initiatives to reform financial market governance to prevent the recurrence of similar crises in the future. The reforms triggered by the financial crisis involved both the regulatory substance – rules, norms, and standards – and the structure of financial governance. (For details, see Mayntz 2012.) Substantive reforms targeted first the most evident, recognized causes of the financial crisis: the incentives for bankers to engage in high risks, the inability of banks to cope with sudden losses, and the behavior of rating agencies. As time went on, derivatives trading and the existence and functioning of the shadow banking sector were addressed. The reforms were piecemeal and selective, and even before sovereign debt and the maintenance of the Euro became major problems, they were judged to be insufficient (Moschella and Tsingou 2013, Admati and Hellwig 2013).

In the course of coping with the financial crisis, the structure of financial market governance also changed – most, though unevenly at the *national* level, and least at the international level. At the national level, early and comprehensive reform initiatives were started especially in the United Kingdom and in the United States, where the Dodd–Frank Act was signed into law by President Obama in 2010. In several countries, regulatory competences were shifted and new agencies were created, both to address systemic risk and to improve consumer protection.

At the regional level of the European Union, the three extant committees that had only coordinative functions were transformed into agencies with at least limited decision-making powers. In addition, a European Risk Board was created (Quaglia 2012). Over the course of time, the European Council, Commission, and Parliament together developed both independent reform initiatives, as well as translating international reform recommendations into directives, subsequently to be written into law by EU member parliaments. This happened, for instance, with "Basel III," the capital requirements reform proposed by the BCBS. While the development of bank capital and liquidity regulation that aimed to prevent another banking crisis made headway in the European Union, the immediately ensuing sovereign debt crisis in the Eurozone made evident the need to also improve crisis management. To this purpose, European governments proposed to establish a Banking Union in June 2012. (Howarth and Quaglia 2014, Schoenmaker 2015). The Banking Union was seen as a further step toward a single European financial market, responding directly to the intensification of cross-border capital flows in the European Union. The Banking Union established a single framework for banking supervision (Single Supervisory Mechanism, SSM), with the European Central Bank as supervisor. A second pillar of this Banking Union is the single bank resolution mechanism (SRM). Banks were to prepare ex-ante bank resolution plans, while in case of bank failure ex-post, resolution measures following a standard procedure were to be taken. The crucial agent in this mechanism, the Single Resolution Board (SRB) became operative in January 2016. The final element of the Banking Union, a common deposit guarantee scheme, had not been agreed by the summer of 2016, largely due to the resistance of Germany, the biggest paymaster which fears the moral hazard effect of such a guarantee. Membership in the Banking Union is mandatory for Eurozone countries, but open to all EU member states; to date, no other country has joined.

The Banking Union is a regional response to the problem posed by
the divergence between a transnationally extended policy field and
a nationally fragmented regulatory structure. This divergence is not
specific to capital flows; it is familiar also from other policy fields such
as trade and pollution, and is generally seen to impair problem-solving.
The financial crisis made evident that, in the field of finance, the
problem of divergence existed at the international level, and not only
the European level. But efforts to adapt international financial governance to the scope of the policy field met with more resistance than the
Banking Union in the EU: At the international level, a corresponding
upward shift of decision-making powers did not occur. There were
some changes in the membership basis of some institutions, but there
was no centralization of competences. The BCBS became an active
reform agent early on, defining stricter capital requirements and leverage ratios for banks, but its function, as that of other standard-setting
organizations, was focused on only a small part of the financial system
in crisis. The establishment of a treaty-based supranational organization empowered to regulate and supervise the internationalized financial system was briefly discussed by a few, but the time-consuming
negotiations needed to create such an organization made this an illu-
sory choice in a situation of acute crisis, quite aside from the question
whether powerful nations would give up competences to such an institution. So, the question arose who would become the "nodal actor"
(Viola 2015) in the fragmented governance system. The G7 that had
occasionally been concerned with financial stability was not specialized
enough, and its club-like membership was too narrow in view of the
quickly expanding crisis. The IMF had no regulatory powers, and only
a limited financial oversight capacity in addition to its main task as
lender to member countries with financial problems. Between 2004
and 2007 IMF surveillance had failed miserably to recognize the build-
up of a major financial crisis, a failure openly admitted in an independent evaluation initiated by the IMF itself (IEO 2011). This failure is
one reason why the IMF did not offer itself as focal or nodal actor
for concerted international crisis management. Another and possibly
even more decisive reason is the preference especially of powerful
nations for voluntary forms of coordination that leave their autonomy
unscathed (Viola 2015). In this perspective, the G20 appeared to be a
more suitable starting point for a concerted international effort at crisis
management than an enhanced IMF.

Before the crisis, the G20 meetings of finance ministers and central bank governors, who often did not attend in person, were low key gatherings that had little impact. In order to establish the G20 as "our premier forum of international economic cooperation" (G20 2009), the G20 heads of government started in 2008 to meet in much-publicized summits. This served the urgently felt need for coordination, without impinging upon sovereign control over financial and economic policy. The G20 heads of government also decided to transform the FSF into a kind of informal G20 staff, now called Financial Stability Board (FSB). The FSB became the focal international coordinator and monitor of the reform initiatives started by the G20, both in summits as in the meetings of finance ministers and central bank governors preceding them. Figure 1.2 gives a rough view of the international structure of financial market governance as it looked after the crisis.

The sovereign debt and related Euro crises that became manifest in the summer of 2011 led to a shift in public attention, but the activities dealing with the reform of financial market regulation continued. The shift of attention to new issues has been most noticeable in institutions with a mandate extending beyond financial market regulation. Financial market regulation is no longer the paramount concern at G20 meetings, though the G20 continue to try and play their role as an "apex policy forum" (Baker 2010). With the third G20 summit in 2009, the stability and resilience of the international monetary system became a new concern, followed later by unemployment and lagging growth (Mayntz 2015). The shift of emphasis from financial regulation to jobs and growth mellowed the earlier reform impetus where stricter standards impacted negatively on the profitability of banks and the functions of financial institutions for the real economy. In fact, the viability of banks has been the reform target most seriously pursued, while other problematic aspects of the financial system, notably the use of sophisticated and "innovative" financial instruments and technologies, have hardly been approached. The viability of banks is also not directly related to the control of money flows. Since 2014, the communiqués of G20 meetings and summit declarations have referred to financial regulatory reform as something largely concluded, summarizing its results and listing remaining steps, in particular, the implementation of agreed changes. In the situation of acute financial crisis, G20 summits have been strong in formulating goals, though their effectiveness and even legitimacy have been questioned (see, for instance, Alexandroff and

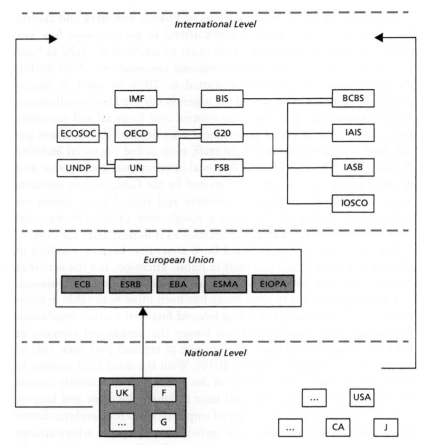

International Level

European Union

National Level

Figure 1.2 Regulatory Structure of Financial Market Governance after the Crisis, 2010.

Kriton 2010). Such criticism is the result of unrealistic expectations; the G20 have never been meant to, nor been able to produce binding decisions, or binding international contracts. The newly expanding agenda of problems demanding international attention may well lead to a widening and dispersion of attention, and thus to lowering the efficacy of the enhanced G20.

In contrast to the G20 and true to its mandate, the attention of the FSB has remained fixed on financial market regulation. It has in fact become the most important international institution concerned with financial market regulation. Though occasionally the FSB has also formulated regulatory "Principles," its role is essentially limited to monitoring and pushing for the adoption and implementation of rules that have been developed by the delegates of nation states or experts with a national passport in bodies such as the BSCB, IOSCO, or the IASB. In its November 2015 report to G20 leaders, the FSB details the extent to which the implementation of reforms in more demanding areas, notably ending too-big-to-fail, making derivatives markets safer, and transforming shadow banking, have been achieved. (FSB 2015)

As a true network organization, the FSB counts both countries and international organizations as members. Its Steering Committee is made up of nation state delegates from finance ministries, central banks, and supervisors. Among the international organizations that are members of the FSB there are the different standard-setters, but also the OECD and IMF. From the first summit onwards, the G20 leaders asked for the collaboration of the IMF. G20 leaders voted to increase IMF resources, and asked for changes in the representation of different countries and regions in the IMF decision-making bodies, called quota reform. The division of tasks between IMF and the future FSB was elaborated in a letter sent in November 2008 from the FSF chairman Mario Draghi to the IMF's managing director: While the FSB was to be responsible for elaborating and coordinating policy, the IMF was to survey and assess its implementation (Knight 2014, 9). Due to foot-dragging by the United States, it took until 2016 for the quota reform to become effective, but the IMF started immediately to support G20 efforts by strengthening its surveillance and deepening its analytical work, supplying on a regular basis surveys of the global financial system in the form of Financial Stability Reports, and detailed assessments of individual countries' financial sector in the Financial Sector Assessment Program (FSAP). In this way, the IMF became an important collaborator of FSB and G20, but not the focal actor in the management of the financial crisis and the ensuing reform of financial regulation.

The changes triggered by the financial crisis and by the ambitious reform plans of the period immediately following it have led to the expansion of the geographical scope of the club-like international governance institutions. The G20 summits have effectively replaced the G7, and standard-setters like the BCBS have become more inclusive. Relations between heterogeneous international institutions have tightened; they have also become tighter between institutions at the

international, the European, and the national level concerned with
financial market governance. As time went on, substantive reforms
thus started to become vertically a bit more coordinated than they
were before. This holds in particular for member countries of the
European Union. The dominant players, however, are still the different
nation states. This is mainly due to the fact that instead of one supra-
national organization controlling financial market governance, heads
of government and national delegates play the prominent role in
policy-making and standard-setting in club-like, self-selected bodies.
But the dominant role played by nation states in financial governance
is also due to the fact that a harmonized international governance of
financial markets depends more than ever on the faithful implementation of rules agreed at the European or international level. When the
G20 heads of government summarily admonish "jurisdictions" to
adopt and put into practice what they have agreed at a summit meeting, it is to nation states and the European Union that they refer. The
European Union is indeed empowered to legislate, formulating binding
norms for its member states, but these norms are not simply adopted
from international templates. They have generally been formed in a
process of negotiation among delegates of nation states, delegates who
act as national patriots, representing what their governments and
parliaments consider to be in the national interest.

Different countries have different interests, and these interests are
not generally supportive of stricter regulation. In general, national
governments try to protect their own financial industry, whether
this means shielding big banks from serious losses or warding off
new regulations that would put a harness on a flourishing financial
industry. In supranational organizations, the professional staff dominates in the development of policy, even if its adoption is subject to
the approval of a plenary of national representatives; supranational
organizations, moreover, also administer their programs themselves.
(Barnett and Finnemore 1999). In financial market governance,
policy is made and standards are defined in negotiation between
heads of government or national delegates in club-like bodies without legal empowerment. If the negotiators in such bodies pursue
different particularistic interests, the ability to agree on a policy or
standard is limited. If agreement is precarious, a decision costs more
time, and the negotiators must be pragmatic, trying to satisfy as far as
possible the different interests represented at the negotiating table.

Inevitably, this means making compromises, or to agree on the level of the lowest common denominator.

Once a policy or a new rule is finally agreed upon at the international or the European level, there remains the problem of its adoption and enactment. The ability of national representatives to commit the governments, central banks, or supervisory institutions they represent in negotiations to abide by the rules they formulate is strictly limited. Often the institutions whose representatives have participated in the formulation of a new policy or standard are not bound to comply with it. In democratic states, finance ministries, central banks, and national supervisory agencies whose heads or representatives have agreed to a new rule in international negotiations are subject to decisions taken by government and the parliament. Possibly in recognition of this fact, only the FSB formally demands compliance from the countries that are its members, with any rules adopted by its plenary. But there are few such rules, and compliance still depends on the goodwill of the member governments. The BCBS and IOSCO do not commit their member institutions to comply with any rules or standards they produce. The BCBS even points out explicitly that its standards have only the character of recommendations and need to be adopted and written into law by its member jurisdictions.

The effectiveness of international, including European, financial market governance is strictly limited by the sovereign powers of the states that must implement reforms demanded by the G20 and devised by international standard setters. The guiding logic of the policy processes involved in postcrisis regulatory reforms has therefore not been problem-solving, but at best bargaining among powerful nations. But since these same nations participate in the development of transnational norms, there exists an uneasy balance between sovereign states and the international community, including European institutions. States have lost more competences in the EU, which does have legislative powers. For better or for worse, the United States has today more sovereignty than member states of the European Union.

The question is whether more power for international institutions is needed, given the international structure of today's financial system – probably the most "globalized" among all policy fields. Decision-making in bodies like the G20 or the BCBS follows the logic of negotiation, but the internationalized structure of the financial system constrains the participating actors to try and find, in the very interest

of their countries, a viable transnational solution. Would a Global
Financial Government really come up with more effective solutions
to the risks inherent in the global financial market than can be agreed
in international negotiations? This question touches on a century-old
debate about the proper relation between state and market, politics
and the economy. Those who still believe, following Hayek and the
efficient market theory, in the superior efficiency of a self-regulating
transnational market will deny that international institutions of financial governance need more power over sovereign states – whereas
followers of Keynes and Polanyi who emphasize the negative consequences of laissez-faire will opt for more international control. Economists tend to embrace the first alternative, political scientists like myself
the second – the issue, I fear, is still undecided.

References

Admati, Anat, Martin Hellwig, 2013, *The Bankers' New Clothes: What's
    Wrong with Banking and What to Do about It.* Princeton: Princeton
    University Press
Alexandroff, Alan S., John Kirton, 2010, The "Great Recession" and the
    Emergence of the G20 Leaders' Summits. In: Alan S. Alexandroff, Andrew
    F. Cooper (eds.), *Rising States, Rising Institutions: Challenges for Global
    Governance.* Washington, D.C.: Brookings Institution Press, 177–195
Baker, Andrew, 2010, Deliberative International Financial Governance and
    Apex Policy Forums: Where We Are and Where We Should Be Headed.
    In: Geoffrey R. D. Underhill et al. (eds.), *Global Financial Integration
    Thirty Years On.* Cambridge: Cambridge University Press, 58–73
Barnett, Michael N., Martha Finnemore, 1999, The Power, Politics and
    Pathologies of International Organizations. *International Organization*
    53 (4), 699–737
Busch, Andreas, 2009, *Banking Regulation and Globalization.* Oxford:
    Oxford University Press
Davies, Howard, David Green, 2008, *Global Financial Regulation: The
    Essential Guide.* Cambridge: Polity Press
FSB Financial Stability Board, 2015, Implementation and Effects of the G20
    Financial Regulatory Reforms: Report of the Financial Stability Board
    to G20 Leaders. FSB 9 November 2015
Goodhart, Charles A. E., 2007, Financial Supervision from a Historical
    Perspective. In: Mayes and Wood op. cit., 43–64
G20 Group of Twenty, 2009, Final Summit Declaration: Pittsburgh Summit,
    2009. G20

Helleiner, Eric, Stefano Pagliari, Hubert Zimmermann (eds.), 2010, *Global Finance in Crisis: The Politics of International Regulatory Change.* London: Routledge

Howarth, David, Lucia Quaglia, 2014, The Steep Road to European Banking Union: Constructing the Single Resolution Mechanism. *Journal of Common Market Studies* 51 (1), 103–123

IEO Independent Evaluation Office, 2011, *IMF Performance in the Run-Up to the Financial and Economic Crisis: IMF Surveillance in 2004–07.* International Monetary Fund

Knight, Malcolm D., 2014, Reforming the Global Architecture of Financial Regulation. The G20, the IMF and the FSB. CIGI Papers No. 42, September 2014

Lütz, Susanne, 2009, Geld regiert die Welt, oder: Wer steuert die Globalisierung der Finanzmärkte? In: Volker Rittberger (ed.), *Wer regiert die Welt und mit welchem Recht?* Baden-Baden: Nomos, 73–95

Major, Aaron, 2012, Neoliberalism and the New International Financial Architecture. *Review of International Political Economy* 19 (4), 536–561

Mayes, David G., Geoffrey E. Wood, 2007, *The Structure of Financial Regulation.* London: Routledge

Mayntz, Renate (ed.) 2012, *Crisis and Control: Institutional Change in Financial Market Regulation.* New York: Campus

2015, International Institutions in the Process of Financial Market Reform. In: Renate Mayntz (ed.), *Negotiated Reform: The Multilevel Governance of Financial Regulation.* New York: Campus, 37–63

Moschella, Manuela, Eleni Tsingou (eds.), 2013, *Great Expectations, Slow Transformations: Incremental Change in Post-Crisis Regulation.* Colchester: ECPR Press

Quaglia, Lucia, 2012, The European Union and the Post-Crisis Multilevel Reform of Financial Regulation. In: Renate Mayntz (ed.), *Crisis and Control: Institutional Change in Financial Market Regulation,* New York: Campus, 97–119

Ruggie, John Gerard, 1982, International Regimes, Transactions, and Change: Embedded Liberalism in the Post-War Economic Order. In: *International Organization* 36, 379–415

Schoenmaker, Dirk, 2015, Firmer Foundations for a Stronger European Banking Union. Bruegel Working Paper 2015/13, November 2015

Viola, Lora Anne, 2015, The Governance Shift: From Multilateral IGOs to Orchestrated Networks. In: Renate Mayntz (ed.), *Negotiated Reform: The Multilevel Governance of Financial Regulation.* New York: Campus, 17–36

2 | Coping with the Dangerous Component of Capital Flows and Asia's Ineffective Cooperation

IWAN AZIS

Free flows of capital became a standard sermon of the International Monetary Fund (IMF) and other international financial institutions (IFIs) since 1980s.[1] It is at the heart of financial and capital account liberalization (KAL) that promises a better way to allocate capital, greater opportunities to savers and investors, and ease of financial innovation, all of which can lead to higher economic growth. KAL is also expected to build discipline to secure macroeconomic stability.

The evidence confirms that many countries have indeed experienced a jump in economic growth post-KAL. But most of them subsequently experienced instability. Some even failed to escape from a crisis. It is no coincidence that the frequency of financial turmoil reached an all-time high during the 1990s, starting from the Exchange Rate Mechanism (ERM) crisis in Europe in 1992, the tequila crisis of Mexico in 1994, the Asian Financial Crisis (AFC) in 1997, the Russian crisis in 1998, and the Long-Term Capital management crisis in the United States during the same year. The game changer, however, did not begin until the 2008 Global Financial Crisis (GFC) erupted.

Capital flows have played a major role in the AFC and the GFC. In both episodes, the shock was preceded by massive capital inflows. The contagion of the crisis was forceful. In the GFC case, it started with the US subprime crisis before the spillovers were felt globally. In the case of AFC, the trouble began in Thailand before spreading to other Asian countries. The early hope for Asia's cooperation in financial safety nets following the AFC turned out to be a disappointment. The utter failure of global regulations as discussed by Mayntz in Chapter 1 and the emerging "financial nationalism" in advanced economies (AE) do

---

[1] The catch phrase "Washington Consensus" introduced by John Williamson (1990) reinforced the argument favoring unrestricted capital flows.

not bode well for efforts to reduce the risks of capital flows.[2] It is argued in this chapter that as long as capital flows and the risks persist, it is imperative for individual countries to cope with the problems by putting a damper on some components of capital flows.

Asian Financial Crisis (AFC)

The 1997 AFC marked a turning point in Asia. The praise towards the region's economic performance before summer 1997 appeared in many articles, books, and reports, including those published by the IMF, the World Bank, and the Asian Development Bank. They failed to predict correctly where the Asian economies were heading for. Even when the signs of trouble and contagion had clearly emerged, in late 1997 the Fund continued to predict no major crisis in the region.[3] As soon as the 1997 crisis broke out, these institutions began to propagate a sharply different analysis. All of a sudden, the very same countries previously praised for their policies and remarkable performances were swiftly coined as economies with misplaced development strategies (Azis, 2005).

Confronted with such an embarrassing contradiction, the IFIs were quick to claim that they *saw* the faults and had *reminded* the governments about weak banking systems, flawed institutions, and widespread corruption. The role of frictionless capital flows under KAL in causing the crisis, however, had never been questioned. It took a major shock of the scale of 2008 GFC to wake them up to the reality of capital flows. After decades of preaching the virtues of cross-border capital flows, the IMF has now conceded that some restrictions on capital flows can help protect the economy from financial turmoil (IMF, 2012). Experts now acknowledge that the "First Best"

---

[2] Emerging "financial nationalism" is discussed among others in James (2009) and Azis and Shin (2015b), and Azis (2016).

[3] In its *World Economic Outlook 1996*, the IMF's comments on Asia reads: "the prospect of a fourth consecutive year of very high growth was welcomed." The Fund's forecast for 1998 were: 3.5 percent, 6.2 percent, and 6 percent for Thailand, Indonesia, and Korea, respectively (IMF, *World Economic Outlook 1997*). These three are the most severely hit countries during the AFC. Such forecast was way off from what actually happened: −9.4 percent, −13.7 percent, and −5.8 percent, respectively. The World Bank's forecast was equally off. But the most overly optimistic was that of the Asian Development Bank: 6.6 percent, 7.9 percent, and 6.9 percent (ADB's *Asian Development Outlook, 1997–1998*).

approach of financial liberalization – where frictionless flows are
venerated – is faulty and should be replaced by an alternative approach
where financial regulation is given far greater importance and capital
controls are no longer taboo (CIEPR, 2012). Central to the shift is
the need to maintain financial stability and macro-prudential policy
(Azis & Shin, 2015a).

We know now that the major culprit behind the 1997 crisis was
the excessive borrowing by the private sector that caused a double
mismatch: debt in foreign currency versus spending and returns in
local currency (currency mismatch); and a large share of debt was
short-term – less-than 1-year maturity – used to finance long term
projects (maturity mismatch). While the region's relatively sound macro
fundamentals may have supported the debt surge, the trend was made
possible by a regime of free flows of capital following KAL. Over-
emphasizing the role of the earlier and undermining the risks of the
latter, in "The East Asian Miracle" the World Bank claimed that
"favorable feedback from other policies enabled the four HPAEs that
did borrow abroad – Indonesia, Korea, Malaysia, and Thailand – to
sustain debt better than other developing economies." Note that HPAE
stands for High Performing Asian Economies, and the publication was
in 1993, the year when private debt began to surge. The rest is history.

The Fund's recommended policies after the crisis focused on factors
unrelated to KAL and capital flows: to create greater transparency
in financial markets, and fix institutional factors such as minimizing
state intervention, dismantling state-owned enterprises, and removing
corruption (Stiglitz, 2007). On the macro side, the IFI's recommended
a standard prescription: fiscal austerity, monetary tightening, and no
bail-out of distressed firms/banks, which essentially favored creditors
and punished debtors. Again, questions over the risks of free flows of
capital never took a center stage.[4] Delayed recovery, worsened socio-
economic conditions, and growing instability were the outcome of
such misplaced analysis and policies.

The Fund also insisted that countries in crisis had to do away with
most State intervention including activities by the state-owned enterprises (SOEs) despite the fact that they were far from the reasons
that caused the crisis. The two largest Asian countries, India and
China, had a large share of SOEs, but they resisted capital account

---

[4] See also Andreas Nölke's Chapter 7.

liberalization and both were spared the crisis. The Fund's standard prescriptions of no bail-out and fiscal-monetary austerity ignored the fact that different type of crisis requires different measures. They may be appropriate for a first-generation crisis like in Latin America during the 1980s but not for the AFC. Socioeconomic conditions deteriorated fast. In the case of Indonesia, massive demonstrations followed by arson and looting forced President Suharto to bow the public pressure and resigned. It is also interesting to note that in the 2007–8 crisis, the policy response of the United States was the opposite of those prescriptions (bailing out financial institutions, loosening the fiscal stand, and easing monetary policy).

Regional Cooperation

A turning point in Asia's regional cooperation came after the AFC. Out of the disappointment with the IMF's handling of the crisis, authorities in thirteen countries (later known as the ASEAN+3 – 10 ASEAN countries plus China, Japan and Korea) made an attempt to cooperate more closely. An early proposal initiated by Japan to set up an Asian Monetary Fund (AMF) was shelved because of the rejection by the United States, which argued that Asia's capacity to provide resources for a regional financial safety net in terms of both financial resources and capacity to do surveillance was limited.[5] A lack of China's support for the AMF (because they were not consulted by Tokyo beforehand) was another factor. Many suspect the real reason for rejection was a fear of duplication and competition that could undermine the IMF's role and credibility. That, however, did not stop authorities from pursuing further cooperation.

Beginning with a series of bilateral swaps, in 2010 a new arrangement of regional financial safety was set up, known as the Chiang Mai Initiative (CMI), which was eventually multilateralized, hence CMIM.[6] This multilateral currency swap arrangement marked the beginning of a more institutionalized cooperation (Azis, 2011). The woes of double

---

[5] Such an argument clearly ignored the fact that financial resources and capacity can be built overtime.

[6] Swap is an arrangement where a foreign central bank agrees to sell a specified amount of its currency to the central bank of another country in exchange for the currency of the latter (usually hard currency such as US dollar) at the prevailing market exchange rate.

mismatch and banks' limited capacity to finance the badly needed infrastructure (hard and soft) led the authorities in ASEAN+3 to focus on the development of a local currency bond market through the Asian Bond Market Initiative (ABMI). One of the ABMI's creation was the Credit Guarantee Investment Facility (CGIF) designed to facilitate the use of local currency bonds for infrastructure development. The Asian Bond Market Forum (ABMF) is another initiative intended to serve as a common platform for pursuing standardization of market regulation and practices (Azis, 2014a). These initiatives reflect a clear intention to do away with short-term borrowing in foreign currencies, as well as to facilitate efforts to recycle regional savings (since the AFC, the region has transformed from excess-investments to excess savings).

Interestingly, this stronger cooperation emerged amid geopolitical tensions and growing rivalry among the "+3." Individually, each of the "+3" (China, Japan, and Korea) also intensified their efforts to strengthen cooperation with ASEAN countries, resulting in more trans-actions and greater cross-border flows. A trend is likely to emerge where overseas direct investment by the "+3" will increasingly use local currencies.

But as far as financial cooperation is concerned, not everything is as rosy as expected. The safety net provided by the CMIM is far from what it should be. The progress has been slow, and the process often collides with flagging political will. As a result, rather than using the CMIM facility, most countries opted for bilateral swaps, including with non-members. For example, during the heightened financial stress in 2008, Korea and Singapore approached the US Federal Reserve, each asked for US$30 billion "swap" lines of credit. ASEAN countries also did not use CMIM facilities; they too preferred the bilateral swap arrangements.

Optimists argue that it is because the region has done quite well that no external help including from the CMIM was needed. But the fact is, some had looked for swap arrangements. Also, discussions with policy makers in the region indicate that some may have been taking advan-tage of the CMIM facility had it been ready and not suffering from fundamental inconsistencies. One of such inconsistencies is the adop-tion of the IMF-link, where only 30 percent of CMIM borrowing quota can be taken without linking it to IMF programs. This is clearly inconsistent with the *raison d'être* of CMIM. Given the short-term nature of the facility (ninety days), and recognizing the fact that the effect of any attached conditionality will last much longer, adopting such a link makes very little sense. Not to mention that borrowing from the IMF sends negative signals to the public and markets alike (IMF *stigma*).

Questions are also raised as to the small size of financial resources committed by member countries (only less-than 5 percent of total ASEAN+3's foreign reserves). Not less fundamentally, the notion that only some ASEAN countries – not the "+3" – are the likely users of the facility is clearly misguided. It undermines the risk of contagion that the "+3" may be hit with, even when the crisis originates in ASEAN countries. As an analogy, one can think of the European Financial Stability Facility (EFSF).[7] Imagine if in designing its facility, the EFSF used the assumptions that during a crisis only some members, say periphery countries, and not other members, can use the facility when the crisis originates in Eurozone periphery. That would reflect a dangerous and absurd assumption that crisis in the periphery will never create contagion to nonperiphery countries. The essence of a regional financial safety net is precisely to minimize the possibility of contagion.

Global Financial Crisis (GFC)

The importance of financial safety nets cannot be over-emphasized especially with the growing uncertainties in global financial conditions following the GFC. As the fall in the housing market (subprime crisis) in the United States spread across border, following the fall of the Lehman Brothers, global banks operating in the United States, particularly those headquartered in Europe, were forced to deleverage. A large sum of money raised by these banks in the US money market was invested in emerging markets (EM) especially in Asia. Thus, the deleveraging squeezed EM liquidity. When the global markets eventually took a severe hit, market confidence reached an all-time low. At the same time, global trade also collapsed. What started as a domestic subprime crisis in the United States ended with the GFC.

For emerging Asia, the low interest rates in AEs since mid-2000 have caused a surge in capital inflows. At first, most of the flows wound

---

[7] The European Financial Stability Facility (EFSF) was set up in 2010. It issues bonds, but not loans, as a temporary solution for Eurozone members hit by a crisis.

up in the banking sector (bank-led flows). The subsequent quantitative easing (QE) policy, which is essentially a large-scale asset purchase program to halt the precipitous fall in the US asset prices, created an even more significant spillover in the region. While bank-led flows continued, after the QE another round of inflows came through the capital market especially the debt market (debt-led flows), driven primarily by search-for-yield amid low returns in AE. Despite a lot of talk about policy coordination and cooperation, including in the G20, the QE policy was taken unilaterally, irrespective of its spillovers to other countries (an emerging form of "financial nationalism").

This was not the sovereign country's "fault" (i.e., the Fed). It is rather the responsibility of the IMF (notably) to counter "spillovers" given the IFIs' main responsibility is to maintain global economic stability. By definition, they should persuade countries to avoid adopting policy that will create negative externalities to others. QE falls in this category. Chapter 1 also shows that the original purpose of establishing the IMF, WTO, and World Bank was precisely to maintain world stability. Past episodes demonstrate that they did it quite forcefully to "less strong" countries, e.g., the WTO punished China and others for protection and deliberate currency devaluation; the IMF pressed developing countries to remove any controls on finance and capital. But when it comes to policy taken by the United States and other "strong" countries they seem not "to see" the negative externality to others. Yet, the effect on the rest of the world is clearly significant.

Indeed, the size of capital inflows to emerging Asia has been larger and more volatile than during the pre-1997 period. As a result, there was a large expansion of liquidity. The depressed cost of borrowing spurred credit creation and economic growth. But at the same time, it also elevated the overall risks of financial instability.

With plenty of liquidity and the low cost of borrowing, banks and other institutions shifted their preference toward risky investing. Banks used the inflows-driven liquidity to expand credits for risky sectors like property and real estate, and to invest in financial assets such as securities and equities rather than investing in productive activities. In some countries, this led to property and financial bubbles.

When capital inflows subsequently flocked to the capital market, fund managers played as the protagonists. Facing pressures on short-term performance, most of them preferred quick returns and were more willing to tolerate riskier investment. Increased reward on the upside and reduced penalty on the downside provided further incentives for fund managers to be pro-cyclical. In the public sector, the low cost of borrowing also motivated governments to raise debt, including foreign currency debt. Everyone took advantage of the cheap money and fast growing financial sector during the "party" time. Everyone danced with the tune.

But this also helped to exacerbate the skewed distribution of wealth and income ("Piketty moment") as only a tiny portion of the population – mostly urban-rich – owned or had access to the fast-growing financial sector; and the economy's capacity to generate employment (measured by "the employment elasticity") declined, because the growing preference for financial assets implies a far lower investment in factories, machinery, infrastructure, and other job-creating activities (Azis, 2014b). In retrospect, the (privately) rational behavior of agents was far from socially optimal.

Nonetheless, the capital inflows-driven growth of financial sector improved the standard macroeconomic data including the GDP growth in emerging Asia. But the risks of financial instability also increased. The episode during summer 2013 provided a clear evidence when the then Fed chairman Ben Bernanke floated the idea of gradually reducing or "tapering" the QE. His remarks immediately sparked a sell-off in the US market. The effect then spread quickly to all emerging markets including in Asia where some capital began to leave, causing the currencies, bond, and equity prices to move sharply. All these occurred despite the fact that there was actually no change in the US policy.[8] At least not yet. As the Fed eventually raised the rate in 2014, outflows surged in 2015. As a result, for the first time since 1988 the recorded net capital flows in all emerging markets turned negative.

Putting A Damper

The lesson from the AFC, the GFC, and most crisis episodes for that matter, is that capital flows could be very risky. Some components easily deceive recipients by creating a perceived strength while at the same time raising the debt and encouraging risky behavior,

---

[8] In reality, bond purchases as part of QE did not end until more than one year later (October 2014), and the first reversal of US federal fund rate occurred only more than two years later (December 2015).

all of which makes the system vulnerable to flows reversal. There are hence plenty of reasons to put a damper on those dangerous components.[9] Doing so is equivalent to discouraging risky behavior. It has been clearly shown that risky behavior will not only raise the probability of a crisis but also worsen the income inequality since the latter depends critically on how agents manage and use the inflowing capital (Azis, 2014b).

An example of risky component of capital inflows is bank debt (bank-led flows). The growth of such inflows enlarges banks' liability and hence banks' balance sheet. As a result, in conducting their operations banks are no longer constrained by the size of core and traditional source of liquidity such as savings and deposits. Additional sources of liquidity from capital inflows-driven debt, or noncore liability, allow them to be more expansionary and more risk-taking. As discussed earlier, this could threaten financial stability. It is on this component of inflows that a levy is proposed to be imposed. With such a levy, debt is expected to be lower, so are the incentives for risky behavior (a kind of crisis prevention). But imposing a levy on banks during good times can also strengthen the authority's capacity to manage a crisis during bad times, as they can use the money from the levy to bail out failing banks, a kind of safety nets for crisis resolution.

Having gone through banking crisis, countries like the UK, Germany, France, and the US realize the merit of imposing a levy. In the G20 forum, they are the proponents of imposing a global bank levy too. On the other hand, those rarely experiencing banking problems, Canada and Australia, for example, may not see the importance of it as reflected in their persistence to water down the proposal. For an emerging Asia who are among the major recipients of capital inflows, it is important to consider such a measure because of their relatively open capital account system. To the extent bank-led flows cause banks' risky behavior and the latter tends to exacerbate the income inequality problem, the region could reap additional benefits from implementing the measure.

Outcomes from the Korean experience are noteworthy. Hit hard by the 1997 AFC and the 2008 GFC, the source of vulnerability in both

---

[9] After decades of promoting unrestricted capital flows, the IMF has finally acknowledged the merit of capital controls of this sort (Ostry et al. 2012; Gosh et.al. 2016).

cases was a rapid build-up of short-term foreign currency debt driven by capital inflows resulting from cheap and abundant money. The evidence was clearly displayed by the rapid growth of Korean banks' liquidity from debt, not from the core sources such as savings and deposits; hence, rising noncore rather than core liability. Realizing the risks of such a trend, in 2010 Korea announced the imposition of levy on noncore liabilities. The new measure was eventually adopted in 2011. This was taken after implementing other measures (e.g., imposing a leverage cap on the notional value of foreign currency derivatives contracts that banks could maintain). The levy rate was set at twenty basis points for short-term foreign exchange-denominated liabilities of up to one year, falling to five basis points for liabilities exceeding five years. Unlike the levy in the United Kingdom, the proceeds in Korea were held in a special account under the Exchange Stabilization Account managed by the finance ministry, because the main purpose is to maintain financial stability, although they can also be used as part of official foreign exchange reserves.

The impact of the levy imposition in Korea shows that total inflows did not fall but the composition changed towards a much lower share of short-term inflows; hence a lower share of non-core liability. Based on a panel study comprising forty-eight economies, Bruno and Shin (2014) found that in contrast to other economies, after a levy was introduced, capital flows into Korea have also become less sensitive to global supply-push factors.[10]

In general, however, understanding the mechanisms of how a levy on bank-led flows affects banks' operation is important, particularly for the purpose of determining the levy rate. Obviously, a country's stage of financial development and structure matter. For the levy to be effective, the preferred rate could be different for different countries. To shed some light on this, a stylistic model can be used. The details of such a model is presented in the Appendix. What follows is the intuition behind the model.

---

[10] Other ideas are Fantacci and Gobbi's Chapter 4 on Keynes's "bancor"; another is Tom Palley's Asset-Based Reserve Requirements that aims to give central banks powers to raise or lower the amount of dangerous/safer loans, respectively, for asset trading. It is discussed in Chapter 9 on inequalities; the Tobin Tax in the Introduction is a way to reduce high speed trading, not long-term investment. Neither brings much revenue, nor has success, unlike this proven Korean scheme.

In deciding their operations to generate highest revenues, banks decide the size and composition of their balance sheet. While that may give the best outcome for individual banks, nevertheless it may not be optimal for the entire financial system and societal interest. For example, when the costs of money are low due to massive capital inflows, individual banks may wish to raise debt, hence inflating the size of the balance sheet, to enable them to expand operations that will boost revenues. But the resulting credit boom can lead to bubbles and heightened vulnerability (e.g., credits to risky sector). When the bubbles burst, the internal buffer may not be adequate to cover the loss. With the presence of systemic risks, often undermined in standard vulnerability indicators, the entire financial system is affected and a crisis may ensue. Thus, what may be best for individual banks can actually contradict with societal interests by elevating the risks of financial instability.

The proposed levy is intended precisely to minimize such risks. But the size of the levy has to be determined carefully by considering the prevailing economic cycle and the market conditions; not one size fits all. To begin with, the decision of individual banks about their operations is influenced by the following factors: the leverage costs, interest rates, returns on assets, the balance sheet position, and the cost to meet the rules and standards such as the capital adequacy ratio (CAR). Concerned with the potential systemic risks, policy makers, and regulators need to make sure that the resulting decision by individual banks will not jeopardize financial stability. Thus, they need to figure out some sort of benchmark level of banks' operation that will ensure such stability, and design a corresponding policy instrument to achieve it. In essence, what they try to minimize is the so-called "loss function," which is the difference between the level at which individual banks prefer to operate and the benchmark level (similar to the logic of avoiding "too big to fail"). If a levy is the intended instrument, policy makers need to determine the rate. In so doing, they will have to consider the prevailing economic cycle.[11]

Obviously, there is a question of what is the money from the levy for. Two distinct views are notable. The first is to treat the levy as an

---

[11] If a bank levy is to be imposed at the global level, as has been considered in the G20 forum, the size of the levies is likely to be smaller than otherwise to keep a reasonably level playing field. A global agreement is also needed to avoid double taxation when a bank from a country imposing a levy has branches in another levy-imposing country.

instrument of insurance scheme; the second is to treat the levy as an instrument to deter and discourage bank-led flows altogether. While both are valid, the problem with the first view is that there is a risk the levy will make banks see that raising debt is no longer risky because it is insured, and consequently it fails to reduce bank debt. At any rate, the money raised should not be part of government revenues in the regular budget; instead it should be channeled into a special fund that could be used to pay for the cost of cleaning up future banking crises (financial safety nets).

Closing Remarks

Episodes of crisis including the AFC and the GFC clearly show that unrestricted capital flows can be dangerous. The key point of the analysis in this chapter is that a levy can act as an additional lever to dampen the growth of bank-led flows, one of the dangerous components of capital flows. While the scheme has been discussed also at the global level through various fora including the G20, each country should set its own standard. Imposing a levy at the national level can be part of comprehensive efforts to secure financial stability in the midst of massive capital flows. It is a part of macro-prudential policy; at the same time it is also a form of domestic financial safety nets.

Given the spillover effects of AE's unilateral policy and the risks of contagion while regional cooperation such as the CMIM remains far from effective, for emerging Asia the proposed measure makes a lot of sense.

Appendix

Increased capital flows driven by the ultra-easy money policy in AEs bring down the cost of borrowing q. This gives incentives for banks to increase foreign currency borrowing (recorded as the noncore liability, labeled L^{NC}, in the balance sheet). With growing debt-led flows, banks' capacity to lend can increase beyond whatever savings and deposits (the core liability, L^C) that they have. The unit cost for L^C is w. Banks have also to pay the cost for keeping a certain level of capital adequacy ratio CAR as part of the standards imposed by the authority, the unit cost of which is v. Hence, given the returns on asset r, the banks' total net returns are the difference between gross returns $r.A$ and the total costs incurred by them:

$$r.A - q.L^{NC} - w.L^C - v.CAR.A$$

If levy (l) is to be imposed, there will be additional costs. How much would that be depends on the bank' relative size or asset size A/Y where Y is the level of national output, since the growth of banks' asset is driven primarily by noncore liability or bank-led flows. Considering the potential systemic risks, the imposed levy is expected to be progressive. Thus, the total costs of levy are specified $0.5\ (l.\ A^2/Y)$, that is, the levy is higher when banks expand too rapidly. Hence banks' total net returns to be maximized subject to the balance sheet are:

$$Max\left[r.A - q.L^{NC} - w.L^C - v.CAR.A\right] - 0.5\,l^{A^2}\big/{}_Y$$

where the balance sheet is $A = L^{NC} + L^C + CAR.A$,

the solution of which is ${}^{A^*}\big/{}_Y = \dfrac{r - q + (q - v).CAR}{l}$

This is what banks decide in terms of their level of operation. From the policy makers' perspectives however, that may not be in line with the level that will not jeopardize financial stability because the banks' decision does not take into account the growing systemic risks. What the policy makers try to do is therefore to minimize the so called "loss function" which is the difference between $(A*/Y)$ and the benchmark level set by policy makers denoted by $(A/Y)^T$. In square terms:

$$Min_l \left[{}^{A*}/_Y - {}^{A^T}/_Y \right]^2$$

How is $(A/Y)^T$ determined? Policy makers may want to consider the prevailing economic cycle such as how far the current level and growth of the economy deviates from the potentials. A particular rule can be used. Denoting the level gap (also known as the output gap) by $YGAP$, and the growth gap by $gYGAP$, the following rule can be applied: when the economy is right on the potential path (no deviation), the benchmark level is $(A/Y)^T = \theta_1$. If it is lower (higher) than the potential path, the level should be lower (higher) than θ_1:

$$\left({}^A/_Y \right)^T = \theta_1 \text{ if } YGAP = gYGAP = 0$$
$$\left({}^A/_Y \right)^T < \theta_1 \text{ if } YGAP > 0; \text{ and } gYGAP > 0$$
$$\left({}^A/_Y \right)^T > \theta_1 \text{ if } YGAP < 0; \text{ and } gYGAP < 0$$

When the prevailing economic condition is overheating (the level and growth of output is greater than the potential level), the benchmark needs to be adjusted downward, and vice-versa. In general, therefore, the benchmark level can be written: $(\theta_1 - \theta_2.YGAP - \theta_3.gYGAP)$ where parameters θ_2 and θ_3 represent the adjustment part. In particular θ_3 reflects the speed at which the gap between potential and actual growth of output is closing.

Thus, after acquiring information about the level of operation banks wish to conduct $(A*/Y)$, the optimal size of levy $(0 < l < l_{max})$ that policy makers may impose will be governed by:

$$Min_l \left[{}^{A*}/_Y - (\theta_1 - \theta_2.YGAP - \theta_3.gYGAP) \right]^2$$

Or, through substitution,

$$Min_l \left[\frac{r - q + (q - v).CAR}{l} - (\theta_1 - \theta_2.YGAP - \theta_3.gYGAP) \right]^2$$

the first-order conditions of which is

$$-2\left[\frac{(r-q+(q-v).CAR)}{l^2}\right]$$
$$\left[\frac{r-q+(q-v).CAR}{l}-(\theta_1-\theta_2.YGAP-\theta_3.gYGAP)\right]=0$$

The solution for the optimal level of levy is:

$$l^*=\frac{r-q+(q-v).CAR}{\theta_1-\theta_2.YGAP-\theta_3.gYGAP}$$

It is clear that the proposed size of levy l^* is not "one size fits all" since it is not independent of the market conditions (reflected by r, q and v), the prevailing rule of CAR, and the size of banks' operation (A^*/Y) that gets larger when capital inflows surge.

References

Azis, Iwan J (2005). "IMF Perspectives and Alternative Views on the Asian Crisis," in P. Gangopadhyay and M. Chatterji (eds.) *Economics of Globalisation*, Ashgate, England.

(2011). "Assessing Asian Economic Integration with Cautionary Notes," *Journal of Northeast Asia Development*, 13, p. 17–42.

(2014a) "Capital Market in the Context of Financial Safety Nets," in *Asian Capital Market Development and Integration: Challenges and Opportunities*, Oxford University Press.

(2014b) "Integration, Contagion, and Income Distribution," in Nijkamp, Peter; Rose, Adam; Kourtit, Karima (eds.) *Regional Science Matters*, Springer.

with Hyun Song Shin (2015a). *Managing Elevated Risk: Global Liquidity, Capital Flows, and Macroprudential Policy – an Asian Perspective*, Springer.

with Hyun Song Shin, eds. (2015b). *Global Shock, Asian Vulnerability and Financial Reform*, Edward Elgar.

(2016) "Four-G Episode and the Elevated Risks," *Asian Pacific Economic Literature*, Wiley.

Bruno, Valentina and Hyun Song Shin. (2014). "Assessing Macroprudential Policies: The Case of South Korea." *Scandinavian Journal of Economics*. 116(1). pp. 128–157.

Committee on International Economic Policy and Reform (CIEPR) (2012). *Banks and Cross-Border Capital Flows: Policy Challenges and Regulatory Responses*, Washington D.C., September.

Ghosh, Atish R., Jonathan D. Ostry, and Mahvash S. Qureshi. (2016). "When Do Capital Inflow Surges End in Tears?" *American Economic Review*, 106(5): 581–85.

International Monetary Fund (IMF), (2012). *The Liberalization and Management of Capital Flows: An Institutional View*, Washington D.C., November 14.

James, Harold (2009). *The Creation and Destruction of Value*, Cambridge, MA: Harvard University Press.

Ostry, Jonathan D., Atish R. Ghosh and Anton Korinek (2012). "Multilateral Aspects of Managing the Capital Account," *IMF Staff Discussion Note*, September (Washington, DC: International Monetary Fund).

Stiglitz, Joseph (2007). "10 Years after the Asian Crisis," *Daily Star*, July.

Williamson, John, ed. (1990). *Latin American Adjustment: How Much Has Happened?* Washington, DC: Institute for International Economics.

3 | How Mobile Capital Plays Off Democracy
The Euro and Other Monetary Federations

JOCELYN PIXLEY

Capitalist money often seems an innocent token for meeting people's desires in markets, yet it is based on flimsy relations of debts–credits shared between financial sectors and governments. The global financial crisis (GFC) started in 2007 when UK and US global banks bankrupted each other and money nearly disappeared. Their governments acted, but mobile capital networks were extensive; European banks were in this with the others. Amidst capital withdrawals, panic and likely world recession, financial sectors' attention shifted, hysterically, to the Euro and each member state. Long oblivious to consequences, their institutional petulance wreaked havoc on the main debtors, firms and households, while governments saved banks.

Banks have not changed, we saw (Chapter 1), and took similar paths with the Euro crisis as with the Asian Financial Crisis (AFC) of 1997 (Chapter 2). The Euro, then ten years old, became the single (simplistic) focus, averting eyes from the same financial centres that created the AFC then GFC. Having sold debt for purposes with no lasting benefit, such as property bubbles, banks thereupon proclaimed 'Europe' as the alleged problem. Market players (banks, funds) panicked, desperate to recoup losses and pick over carcasses. This panic again demonstrated that market assumptions about money as a handy thing, a commodity for productive investment and exchange is one-sided. Money's social relations involve unstable options. US banks sold packaged debt for bubbles. Afterwards, lurid stories, serious distress and blame-casting swirled about the European Union, as it had about Asia, the United States and the United Kingdom. What was this 'thing' called the Euro?

This chapter deals with the social mechanisms of money behind the devastation for European member states: soaring unemployment and suicide rates, foreclosures, industrial collapses and deflation. Huge benefits accrued to banks: higher interest from member-states, higher debt values and bank bailouts, some of which were masked. Stepping back from the decade's gloom, I compare the European Monetary Union (EMU) with the US, Australian and Canadian monetary federations. I include the United Kingdom, often taken to be a mono-state with full monetary sovereignty.

In contrasting the EMU-Euro with old, messy, often terrible experiences of the US$, CAN$, AU$ and UK sterling, this chapter accepts fully Renate Mayntz's account of the dearth of *global* governance and over-reliance on market 'solutions'. Later chapters amplify these, and the US hegemonic currency (cf. the Euro) is explored in Chapter 6. Mine is a view of the Euro from an outsider of an old democratic federated country regarded as a nobody in world financial affairs (luckily, I think). Money is 'a space of exception', as Geoff Mann (2013) says; however, the monetary stories of Australian or Canadian full capitalist money and labour systems that are, or were, subversively egalitarian are *modest* counter-exceptions.

I give thumbnail sketches of the social forces involved in the full monetary unions, not the complexities of each EU member state. I explain what monetary federation has fitfully entailed with these diverse examples of compromises and divisions. Analyses of social-political conflicts over state money and bank money production are rarely applied anywhere, therefore, there are no hard and fast *rules*, whether of the dire monetarists or the civil, kinder Keynesians. The Euro is no more about *mistakes* than sterling in the 'UK', or dollar in Canada, or profit seeking banks playing off countries and provinces everywhere.[1]

The Allegedly Flawed Euro Monetary Federation

The coherent criticisms of the Euro are that EU member states voluntarily surrendered their monetary sovereignty. Critics were mainly English chartalists, that is, with a state theory of money that criticizes pro-market distinctions between fiscal and monetary policies as fiction.

---

[1] Poking fun at all banks, Admati & Hellwig *The Bankers' New Clothes* 2013 look at 'what is wrong' (not fully, but amusingly). See Josh Ryan-Collins, 2015 on Canadian debates; Australia's situation is regressive but its central bank is subversive: both offer hope to Europeans. See Ingham, 2011 on conflicts to control money production.

Monetarists loved the Euro idea. If this is surrender to mobile capital, I suggest it is widespread in all jurisdictions, and favouritism to finance is hardly voluntary.

Euro member states no longer have a sovereign currency to manipulate, with its damages and bonuses for different social groups and sectors. Impoverished Yorkshire never did. Money always distributes up and down, whether with external exchange rates or internal central bank rates. That remains perennial in federations and mono-systems. If there is 'fair' redistribution, central banks can lend to distressed areas (as in Canada). Taxes can shape sectors needing a slow down or encouragement, and (in all three federations) fiscal transfers are ruled by economic ups and downs of each state/province. My argument is a Treasury's power to devalue/revalue is not like social and economic policies to compensate differences. Europe has the oldest, most social democratic parties of labour; but a EU break-up to devalue against Germany, when the EU 'rest' must import Germany's capital goods, is hardly sensible, we see.

Before moving to central banks and democratic processes, I make three initial points. Among the democracies, no federation is better (or worse) than mono-states in controlling global financial threats so, in that regard, I do not see the EU as especially doomed; remedies are possible. Second, money is a social relation, not a technical commodified thing to be manipulated via the 'US one best way'. Third, the inordinate reliance on monetary policy is not economic, but politically advantages financial sectors. Independent central banks are allegedly free from elected governments, though are not, in ways hidden to the public. With the European Central Bank (ECB), granted, it is unclear what its independence is from when there is no European treasury. Yet everywhere monetary policy favours the pecuniary classes, and *creates* winners and losers. Central banks can create depression-crushers via fighting wage and price inflations but can do virtually nothing against asset and bank-money inflations. Other than not prolonging depressions with high rates, *reflations* or Quantitative Easing foster asset bubbles but cannot get economies out of deflations; treasuries and other centralized institutions can help – or make depression far worse. After the GFC, Europe (and banks) demanded austerity of member states that made debt's value grow further. Britain's crueler fiscal policy had similar aims.

The EU Expansion to Euro Money

Money-creation of *banks* that all states (and Euro member states) rely upon is at odds with the inordinate praise given to 'creditors'. Orthodoxy says that savers depositing 'their' money in banks are the untouchable creditors who make loans possible via innocent bankers. But banking practice (see Introduction) is to 'deposit loans' in the whole banking system. Loans – banks' source of profits and recently via trading assets and financial claims, 'securitized' IOUs (Admati & Hellwig 2013: 86) – are often directed to asset trading, to consumer debts and property bubbles, not productive ventures. Hyman Minsky pointed out banks are merchants of debt and instability is permanent. Creditors, or rather guarantors or gamblers on future loan servicing, cannot profit without debtors. Neither bankers nor politicians want to see this.

For years, the EU gathered for diverse reasons. Pan-European proponents aimed for cultural, political or trading unions, such as the 1929 French and German peace plans of Briand and Stresemann; doomed (Tooze 2014:491–3). Postwar, the 'imaginary' money union fostered mutual promises, like Keynes's bancor that Fantacci and Gobbi (next Chapter 4) describe, and a Common Market. Of note, the *Community* was no mere economistic idea, nor vaguely cultural; it had social democratic aims to further peace, justice and diversity.

Nevertheless, as positive ideas of an EU developed, in the United Kingdom and United States a mean-spirited approach emerged in the late 1970s that, above all, relinquished the wartime–postwar 'financial repression' and union truces to pushing profit for the dominant money centres, Wall Street, the City, *rentier* classes and US war machine. That US and UK central banks were temporarily progressive (30–40 years), far less than others in the OECD, made the switch easy! Monetary policy was 'maestro' again for Bank of England (BoE) and Fed 'technocrats'. Also, London bankers were long involved in Europe.

Early in those 1970s, EMU-Euro ideas magnified out of defensive attempts to ease pressures from the hegemon US$ of President Nixon's inflation-deflation switches and decision to float the dollar. Germany and France were dissatisfied with 'America's geopolitical leadership' and dollar weakness, until Volcker drastically *stopped* the US economy in 1980. The harsh Bundesbank lost briefly (Oppenheimer 1998: 60) to

Helmut Schmidt and German industrial lobbies wanting reflation.
In 1978, the European Monetary System had its key features agreed
in the European Commission, but Wall Street was spreading. There
is much debate as to how far the EU aimed ambitiously for a Euro
challenge to the US$ hegemon, which was not to be (Chapter 6).
A key consideration remains to what extent the monetary union has
been Europe's biggest problem since the GFC, with the inability of
member states to devalue as in the past. Surely austerity, delicate
fiscal transfers, fair wages and lack of a 'stern' financial union *against*
banks are part of the story. One orthodox argument was that the
EMU would make significant savings in transaction costs, but savings
have been 'fairly small on any estimate' (Forder 1998: 39).

Wall Street rose further with Nixon's dollar float, and a quantity
view of money returned, which held that governments were the sole
source of 1970s inflation through their 'excessive' money creation.
Eyes averted from fractional reserve *bank money creation*, as well,
from trade unions wage demands, corporations price rises and private banks asset inflations, except that central banks, notably the
US Fed and Bundesbank raised interest rates against the wage-price
spiral. As stagnation set in from 1980 onwards, UK and US bank
money creation expanded. In fact, neoclassical assumptions against
'irresponsible' EU governments ignored that financial markets might
'lend too much' and that money markets can be incompetent too
(Forder 1998: 40). High-Powered Money (HPM), that is cash, meaning state notes/coins, the more trustworthy money via the coercion
of taxes than bank money, dropped. At present the ratio is 3:97
state:bank money (UK) from roughly 50:50 before 1970 to earliest
records.[2]

Jacques Reland (1998: 103) repeatedly suggests that financial globalization was a greater loss of European sovereignty than EU constraints.
'To the extent that capital is internationally mobile, it is a problem' in
any case (Forder 1998: 39). A 1987 OECD report urged France to
make Paris a major finance market, while also limiting money financing
of the public deficit (Reland 1998: 86; 92). In 1988 President
Mitterrand 'uncritically accepted' the complete liberalizing of capital
movements in the EU and, Reland argues, reliance on foreign capital

---

[2] See Introduction; Haldane 2010, other measures; 3:97 ratio is in British and
Australian records (Ryan-Collins et al 2011; RBA data)

had more impact on French economic policy autonomy than the Maastricht Treaty of 1991. Worse, the Treaty's terms created a deflationary bias. With the liberalizing of cross-border banking, member states held on 'to national institutions for regulation, supervision, resolution, and insurance that were too small to safeguard the banks and insurance firms that emerged in Europe's integrated financial space', argues Jones (2015: 45). How much this absence mattered we cannot know. The City and Wall Street had 'financial unions', which had deregulated to competition on financial markets, 'light touch' and feeble supervision. Interbank borrowing with market rates, money fund markets and private credit rating agencies were said to be more efficient than the authorities, until the world's largest ever bailout, by the UK treasury of the Royal Bank of Scotland (RBS). US and UK authorities had been, only hindsight said, asleep at the wheel.

Mobile capital roamed across Europe and Southeast Asia, with partial exceptions (including Australia and Canada). Euro member states' treasuries must borrow (issue bonds) from the wholesale money markets or big banks, not from either their own central bank or *de jure* by Treaty from the ECB (like other federations). There is a development bank, true, for regions, but banks like RBS could trade anywhere, picking and choosing 'innocently'.

Bailouts of EU banks

After the GFC, European northern states openly bailed out local problems, such as Landesbanken with €18 billion, billions more to Hypo in Germany and Dexia in France (Admati and Hellwig 2013: 11; 324). The larger crisis was deregulated big banks, and foreign banks selling 'subprime' and other securitized debt. Capital from northern banks of Germany, France and the Netherlands had parked in Ireland, Portugal, Spain (their private banks) and Greece (the state). When 'subprime' et al. collapsed, that squeezed core EU banks badly. In 2010, bond traders had a hand in forcing austerity by shorting member states' debt (bonds). The only respite from the 24/7 gambling on the Euro was not from authorities but when traders took a 'group ski holiday' (Authers 2010: 18). These 'traders' were blandly called 'investors'; only the *New York Times* revealed the main dealers of EU member states' debt were J. P. Morgan Chase, some New York–based anonymous hedge funds and the US 'bond giant' Pimco (Bowley and

Ewing 2010). In Greece, the first to short its debt was the firm that concocted a secret, rapacious deal ten years before, GS&Co.

In contrast to colossal UK and US bailouts, very little is clear about how the big private EU banks seemed to get off so lightly. Streeck (2014: 152–4) argues the technocratic peak used camouflage, technical tricks but in a situation of confusion, not necessarily conspiracy. (Yet UBS was worse in Switzerland.) Banks would not endure a haircut, nor be nationalized, but discreetly rescued with public funds. In 2010, the IMF, EU and ECB lent the Greek government €110 billion to pay its 'creditors', that is, banks engaging in money creation. Cassidy (2015) cites Karl Otto Pöhl, former head of the Bundesbank, that the bailout "was about protecting German banks, but especially the French banks, from debt write-offs." Steil and Walker (2015) show how in 2010 French banks had the largest exposure to Greece, Germany next. This lending enabled Greece to avoid defaulting on these banks, they say, and saved France from bailing out its banking system. France then offloaded €8 billion in "junk debt" to Italy and Spain, landing them with the exposure to Greece. And when German banks pulled money out of Greece (Bloomberg Editors 2012), all euro area central banks lent to the Greek central bank, leaving all responsible for Greece. Dangers in French and German banks' balance sheets were thus shifted to the entire EU's taxpayers, but it took time for these secrets to be revealed.

The 2010 collapse of consensus unravelled the status of the Euro as a 'standard' (thus not a 'commodity') and threatens further the democratic EU ideal. The Euro as a *market currency* was shown as a divided not unified standard: whatever the Forex or bond traders guessed about the Greek Euro or the German Euro must be correct, although in hindsight those judgements were mindless both pre-GFC when traders assumed wrongly the euro had one value across the EMU, and post GFC, to frantically switch (going long or short) on the euro's 'value'.[3]

---

[3] Admati & Hellwig on UBS. See also Jabko 2015: 78–81. Note that Ireland's bank bailout was public. Bank bond trading was 'wrong' in that it 'overshot' the value of the 'Greek' Euro, assuming the Euro was the 'same', and post-crisis 'undershot' its value through exaggerating the previously ignored Greek state debt (Gibson 2009 shows). Designers put the Euro at the mercy of markets – 'going long or short' are bets on rising or declining 'values' respectively. Irish, Portuguese or Spanish troubles are relevant to other contrasts (Chapters 1, 5 and 6) in Asia (Chapters 2 and 7).

The 1980s CBs and Role of the ECB

Stepping back, the Washington–Wall Street Consensus had tried to impose its global straitjacket (Azis, Chapter 2 on Southeast Asia; cf. Nölke, Chapter 7 on China and India, minimally), while crashes from capital flows-flights rose. All central banks lost control over global finance *at least* by the 1990s: that includes the extent of bank-money expansion and the scale of flows (D'Arista 2009). New freedoms for global banks enhanced the far older "state debt and money creation mechanism which is operated by the state treasury, central bank and banking system" (Ingham 2011: 287). What that involves is that banks (bond traders) can assert a plebiscite over state debt at whim – or as monetarist Allan Meltzer (2013: 224) threatens, the 'interest rate and the exchange rate at which the market will willingly hold the government debt'. In the EMU, then, the ECB arrived just when few central banks could control global banks, and just as bond traders could pick off EU member-states' debt or Thailand's to make fortunes.

The EMU's timing was inauspicious. Worse, the 1980s' lobbying pan-globally for 'independent' central banks forbad monetizing state debts, only bank debt (quietly). Finance sectors (or the IMF) could threaten loan withdrawals if central banks did not fall into line. That was fixed into EMU rules, yet every central bank anyway buys state debt; markedly in the GFC mostly to save banks not people; Wall Street not Main Street. The ECB did likewise.

Ignoring Germany's corporatist system, the Bundesbank was the model for the 'independent' movement *everywhere* not only the ECB. Its sole aim was price stability. Like the rest, it ignored the savage deflation of 1930–33 with crippling levels of unemployment. That memory only nagged the Bundesbank's early years, until the focus narrowed to the 1923 hyperinflation and Nazi takeover of the Reichsbank. Jörg Bibow (2015: 15) cites Walter Eucken's denunciation of all three episodes. By the time of David Marsh's history of the Bundesbank, there is one remark about the 1930 "Hunger Chancellor" Brüning (not his grim tag) and Reichsbank president ('arch-conservative') Hans Luther's tough deflationary policies in 'exacerbating' the depression (Marsh 1992: 107). Marsh makes little comparison to the UK 1920s grim recession to depression (although a *Financial Times* journalist); and mentions the Rentenmark during Germany's 1923 hyperinflation horror. However, the Rentenmark was really a miracle cure (Orléan 2013) – which later occurred in France. These cures, in days, not weeks, were called miraculous at the time, to show that inflation, not just hyperinflation under which money-holders lose everything, is relatively easy to halt. After the 1970s, not only in the Bundesbank to ECB, many authorities hectored about hyperinflation as cover for *rentiers* to bask on unearned income from stagnation.

In Anglo-America, wages were crushed and unions delegitimized; in Germany, SPD Chancellor Schroeder in the 1990s attacked wages not unions. Monetarism *with* the Laffer curve regressive tax cuts, which increased state debt, attracted governments of US Republicans and UK Tories and, eventually, overwhelmed those of social democrats and labour. Markets in all things financial, commodified money again, ganged up against *social* state money creation, and the BoE and US Fed led in state-guaranteed private bank money expansion; to *club the economy*; to promote deflation. Bank money took off, but whatever Maastricht or formal independence rules are set for central banks, they always monetize government spending just like bank advances. They must buy government bonds (state debt) with which banks can use as cash.

Similarly, hidden problems of the Euro are not insoluble. The ECB was engulfed through the main EU governments' bowing to markets for central banks to *tighten* borrowing (costs) with Inflation Targets, excluding asset inflations. Everywhere, bond vigilantes demanded these deflationary targets of CBs in the 1990s (of dot con inflation infamy). The Bank of Canada and Reserve Bank of Australia were the *sole* CBs that refused to take this ominous target so seriously as to maintain the permanent stagnation of elsewhere.[4] Independence we saw aimed to forbid monetizing of government debt, only of banks secretly.

Maastricht threatened EU member state debts ('no bailout'), but which *banks* would be monetized? Just as other central banks were forbidden overtly to monetize state debt, but did so by the back door to monetize private bank debts, the ECB also did so, it seems. The ECB at its founding (2001) had raised interest rates which depressed many economies. To what avail? It made member states desperate, notably

---

[4] 'Clubbing the economy' was a phrase I learned from junior Banca d'Italia officials, in 2013. RBA see Grenville 1997; BoC in Kuttner 2004. Inflation Targets *only measured* CPI, not bank money inflation for consumer debt or asset inflation. They exploded lucratively as jobs languished.

those without the *inflexible* labour systems of the 'German north'. Member states are not allowed to use their national central bank for emergency liquidity. The Euro compared to the symbiotic US$ *posed* as pure private money. Geoffrey Ingham's formulation on monetary sovereignty suggests this 'monetary space' need not be national but *some authority*, and not via market assessments alone – the Euro – must make and sustain viable money, or else this 'space' is likely to be unstable. What makes the EMU so problematic?[5]

The large French and German banks had consolidated and stepped in to create the money for spending by member states and banks on property bubbles. It is clear by 2012 that the ECB did monetize more member-state debt. As Streeck puts it, the ECB's new head Draghi in 2012 lent €1 trillion, at 1 and then 0.75 per cent interest to the banks; then bought 'unlimited quantities' of crisis states' bonds, first only from banks, not initially from governments. There were 'non-recoverable fiscal subsidies' to enable insolvent states to meet obligations to alleged creditors. Also camouflaged were inter-state transfers or potential transfers to national central banks balances with the ECB. Streeck gloomily points to 'an unshakeable faith in the governability of Europe from above' (2014: 155). So?

This was common. Armed with global 'bankster' details, it is hardly *shocking* to see Greece's secret loan in 2001 from the ubiquitous Goldman Sachs was concocted while Mario Draghi, incidentally, headed GS&Co Europe. Bloomberg called it 'a sexy story between two sinners'.[6] Northern Europe later luxuriated in moralism at Greece, although not at Draghi or bank CEOs like Ackermann of Deutsche Bank, or Draghi's colleague Hank Paulson running GW Bush's US Treasury, who fudged to Congress his bailouts managed with the privately-owned US New York District Fed (J. P. Morgan et al.). Yet a Nicolas Veron (2017), talking down to a Berlin business school, is scandalized about the way Greece hid its deficit and its head of

---

[5] Jabko 2015: 79–80 discusses 'no bailout'; see later Hancké 2013 on EU labour markets
[6] Australian journalists filmed retired 'family reasons' NSW Premier race to revisit Deutsche Bank, Sydney that received 'contract work' for NSW. A 'boyish' Premier, transformed in his merchant banker uniform: black shoulder bag, dark glasses, he got a $2m pa job; 2017. Bankster was an American 1930 take on Wall Street when Mafia gangsters were rife, revived 2008. On Draghi: Bloomberg 2012; Streeck 2014:132.

statistics was sued for revealing it. He ignored the equally nefarious part of GS&Co Europe and masked bailouts of BNP Paribas and Deutsche Bank. The revolving doors was perfected in the BoE's 1694 nexus. Insider trading was the 'done thing'. The Bismarck family is one of Germany's richest, from Otto's dealings with Bleichröder, the banker who funded the unification wars.[7]

Austerity Was an EU Fiscal Policy!

Jörg Bibow remarks the 'peculiar divorce of monetary and fiscal powers in Europe's currency union is a precarious outcome for all parties concerned'. It was *peculiar* to me because austerity is fiscal policy (UK, etc.) but contradicts current BoE, Fed and RBA policies. Credit raters see that austerity – demanded by Whitehall *or* a Troika, probably hard bargains between France *versus* Germany – ruins the credit worthiness of member states (and democratic decisions), a centralizing feature brushed aside so far.

   Given the Eurozone's problems, I think bewailing a fiscal union is a fudge. Envisaged in Veron's jargon as a system of 'debt issuance and revenue collection' at European level, fiscal union apparently means a 'size-bound financial firepower' with the 'ability to issue debt' of the European Stability Mechanism, and 'a limited-purpose levy on European banks to feed into the Single Resolution Fund', to be 'fully transnational' by 2024. Why a 'limited' levy, or 'size-bound'? Why 2024? Since June 2017, decent changes look possible. The European Investment Bank's 'financial capacity' and EU's own resources, like 'customs duties and sugar levies' (Veron, 2017), could expand into fiscal transfers under democratic rules and via constitutional referenda, as in old federations. The EMU has one fiscal policy (like Britain), to impose austerity on all member-state treasuries, which depresses economic activity and increases state debts. Debts, growing in value, to whom? To the same finance sectors that started the fire.

   Wolfgang Munchau of the *FT* (2016) was critical of an EU 'establishment' which has learned nothing and still listens to inadequate ('post-real') macroeconomists. He urged the EU to solve the 'out-of-control' finance sector, 'uncontrolled flows of people and capital', and unequal income distribution. As well, Merkel needed to reduce

---

[7] Blinder 2013 on Paulson; Stern 1977, on Otto's family fortune. Veron is utterly typical.

Germany's excessive current account surpluses and 'dogma' on fiscal surpluses – so Germans can buy from the EU. I cannot see this 'incompetent crisis management' is worse than America or United Kingdom.

Fiscal Transfers and EU Labour Markets

In 2015, ECB president Draghi wanted to *force* member states to stay in the Eurozone. Further fiscal transfers were not proposed, instead Draghi wanted the same technocracy to centralize authority to Brussels over labour relations laws, product market regulations, family policy, possibly housing and pension rules. It implies copying nefarious (elected) Presidents and Prime Ministers elsewhere who crushed unions and privatized mutually-owned pension funds. This 'sovereignty' would be 'exercised jointly' Draghi said ominously (Sandbu 2015). 'Brussels' sounds like the Troika. The IMF is run by the US's voting supremacy, so wait for Republican Congress fingers on IMF loans. The US may wrench all possible IMF funds back via 'conditions': I can see Greece being required to fund a few US nuclear bombs, while China owns most of Piraeus.

Draghi's proposal may die. But let us take the labour market alone. Today, the EMU has only competitive unit cost reduction against wages and jobs as a worst 'strategic' option (given the jobless), to *prove* the Euro's value. Purchasing power varies in the rich north and 'the rest'. Munchau (2017b) excoriates Germany's suppression of real wages of workers (a form of currency manipulation). Bob Hancké (2013) shows the ECB's advent *divided* flexible labour markets of the 'rest' from non-flexible *organized* labour systems of the 'D-bloc'. The 'unionized north' checked wage inflation with the corporatism led by IG Metall; meantime 'the rest' was so flexible, disorganized, that service sector wages (surgeons) kept rising against the new ECB's harsh interest rate policies that (surprise, surprise) benefited northern capital goods export sector to disadvantage 'the rest'. Thus, the Euro was unstable. Then came the EU 2010 crash, and Polish workers (etc.) fled to work in the United Kingdom. Since Brexit, they flee anywhere else, because of pound sterling's 'value', not just English hostility.[8]

---

[8] Munchau 2017b on German currency manipulation via wages; Hancké 2013 *passim*. Also for wage rise proposals www.socialeurope.eu/2016/11/wages-economic-performance-three-fallacies-internal-devaluation/

Banking union

France and Germany are tough on credit cards, mortgages are rare: the opposite in Ireland, Greece or Spain. There was no authority to control EU-wide bank advances and prudential matters: that is changing. So far not for the better since, from 2012, the EU moved partially to ban any assumption of bailout rather, to 'bail-in', i.e., 'burden sharing' or 'resolution' of private banks (Veron 2017).

Those critical of the EMU's banking union argue 'bail-in' is 'simply the latest step in the EU's post-crisis creditor path of austerity and asymmetric adjustment; that could potentially put the final nail in the EMU's coffin'. Trying to 'mutualise' costs of bank resolution is a disaster (see later, Australia). Concentration of capital in the D-bloc (from mergers), means that *'a banking union is likely to exacerbate, rather than reduce, core-periphery imbalances'*. Bail-in rules make countries susceptible to bank-runs with self-fulfilling panics, and periphery countries are experiencing massive capital flight towards core countries in fear of bail-ins and bank failures (Fazi 2016, cited in Zaccone 2016).

The City is a large provider of financial services in the Eurozone, such as settlement and clearing of bank money-creation, which continues. Thus, the EMU's main financial centre is *outside* Eurozone borders. 'There is a clear potential for blackmail here' to enhance Brexit's terms, warned Munchau (2017a). Well, I'd be worrying far more because no new London rule is 'enough to stop another Libor scandal'. Barclays has a Qatari fraud case, and rigged the London Interbank Offered Rate (Libor). Market lending rates, even when not corrupted, undercut and removed bank assessments of recipients of advances.

However! The EU Parliament was worrying in February 2017. More might come. It democratically directed the EU Commission to investigate a fabulous idea that aims to rule out 'untrusted' City banks and other 'high impact' foreign mobile capital that basks in 'light touch' or 'regulatory bonfires'. *Financial Times* or *New York Times* journalists are sick of hearing about the 'culture of banking' in the United Kingdom and United States, since it is line management that produces 'rogue traders'. Unless ideas like 'equivalence' are implemented, the EMU further faces a break-up.[9]

[9] Brunsden & Fortado *FT* 2017 on Brussels tough on equivalence; Kotlikoff, 2012 on Libor; and Gibson, 2009

Comparing with Other Federations or Faux Federations

Capitalist money has been a major (primary?) force in the federations of the United States, Australia and Canada too, in diverse ways rarely noticed. All had inauspicious beginnings in uniting, interspersed with disintegrations and financial crises. After a few hundred years or so of conflicts over money, none has a settled landscape. This brief sketch can only pick examples of relevance to the EMU. All have endured financial attacks on state spending for development and social services, resolved more and less fairly. The US political system was never a social democracy, Australia's possibly was, Canada maybe the most. Neither has a central bank structure like the US Fed, which promotes Wall Street since its 1913 design and finances America's nuclear arsenal *sotto voce*. War finance is lucrative to banks (we see, Chapter 4) yet divisions are not only from the US's extreme inequality. Regardless how far the States is *united*, Washington DC and Wall Street elites loathe countries that dare poke fun at an empire as narrow and provincial as the last, British. Given Wall Street's global reach, its efforts at controlling the production of money away from other nation states are often brutal.

Despite America's size and might, Canadians and Australians take a dim view of banking, finance, and both empire snobberies. Once the US$ became hegemon over sterling after World War I, the significance of republicanism fell off. Australians loathed the gold standard and banks from at least 1817. Both rejected the imperial BoE and faux domestic US Fed models during the Great Depression, and built central banks neither slavish to their banks or states. The BoC and RBA have been harsh on all kinds of inflations *and* deflation, and keep fragments of social development of the 1930s or earlier. US "exceptionalism" is a dreary fact of capitalist monetary life that requires groveling even when wealthy (OECD). Australia is comparable *per capita* to the USA and UK for 200 years, Canada more recently. Neither had horror GFCs, yet both have occasional secession threats, French Canada the most.[10]

Yet in the UK, Scotland often wants to leave. The "United Kingdom" is a murky, closed affair with crushing poverty in regions

---

[10] On wealth comparisons: McLean 2013. Both have bank controls, Canada's best; in Australia's 2008–09 stimulus, the RBA gave a 'helicopter drop' of a cheque to each Australian household.

long conquered by lower England rulers, more public since the 2016 Brexit vote. UK's imperial desires are as defunct as Roman Emperor Hadrian's, who luxuriated in his Athens villa not England's damp, directing construction of his Wall. The Scottish idea of a shared monetary federation is offensive to London. Few see the UK is a *failed federation* with no constitution. Its Parliament's absolute monetary sovereignty rules the Kingdom but implicitly, the Bank of England, City and Treasury are like the EU's brand-new Troika or US Congress–Treasury–Wall Street–Fed. For England's despised outliers, the EU gave hope. Europe's concept of 'the people's sovereignty' is unknown in UK law, and given the City has long held a malign global power. Anything can happen but globally, the democratic deficit has grown since the 1970s, in all kinds of political-territorial formations. One needs, therefore, to distinguish these depressing trends from specific EMU questions.[11]

Although the UK is taken as a 'finance-monetary' benchmark (by the English), the origins and extant aims of state-capitalist money in London are totally undemocratic (the BoE's postwar nationalization made little difference). Studies (Ugolini 2011, Epstein 2006) show few BoE copy-cat central banks in nineteenth century Continent or Japan. They aimed for economic development and later, the UK 'Dominions' included progressive redistribution to enrage the BoE. Only the US Fed copied, and competed with, the UK's huge empire on the back of this incredible (secret) money creation, via the BoE the banker to the Crown and to City merchant-bankers. The rich centre rarely maintained UK's industrializing regions (so punishing labour) Geoff Ingham shows, while Empire and the City spread their wings globally. Forget that empire now, or moral duties to its underdeveloped ex-colonies (or others to their spheres).

The cruelty on display when the EC 2011 'compact' imposed a pure fiscal policy of austerity, barely matches UK Treasury's vicious stupidity.[12] Did the 'empires' not long for, and promote EMU collapse?

[11] Yorkshire trusts no one south of Sheffield; Ireland had 600 years of oppression like indigenous peoples of settler countries. Ascherson 2016 discusses UK (unwritten) constitutional doctrine of the 'absolute' sovereignty of Parliament, whereas Brexit's *apparent* claim for 'the people' is 'un-English' and paradoxically European (or Canadian, American, Australian).
[12] Bibow 2015: 45; Jabko 2015: 80–1, a stability 'mechanism', 'ESM' agreed by 25 member states in late 2011 to budgets 'balanced or in surplus'; with Treaty *revisions* early 2011, not to the ECB, but for 'ESM' 'last resort'. Referenda are for constitutional changes.

Brexit showed, first, Whitehall was never interested in stagnant UK regions. Its then Chancellor, that is, treasurer Tory George Osborne, said 'we' can 'no longer' molly-coddle the north of England. Thatcher compared the state budget to a household's decades before Merkel. Second, when Brexit won 2016's weirdly called referendum (a 50–50 plebiscite),[13] it was interpreted as against the City–Whitehall–BoE establishment *and* the EU Troika's *red tape*. How could Brexit voters have foreseen that the new Prime Minister, Theresa May, would claim 'Crown Prerogative', not even the clipped Crown's constitutional power in Parliament? (She failed on that in court.) This fake non-federal United Kingdom – with 'four nations' say, in the United Kingdom's National Health – directed monetary sovereignty for financiers of one 'nation'. The BoE always applied inequality to damn the most blasted regions further (Dow & Montagnoli 2007). UK Treasury's devaluations and revaluations likewise give unequal outcomes for imports and exports, small business and the City.

Moving from the so-called United Kingdom back to America, the disastrous story of the EMU in 2010 onwards has similarities to the United States's 1837–44 first 'great' depression. States, not the US Administration raised loans from London for development and plain pork barrelling. As in the EMU, City banks made cozy profits until eight US states defaulted on London, including New York State (others paid up), but high unemployment and violence ensued. Despite US Congress control of the currency, US Treasury had no central income taxes, just customs and excise (as in Australia 1901–43, or the EC). US Treasury was so short it could not fund a territory war against British Canada, asking London being pointless (Roberts 2012). Whereas 1970s–2010s Wall Street abused the Fed and US$ unification (by 1933), it seems the EMU followed untidy parts of all three federations, under orthodox US–IMF policy and the Bundesbank.

These older federations started with neither unified taxes or fiscal transfers. It is well-known that the US War of Independence's slogan against Britain was 'No taxation without representation', but

---

[13] Voting systems help moderate raw capitalism. The United Kingdom and the United States have insensitive first-past-the-post, where voters' third choice delivers to their 'least-liked' of two big parties. Compulsory turn-out puts the onus, say, on the Commonwealth of Australia to enrol and encourage turn-out (ballots can be scribbled on), and to manage electoral boundaries/districts on strict demographic rules (cf. US gerrymanders).

John K. Galbraith grumbled that turned into 'no taxation *with* representation'. President Lincoln did impose a temporary income tax in the Civil War – another part of the violent US federation struggle – but US Treasury only collected income taxes in 1913.[14] Fiscal transfers to states also developed, to the extent that when unemployment in any US state creates a deficit, funds *automatically* flow there from the Administration. Aid, not loans (Zaccone 2016). Canada has fiscal transfers, partly to 'impose' generous healthcare! The EU has modest transfers from richer to poor economies; reduced in 2015. Some transfers among Member-states are the Structural Funds and Cohesion Fund,[15] a first for "UK" poor regions.

Other aspects of old federations (save the United States) are union engagement in central wage bargaining, not just a unified tax system or fiscal transfers. Played down in the EMU or UK, social justice arrangements combine as democratic bulwarks against finance sectors' crisis tendencies. In Germany's (corporatist) federation, debates about fiscal transfers to the Laender always involve hot political debates, as in Canada and Australia, but transfers were limited in the EMU. The ECB was to do the heavy (unequal) lifting, which no central bank since the GFC can do alone, except via 'breaking the world' as in 1930 (Ahamed 2009) or via the thought-free elites' Brexit.

With routine fiscal transfers from Washington DC, Ottawa or Canberra, rich provinces are no less desperate about bond or currency vigilantes than poorer. Rich grumble about poorer: all three federations took ages to unify these aspects lacking in the EU and UK so far.[16] It is not that the EMU is a 'mistake' so much as too ambitious, too prepared to put all member-states to the mercy of bond traders.

[14] Galbraith 1975; irs.gov.

[15] This is the EU's flagship development Programme which is designed to narrow the gap between the rich and poor parts of Europe (and Prince Charles). More than one third of the total EU budget, €347bn, goes to structural and cohesion funds, which contribute funding to everything from roads and bridges to employee training. Overall, the policy aims to strengthen economic and social cohesion in the EU by reducing differences in development between regions. Most of that spending is to three funds: the European Regional Development Fund (ERDF), the European Social Fund (ESF) and the Cohesion fund. http://lexicon.ft.com/Term?term=EU-structural-funds – http://ec.europa.eu/regional_policy/en/funding/.

COHESION FUND - http://ec.europa.eu/regional_policy/en/funding/cohesion-fund.

[16] Corporatism refers to unions-firms' relations, and was similar in Australia.

Americans loathe their central government: what of the UK? Given technocratic set-ups despise electorates, all monetary arrangements are political.

Do *political* arrangements entail democratic participation? Britain has never held referenda on any constitution nor did Europe *fully*; the US constitution was written and agreed upon by slave owners and bourgeois classes. In contrast, Australia had two full referenda in the 1890s on the constitution under the two-thirds norm. And capitalist money played a large, hated role in Commonwealth debates: New Zealand decided to withdraw after the scandalous 1880s–90s bank bubble-crash in Melbourne that spread into *the great* depression (Australia endured) of that global era. British banks and private buyers of UK Treasury Consols were after higher rates. In Melbourne's disastrous 1890, a *bail-in* ('reconstruction') created this full-fledged Australian depression since depositors lost to banks' benefit (as the EU). Those with deposited loans had to maintain interest payments or default, and Parliamentarian-bankers ensured 'their' bankruptcies didn't occur (Butlin 1961). Some banks limped on for 100 years. To Minsky (1986), rising levels of unserviceable debts are normal functioning events that can lead to debt deflation, and insolvent banks should be run down in an orderly fashion. This neither happened in Melbourne's 1890s, nor in the EU 2010–2015, with 'bail-ins' *and* vast bailouts.

The EMU started with the Euro; likewise, after 1901's union of Australia, banks lost the note issue, and insurance firms regulation centralized to Canberra. In 1911, a Labor Government founded the state-owned "People's Bank," the Commonwealth Bank of Australia (CBA), to outperform capitalist banks for 80 years, until opposing social forces and private banks triumphed in splitting off the CBA (later selling it). The Reserve Bank of Australia (RBA) was a rebadging of the state-owned CBA that retains some egalitarian aims.

Like the EMU, Australian income taxes were still not centralized until 1943's WW2 inflation, via the 'war powers' emergency. Of great relevance to the EMU, Australia's *fiscal equalizer* came a decade *earlier* in 1934. In Depression, federation's *survival* was highly doubtful, which prompted Canberra to ease the tensions of debt deflation. Data for 2005–06 show how, under Australia's fiscal equalizer, the two richest, largest states *per capita* implicitly transfer via Canberra some billions of dollars to the three poorest and smallest, and variably and fairly to others (Coleman et al., 2006:155–60). In 2016, the democratic strength of the fiscal equalizer meant states flatly refused Canberra's (stupid) idea to return them income tax powers (a potential *end* to federation). State politicians far prefer the Commonwealth endures the obloquy of tax collection while they gain the benefits of fiscal transfers and other federal schemes like health. Naturally, publicized federal-state annual debates remain heated, states accused of profligacy (pork barrels; sell-offs etc.). Since this 'fiscal equalizer' was in *deflationary* 1934, money-creation of the central bank is not a problem for writing out cheques to state treasuries, ten years before WW2 unified taxes. Australia's federation was saved.

Canada's large five banks fell into disrepute in the 1920s–30s, and democratic reforms ensued there too. Canada and Australia took a firm hold of their money centres (and notorious BoE) during the 1930s Great Depression (as did FDR's US Administration), with the aim to control private banking to socially useful purposes. Canada's is the most loose 'confederation'. In contrast, in the 1990s EMU formulations, EU's member-states' finance centres had no *crisis* (then) but financial markets and the City dominated. Yet the (reckless) big French and German banks were saved secretly in 2010–12. That was a distasteful aspect of Europe's union, we saw. The United Kingdom's populations suffered from the City's mass rescue; even if with transfers, America's likewise. Austerity plays the role of the "Cross of Gold" that small farm political parties knew in America's nineteenth century (Galbraith 1975; Eichengreen & Mitchener 2003; Ryan-Collins 2015).

On EMU labour market coordination, member-states' trade unions could collectively work out their preferred federated options from below (not via Draghi's rigour). Canada, New Zealand, the United Kingdom and the United States set minimum wages through their legislatures. Australia is unusual in having wages set by a central statutory authority (Wilson 2017: 256). Typically, right-wing govern-ments attack minimum wage settings and unions, but *public* court submissions are put from all concerned. At today's juncture, higher wages reduce deflation and indirectly 'tax' corporate capital, much needed after finance sectors misused 'freedoms'. The implication of Draghi that 'prices', namely concrete social relations of money with multiple distributive impacts, just need to 'adjust' has long under-mined democratic procedures.

The same occurs in mono and federated states: Canberra is selling off 'deferred wage' agreements (a trusted pension sector, successful non-profit, union-run funds) as did Germany under Gerhard Schroeder who broke the wage agreements that entailed wage sacrifices during inflation (Streeck 2014: 66–8). So far, Canadian unions have resisted further labour deregulation. US Congress helped push US wage declines, which haven't *stopped* US employment declining further, markedly since 2000 (Wilson 2017: 250; 259). Employers now engage in wage theft.

Potentials for the EMU

Compared to older, unequal federal institutions in America – Australia nearly, less so Canada – the mono-state UK is as unequal and, without federation, lacks the EU's opportunities to save the EMU. Possibilities that enough far right political parties take power to destroy the EU exist. Yet as EU member-states collectively debate policies, two modest progressive ones could look, first to raising minimum wages across the EU *if* it included unions in negotiations; second, to enlarging fiscal transfers via ECB monetizing. Since the ECB monetized member-states deficits to repay big northern banks, it could do that positively for transfers: for EU-wide projects and ventures with lasting economic returns, dignity and jobs. The EU Parliament can stop fiscal austerity and moderate the vaunting Euro ambitions, the crisis of which made 'poorer' areas poorer. Both give breathing spaces for member-states to decide their welfare state levels, celebrate diversities, and stimulate (taxable) economic activity that enhances cultural and economic strengths (like richly diverse French-British Canada).

Deflation is not susceptible to any miracle cure (unlike inflation). This was well-understood after the Great Depression, even in the US Fed. When Australia's central bank had dual remits for full employment (FE) and price stability, *and* owned its 'commercial' arm, it could order it to reduce inflationary credit, or to expand productive lending in deflation. Central banks cannot *create* full employment, but FE remits ideally prevent their holding interest rates so high as to cause large-scale unemployment (as America's, 1980). The Bank of Canada nationalized in 1938, aims 'to promote the economic and financial welfare of Canada'.[17] With the US

---

[17] United Kingdom is not only 4 bogus 'nations'; also, England's London, west, midlands and northern regions are poorer than many EU (Spain has only

Fed, President Roosevelt's reforms tried to remove Wall Street's control of the Fed, but could not nationalize the District Feds. Yet two Fed chairs Marriner Eccles and McChesney Martin were committed to FE and to 'taking away the punch bowl' before a riot (of bank-money) broke out. They monetized federal state debt. Lost in the USA by 1980, the Fed's dual remit, price stability and FE remains. The Bank of England is unlikely to ever get a FE or 'welfare' remit; nor did the ECB; the BoC's 'welfare' is *foreign* to the US Fed.

EU member states *could* insist on full EMU referenda, one for new ECB remits: FE and open not secret ECB monetizing, another for reversing fiscal austerity *determinism*. After grim EMU activities since inception, this could be popular and give democratic legitimation. Under present deflation, the ECB *could* be ordered to monetize transfers without causing CPI inflation: it is only when various inflations emerge that more unified taxes are needed to retire the transfers' debts. It is not impossible given the EU Parliament has tried to move against reckless bank money creation: *unsolved* everywhere.

Further on EU monetary sovereignty, a key point (Halevi 1995) is Germany exports the bulk of Department I goods to 'the rest'. No EU firm can survive without importing such capital goods, so any devaluation in, say lira is suicide for Italian firms. That is why Germany needs stimulus (its population is bound to like) to buy consumer goods and services from 'the rest' with Euros, so D-bloc exports can be purchased: creditor and debtor states need each other.

To conclude, the Eurozone shows grim possibilities of undemocratic *moralistic* policy in its absence of socially just, economically boosting fiscal transfers, improved (taxable) minimum wages, and banking union *controls* not *gifts*: logically these foster money's stability and jobs. If mobile capital is dependent on monetary sovereignty, but demands profits *sufficient* at cruelly low economic activity (austerity, high ECB rates), things are seriously wrong. The EMU is anomalous to its populations' purchasing power, but not banks, which control money production against states. So is the 'United' States, or the 'Common' wealth of Australia or more so, the 'Dis-United' Kingdom. All have predatory finance sectors; Canada remains better. The majority Republican US

Catalonia as breakaway). On the CBA/RBA, Butlin 1983; on FE, Pixley 1994. The BoC claims, see www.bankofcanada.ca/about/ - beyond price stability, and safety in the financial system remits, to be the "fiscal agent" for the Canadian Government.

Congress is any day to allow, like Canberra, the big banks to rip off their clients again, by weakening Dodd-Frank (Morgenson 2017; Chapter 1). The EU is hardly *alone* with problems then, of mobile capital.

If the EU turns differently, perhaps to a stronger military defence 'union', the worst option is war finance from uncontrolled banks, and less from centralized taxes. World War I proved this so badly that some of World War II was funded by taxes among the federations this chapter examined. War finance and its vast expansion in the United States, postwar, is discussed in the next chapter.

References

Admati, A. and Hellwig, M. 2013. *The Bankers' New Clothes: What's Wrong with Banking and What to Do about It*. Princeton University Press

Ahamed, L. 2009. Lords of Finance: 1929, *The Great Depression and the Bankers Who Broke the World*. London: Heinemann

Amato, M. & Fantacci, L. 2012. *The End of Finance*. Cambridge: Polity 2014. 'Back to which Bretton Woods?', *Cambridge Journal of Economics* 38: 1431–1452

Ascherson, N. 2016. 'England prepares to leave the world' *LRB* 17 November 7–10

Authers, J. 2010. 'Why the bond vigilantes are starting to wake up' *FT* December 12, 2010: 18

Bowley, G. & Ewing, J. 2010. 'Europe's game of cat and mouse' *Australian Financial Review (AFR)* December 10: 17. Reprinted from *NYT*

Bibow, J. 2015. 'The Euro's savior? Assessing the ECB's crisis management performance'. *Macroeconomic Policy Institute (IMK)*, Study, June, 42

Blinder, A. 2013. *After the Music Stopped*. New York: Penguin

Bloomberg The Editors 2012 'Hey, Germany: You got a bailout too', *Bloomberg* May 23

Brunsden, J. & Fortado, L. 2017 'Brussels sets out tough new lines on equivalence' *FT* February 27

Butlin, S. J. 1961. *Australia and New Zealand Bank: The Bank of Australasia and the Union Bank of Australia Limited, 1828–1951*. London: Longmans 1983. 'Australian central banking 1945–59', *Australian Economic History Review* 23 (2), September: 95–192

Cassidy, J. 2015. 'Greece's debt burden: The truth finally emerges' *New Yorker* July 3

Coleman, W., Cornish, S. & Hagger, A. 2006. *Giblin's Platoon*. Canberra: ANU Press

D'Arista, J. 2009. 'The evolving international monetary system', *Cambridge Journal of Economics* 33: 633–52

Dow, S. C. & Montagnoli, A. 2007. 'The Regional Transmission of UK Monetary Policy', *Regional Studies* 41 (6), August: 797–808

Eichengreen, B. & Mitchener, K. 2003. 'The Great Depression as a credit boom gone wrong', *BIS Working Papers* 137, September

Epstein, G. 2006. 'Central Banks as Agents of Economic Development', *United Nations University (UNU-Wider)*, Research Paper No. 2006/54, May: 1–20

Forder, J. & Menon, A. (eds.) 1998. *The European Union and National Macroeconomic Policy*. London: Routledge

Forder, J. 1998. 'National autonomy' in Forder & Menon (eds.) *op cit.*: 28–44

Galbraith, J. K. 1975. *Money. Whence It Came, Whence It Went*. Boston: Houghton Mifflin Co

Gibson, H. 2009. 'Competition, innovation and financial crises', *Open Economic Review* 21 (1): 151–157

Grenville, S. 1997. 'The Evolution of Monetary Policy', in P. Lowe (ed.), *Monetary Policy and Inflation Targeting*. RBA: 125–58

Haldane, A. 2010. 'The Contribution of the Financial Sector: Miracle or Mirage?' Executive Director, Financial Stability, Bank of England. *The LSE Report: The Future of Finance* LSE: 1–38

Halevi, J. 1995. 'The EMS and the Bundesbank in Europe' pp 263–291, in *Finance, development and structural change* (eds.) P Arestis & V. Chick, Aldershot: Elgar

Hancké, B. 2013. *Unions, Central Banks and EMU*. Oxford University Press

Ingham, G. 2011. *Capitalism: With a New Postscript*. Cambridge: Polity Press

Jabko, N. 2015. 'The elusive economic governments' in Matthijs, & Blyth, (eds.) *op cit*: 70–89

Jones, E. 2015 'The forgotten financial union' in Matthijs, & Blyth, (eds.) *op cit*: 44–69

Kotlikoff, L. 2012. 'Vickers is not enough to stop another Libor scandal' *FT* July 9

Kuttner, K. N. 2004. 'A snapshot of inflation targeting in its adolescence', *RBA* 9–10 August 2004. www.rba.gov.au/publications/confs/2004/kuttner.html

Mann, G. 2013. 'The monetary exception: Labour, distribution and money in capitalism', *Capital and Class* 37 (2): 197–216.

Marsh, D. 1992. *The Bundesbank: The Bank that Rules Europe*. London: Heinemann.

Matthijs, M. & Blyth, M. (eds.) 2015. *The Future of the Euro*. Oxford University Press

McLean, I. W. 2013. *Why Australia prospered.* Princeton University Press

Meltzer, A. 2013. 'Comments', in M. D. Bordo & W. Roberds (eds.), *A Return to Jekyll Island*, Cambridge University Press: 219–225

Minsky, H. 2008 [1986]. *Stabilizing an Unstable Economy.* New York: McGraw Hill

Morgenson, G. 2017. 'The watchdog protecting consumers may be too effective' *NYT* February 10

Münchau, W. 2017a. 'Europe will pay unless the Brexit deal is a fair one' *FT* 27 January

2016. 'The liberal elite's Marie Antoinette moment' *FT* 28 November

2017b. 'Peter Navarro has a point' *FT* 2 February

Offe, C. 2015. *Europe Entrapped.* Cambridge: Polity

Oppenheimer, P. 1998 'Motivations for participating in the EMS' in Forder & Menon (eds.) *op cit.*: 58–82

Orléan, A. 2013. 'Money: Instrument of Exchange or Social Institution of Value?' pp 46–69 in Pixley, J. F. & Harcourt, G. C. (eds.) *Financial Crises and the Nature of Capitalist Money.* London: Palgrave Macmillan

2014. *The empire of value.* MIT Press

Pixley, J. F. 1994. *Citizenship and Employment* Cambridge University Press.

Reland, J. 1998. 'France' in Forder & Menon (eds.) *op cit.*: 85–104

Roberts, A. 2012. *America's First Great Depression: Economic Crisis and Political Disorder after the panic of 1837.* Ithaca: Cornell University Press

Ryan-Collins, J. 2015. 'Is Monetary Financing Inflationary? A Case Study of the Canadian Economy 1935–75', *Levy Economics Institute*, Working Paper No. 848

Ryan-Collins, J., Greenham, T. & Werner, R. 2011. *Where Does Money Come From? A Guide to the UK Monetary & Banking System.* London: New Economics Foundation

Sandbu, M. 2015 'Central banks v democracy', *FT*, June 3

Social Europe 2016. www.socialeurope.eu/2016/11/wages-economic-performance-three-fallacies-internal-devaluation/

Steil, B & Walker, D. 2015 'Greece fallout: Italy and Spain have funded a massive backdoor bailout of French banks' *Geo-Graphics, Council on Foreign Relations*, July 2

Stern, F. 1977. *Gold and Iron: Bismarck, Bleichröder and the Building of the German Empire.* New York: Alfred A. Knopf.

Stevenson, R. 1998. 'Fiscal Stones, Glass Houses: Bailout Points Finger Back Toward the U.S.' *The New York Times*, September 26 pp. 1 & C2

Streeck, W. 2014. *Buying time.* London: Verso

Tooze, A. 2014. *The Deluge.* London: Allen Lane

Ugolini, S. 2011. 'What do we really know about the long-term evolution of central banking?' *Working Paper 15. Norges Bank*

Veron, N 2017 'Economic and financial challenges for the European Union in 2017', ESMT, Berlin https://piie.com/commentary/speeches-papers/economic-and-financial-challenges-european-union-2017#.WKfHDcS-OfY.email

Wilson, S. A., 2017. 'The politics of minimum wage welfare states: The changing significance of the minimum wage in the liberal welfare regimes', *Social Policy and Administration* 51 (2): 244–64

Zaccone, J. 2016 'The euro: a gold standard with no exit' *Recent Works* 2/16. www.njfac.org

4 | Mobile Capital as the Ultimate Form of War Finance

LUCA FANTACCI AND LUCIO GOBBI

A basic tenet of war finance is that 'citizens have to pay for the war either from their current or future income' (Cappella Zielinski 2016: pos. 380). Indeed, whether they are financed by forced labour, direct or indirect taxation, domestic or foreign debt, or even outright monetary inflation, wars traditionally imply some, more or less explicit and perceptible, form of resource extraction. Sooner or later the costs of the war are borne by the population through a loss of income, wealth or purchasing power. Now, this homely notion of war finance has been overthrown by the peculiar financial regime that has supported the rise of US global hegemony over the past decades. Since the end of World War II, the military and consensus mobilization that has allowed the United States to impose their primacy has been financed by a form of debt that does not entail any cost, since it is not intended to be repaid, but indefinitely floated on international financial markets. Thanks to the liberalization of capital movements worldwide, the United States have managed to finance persistent balance of payments deficits. Hence our thesis: mobile capital represents the ultimate form of war finance.

The argument is two-fold: as we shall try to show, on one hand, free capital markets emerge as a response to the financial requirements of the cold war; on the other hand, they contribute to the perpetuation of a condition of constant belligerence. We lay the logical and historical foundations of our argument by claiming that the financial condition for peace rests upon the establishment of an international regime that favours the payment of debts (section 1). Despite its original intentions, the Bretton Woods system violated this principle, allowing systematic current account imbalances to be financed, on the basis of non-economic motives, through military expenditure and international aid (2). The cornerstone of the system, namely the convertibility of the dollar into gold, was put under strain by the twin deficits accumulated by the United States in order to finance the Cold War, and more specifically

the conflict in Vietnam: suspension of convertibility sanctioned the
state of war with the establishment of a *cours forcé* on a global scale
(3). Conventional explanations fail to provide compelling reasons for
the ensuing financial liberalization (4). What actually required the
abolition of capital controls was the need to provide an outlet for
international liquidity, stemming dollar depreciation and inflation (5).
International fiat money coupled with free capital markets provided a
potentially unlimited source of funding to face military escalation and
perpetuate warfare without curtailing welfare (6). At the same time,
mobile capital accommodated the build-up of global imbalances,
fostering international frictions and financial instability (7). The res-
toration of peaceful economic relations requires the establishment of a
reformed international monetary system that allows for the payment
of debts (8).

The Financial Condition for Peace

When John Maynard Keynes sketched out his plan for the postwar
economic order, he spoke explicitly of 'financial disarmament'.

If the arrangements proposed can be described as a measure of financial
disarmament, there is nothing here which we need be reluctant to accept
ourselves or to ask of others. It is an advantage, and not a disadvantage,
of the scheme that it invites the member States to abandon that licence to
promote indiscipline, disorder and bad-neighbourliness which, to the general
disadvantage, they have been free to exercise hitherto. The plan makes a
beginning at the future economic ordering of the world between nations and
'the winning of the peace.' (Keynes 1941b: 57)

The plan required individual countries to accept a partial surrender of
national sovereignty, yet 'not more than in a commercial treaty', and
largely compensated by the fact that this would allow to establish an
international order, in which each State would be free to pursue the
prosperity of its own domestic economy, without prejudice, indeed to
the advantage of its neighbours.

Ultimately, according to Keynes, the basic rule of such an order is
that international debts and credits are not accumulated indefinitely,
but are eventually paid out. In the payment, debtors and creditors
are appeased. Peace is etymologically related to payment. 'The original
meaning of pay was "to pacify," and it goes back to Latin pax "peace."

The notion of "payment" arose from the sense of "pacifying" a creditor' (Oxford English Dictionary). A financial system which rests on the systematic non-payment of debts is likely to be inimical to the preservation of peace. Again, Keynes identified the persistence of balance-of-payments disequilibria as a permanent source of social unrest and geopolitical tensions:

The problem of maintaining equilibrium in the balance of payments between countries has never been solved, since methods of barter gave way to the use of money and bills of exchange. [...] [T]he failure to solve this problem has been a major cause of impoverishment and social discontent and even of wars and revolutions. (Keynes 1941a: 27)

If an international monetary and financial system is to preserve peace, it ought to conform to this principle of great simplicity: debts are to be made payable. Keynes (1919) had denounced the peace treaty of Versailles precisely on the grounds that it made the repayment of war debts depend on unpayable reparations.

The Flaws of the Bretton Woods System

Despite all Keynes's efforts, even the international economic order established after World War II only partly responded to the criterion of making debts payable and ensuring peace. This time the winning powers refrained from imposing on Germany unsustainable obligations: in fact, the London Agreement of 1953 not only restructured and rescheduled German debt, but also set repayments in proportion to the actual capacity to pay, subordinating them to the existence of a trade surplus (King 2016: 342). However, as we shall see, postwar reconstruction was eventually financed by a new form of unpayable debt.

The principles of the postwar economic order were drawn since August 1942 in the Atlantic Charter. One of the main pillars was free trade. The liberalization of trade implied the need to stabilize exchange rates, without the rigidities and the deflationary pressures implied by the gold standard. This required nations to finance temporary imbalances on current account and to ensure that such imbalances remained temporary. This was, in fact, mentioned as one of the purposes of the International Monetary Fund in the Articles of Agreement drafted at Bretton Woods: 'to shorten the duration and lessen the degree of disequilibrium in the international balances of payments of members' (Article I (vi), q UN 1948: 943). Various sources of funding were regarded as possible instruments to that effect: loans from the International Monetary Fund; long-term private capital investments; official capital transfers in the form of grants or loans, particularly under the European Recovery Program.

Instead, liquid and short-term capital movements were explicitly ruled out in order to preserve international relations from the instability that speculative capital flows had caused before the war. Moreover, following the logic that was later to be framed in the 'basic policy trilemma', the decision to forsake free capital flows was intended to reconcile a system of stable exchange rates (as a condition for free and fair international trade) and the possibility of autonomous monetary policies by individual states (as a way to promote full employment and prosperity in national economies).[1]

Despite the way it is commonly represented, the Bretton Woods system did not *impose* capital controls. In fact, it *allowed* countries to resort to capital controls as an extreme remedy to defend exchange rate stability. The Articles of Agreement clarify the point in so many words:

Members may exercise such controls as are necessary to regulate international capital movements (Article VI, section 3).

The IMF played a marginal role in financing current account deficits after the war. IMF loans were insufficient, due to the (intentionally) low capitalization of the Fund. In this respect, it dramatically failed to meet its statutory end. On the other hand, private investments were withheld by the scant prospects of return, due to stagnant production and demand. Overall, ordinary funding for current account deficits was inadequate. This made recourse to exceptional alternatives inevitable.

Thus, a large part of the 'dollar gap' was bridged by the Marshall Plan (Triffin 1957). As major creditor country and issuer of global money, the United States willingly accepted the burden of providing debt relief and of financing postwar recovery worldwide, in exchange for the possibility of drawing from an inexhaustible source of funding

---

[1] As recently recognized also by the Economist (2016), Keynes was a precursor of the trilemma later formalized by Mundell (1963).

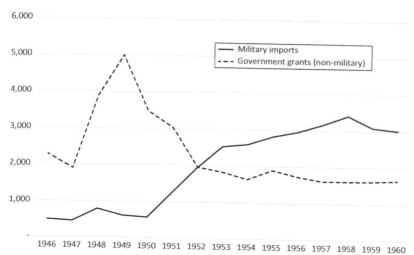

Figure 4.1 US military imports and government grants (millions of dollars).
Source: Federal Reserve Bank of St. Louis (1961), retrieved from FRASER, Federal Reserve Bank of St. Louis. 'United States Balance of Payments 1946–1960',: 2–9. https://fraser .stlouisfed.org/scribd/?toc_id=412711&filepath=/files/docs/publications/frbslreview/rev_ stls_196103.pdf, accessed on June 19, 2017.

for the purpose of both economic and military mobilization (Rueff 1971). The Bretton Woods system, by granting the dollar the status of international currency, allowed the United States to finance indistinctly, and without budget constraints, the pacifying deeds of the Marshall Plan and the military escalation of the Cold War.

In fact, a smaller, but increasing part of the dollar gap was bridged by military expenditure. Europe eventually recovered, and managed to balance its trade with the United States already starting from the early 1950s (Fantacci 2014: 34). And this was achieved only thanks to the European Payments Union, which allowed the recovery of intra-European trade that the Marshall Plan had failed to produce (Amato and Fantacci 2012: 110–120). At that point, US aid was cut back, but military expenditure continued to increase in the wake of the Korean War (Figure 4.1).

In principle, the Bretton Woods system, consisting essentially in a reedition of the gold standard, imposed constraints on both the fiscal budget and the balance of payments of all countries, including the United States. Initially, the military expenditure contributed to keep the US balance of trade in equilibrium, without causing excessive budget deficits (the Korean War was largely financed by taxation, rather than deficit spending). Eventually, however, both constraints were put severely under strain by the Vietnam war. The precarious balance of the Bretton Woods system responded more to military than to commercial logics: it was ultimately disbanded by the financial requirements not of trade but of war.

Cold War Finance and US Twin Deficits

Formally the Bretton Woods system was based on the convertibility of the US dollar, which could circulate as global means of settlement in virtue of its convertibility. And convertibility entailed constraints on monetary policy and on the balance of payments. The Vietnam war broke both. It was financed through monetary expansion and resulted in a balance of payments deficit. Suspension of convertibility was the inevitable consequence.

The Vietnam war was the tipping point: it contributed decisively to turning negative the balance of payments of the United States. Dudley and Passell (1968) estimate that the direct and indirect effects of the war caused a deterioration of the balance of payments for 4 billion dollars in 1967, concluding that 'the United States would have been in international payments surplus in 1967 in the absence of Vietnam War expenditures' (p. 442). Indeed, the overall deficit of the balance of payments in that year was 3.6 billion dollars: according to Dudley and Passell's calculations, if it had not been for the war, the United States would have still had a surplus of 0.4 billion dollars.

Cumulative US balance-of-payments deficits caused American gold reserves to dwindle and dollar reserves abroad to swell until Nixon was forced to recognize the disproportion and suspend convertibility: as always in history, the cours-forcé ratified the state of war – this time, on a global scale.

The 'temporary' suspension, however, became permanent. The situation seems, indeed, to have precipitated in the following years, at least judging from the explosion of US liabilities towards foreign governments and central banks between 1969 and 1972 (Figure 4.2).

Financed primarily by printing money, the Vietnam war inevitably produced inflation, particularly on commodity markets. Inflation, in fact, had started to increase already before the suspension of dollar convertibility, and before the oil shocks (Figure 4.3).

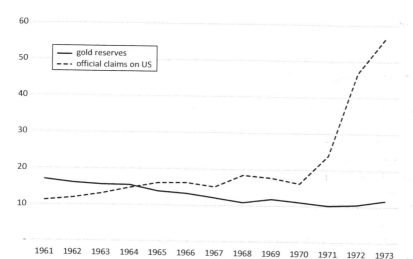

Figure 4.2 US gold reserves and external liabilities (billions of dollars).
Sources: Federal Reserve Bulletin, June 1974; IMF Annual Reports 1971 and 1973

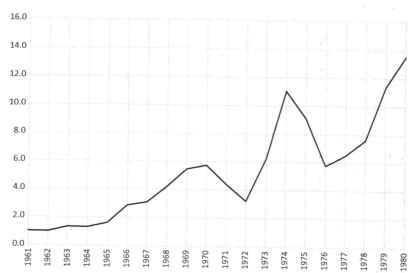

Figure 4.3 United States, inflation rate.
World Bank, Inflation, consumer prices for the United States [FPCPITOTLZGUSA], retrieved from FRED, Federal Reserve Bank of St. Louis; https://fred.stlouisfed.org/series/FPCPITOTLZGUSA, May 31, 2017

The oil shocks were triggered by political turmoil in the Middle East. But this was only the contingent cause. The structural factor that led to double digit inflation across the Western world by the end of the 1970s was the monetization of the twin deficits of the United States: dollars printed and circulated globally to finance military expenditure and the ensuing current account deficit (Fantacci 2014).

Despite the suspension of convertibility into gold, the dollar continued to be accepted as international currency. Why did the end of the Bretton Woods system not imply the end of US monetary hegemony? One reason must be traced in the agreements between Western countries and OPEC to denominate oil exports in dollars: the dollar, no longer convertible into gold, became exchangeable into black gold. The use of the dollar as means of payment on international commodity markets contributed to support the external demand and value of the US currency. However, this was not enough to avoid inflation, caused by a structural excess of money with respect to goods. The ultimate solution to the inflationary pressures came when overabundant dollars were offered an alternative outlet on financial markets. Here, unlike on commodity markets, assets could be produced with the same promptness and ease as fiat money itself. The liberalization of international capital markets may be seen, therefore, as a way to overcome the inflationary pressures caused by the war and to make cold war finance less perceptible and more sustainable.

This argument contrasts with established reconstructions of the oil shocks of the 1970s and of the ensuing crisis of Keynesian policies. Phelps (1967) and Friedman (1977) rightly criticized the supposed relationship between inflation and unemployment known as the Phillips curve, showing, already since the end of the 1960s, that an increase in inflation could contribute to boost employment only if it exceeded expectations. Indeed, the monetization of military expenditure for war in Indochina, by pushing inflation beyond expectations, supported employment. This view also provides a plausible explanation of the stagflation following the oil shock of 1973. However, what the monetarist narrative fails to acknowledge is how, starting from the second half of the 1970s and during the Reagan administration, the liberalization of capital movements became a structural instrument to control inflation under fiscal expansion and tax reductions, undercutting the theoretical and political stance in favour of austerity measures. This claim, however, also departs from traditional accounts of financial liberalization, to which we must now turn.

Factors of Financial Liberalization

The last fifty years have witnessed a gradual, yet relentless process of liberalization of the financial system on a global scale. The liberalization has involved both a deregulation of national financial systems and growing integration between them. It has entailed not just an increase in scale and scope, but a radical change in the character of finance, with a shift towards liquid investments as opposed to long-term commitments: the rise of mobile capital.

What are the driving forces that have led to the increasing liberalization of international capital movements over the past decades? Various factors have been traditionally identified to explain the emergence of global financial markets:

1. technology, and specifically the revolution in information and communication technologies, which has allowed to elaborate data and transmit information rapidly and cheaply on a global scale, supporting investment decisions and the exchange of money and securities across the world (Wriston 1988);
2. neoliberal ideology, and particularly the belief that free, integrated, liquid capital markets represent the most efficient mechanism to allocate savings to the most productive investment opportunities (Bhagwati 1998);
3. policies of deregulation, inaugurated by the right (Thatcher and Reagan) and continued by the left (Blair and Clinton);
4. vested interests of banks and financial intermediaries lobbying those governments;
5. intervention of central banks and international organizations in the function of lenders of last resort, to dampen the effects of the crises produced by capital outflows and at the same time perpetuate the logic of deregulation through structural reforms imposed in exchange for conditional lending (Helleiner 1994).

None of these explanations is sufficient. The first and the last are merely necessary conditions: without ICT the globalization of finance would never have started and without lenders of last resort it would already have finished. Both contributed to making it possible, yet neither made it inevitable or even desirable: 'trends that enable capital mobility are not the same as, nor do they inexorably lead to, rules that oblige governments further to liberalize capital' (Abdelal 2007: 19).

Not even political or ideological motivations, however, seem capable of explaining financial liberalization. In fact, the neoliberal doctrine, together with the policies that it inspired, does not predate financial liberalization. Classical liberal economists, such as Ricardo, even opposed free international capital movements.

> Experience, however, shews, that the fancied or real insecurity of capital, when not under the immediate control of its owner, together with the natural disinclination which every man has to quit the country of his birth and connexions, and intrust himself with all his habits fixed, to a strange government and new laws, check the emigration of capital. These feelings, which I should be sorry to see weakened, induce most men of property to be satisfied with a low rate of profits in their own country, rather than seek a more advantageous employment for their wealth in foreign nations. (Ricardo 1821[2005], pp.136–7)

The idea that free capital movements are a desirable complement to free trade is distinctive of neoliberalism, as opposed to classical liberalism. It only emerges in the 1980s and consolidates with the establishment of the Washington Consensus in the mid-1990s (Harvey 2007: 66, 92).

Even vested interests, particularly those of bankers, had been served equally well in past centuries by other forms of international finance, such as foreign direct investments, without having to resort to short-term loans or liquid portfolio movements. Think of the stable, long-term relationships that characterized the operations of the haute finance in the period of global financial integration, and of international peace, preceding World War I:

> *Haute finance*, an institution sui generis, peculiar to the last third of the nineteenth and the first third of the twentieth century, functioned as the main link between the political and the economic organization of the world. It supplied the instruments for an international peace system, which was worked with the help of the Powers, but which the Powers themselves could neither have established nor maintained. [...] There was intimate contact between finance and diplomacy; neither would consider any long-range plan, whether peaceful or warlike, without making sure of the other's goodwill. Yet the secret of the successful maintenance of general peace lay undoubtedly in the position, organization, and techniques of international finance. (Polanyi 1944 [2001], p. 10)

Since the outbreak of the global financial crisis in 2007, the theoretical fracture between classical liberalism and neoliberalism has started to be acknowledged also by mainstream authors. Indeed, growing global imbalances, asset bubbles and capital flights have induced several orthodox economists to question the rationality of a complete liberalization of international capital flows (see e.g. Blanchard 2016 and Gosh and Qureshi 2016).

The link between international financial architecture and war finance remains still largely unexplored. The role of war finance is neglected not only, as we have just shown, by prevailing accounts of financial liberalization, but also by most literature on the economics of war.[2] Without questioning the relevance of all the factors listed above in fostering the liberalization of capital movements, we intend here to draw the attention on a different, relatively neglected motivation: war finance.

A New Financial Revolution

Money is the sinew of war. In premodern times, wars ended when money finished. Modern paper money was invented essentially to overcome this constraint: the Bank of England was founded in 1694 with the peculiar 'purpose of assisting the marketing of national debt in time of war' (Kindleberger 1984: 52). With the financial revolution of the late seventeenth century, Britain invented a 'metaphysical war chest': an unlimited source of funding in the form of negotiable government debt financed by the market – and hence indirectly by the liquidity created by the central bank through issuing banknotes. It was this financial revolution that allowed Britain to mobilise the resources required to win wars and gradually emerge as a hegemonic power on a global scale (Dickson 1967).

The Bretton Woods system and its demise represent a financial revolution on a global scale. The gold dollar standard, like the Great Recoinage of 1696, sets a fixed parity between the unit of account and a quantity of precious metal of given weight and fineness. The confidence in the parity allows dollar balances to be accepted as reserve assets and payment instruments in lieu of gold, like the banknotes of the Bank of England, but on a global scale. By issuing convertible

---

[2] It is hardly mentioned, for example, in the contributions collected by Garfinkel and Skaperdas (2012). On the contrary, financial historians do recognize the importance of war: 'Financial history cannot escape dealing with war. War is a hothouse and places enormous strain on resources, which finance is used to mobilize. Financial innovation occurs in wartime' (Kindleberger 1984: 5).

paper money, the United States manages to finance both trade and war, mobilizing military forces without depressing productive activities, as the United Kingdom had done since the late seventeenth century.

The suspension of convertibility causes inflation on commodity markets, which has to be staved off by providing an alternative outlet for overabundant liquidity on liberalized capital markets. The English financial revolution relied on the co-operation of three elements: the Treasury, the Bank of England and the Stock exchange. It endowed the United Kingdom with an inexhaustible war chest in the form of irredeemable debts: inconvertible paper money, bank money, and sovereign bonds floated on financial markets (Amato and Fantacci 2012: 183–196). In the same fashion, the new financial revolution is complete only with the liberalization of global financial markets, where dollars and T-bills can be freely exchanged, avoiding the depreciation of both.

From the sterling standard of the late eighteenth century, through the gold-exchange standard of the interwar period to the current dollar standard, the use of national currencies as international money has granted certain countries the 'exorbitant privilege' of unlimited funding for their imperialistic policies. In fact, the country issuing the key currency (essentially Britain in the nineteenth century and the United States in the twentieth century), unlike all other countries, did not have to earn the money required to settle its international engagements, but could afford to print it (Rueff 1971, De Cecco 1974, Eichengreen 2012).

Open-Ended Finance for a Never-Ending War

The liberalization of global capital markets is the answer to inflationary pressures caused by an old form of war finance and, at the same time, it is the prelude to a new form, characterized by blurring distinctions between money and credit, war and peace.

Global finance, as it has gradually emerged over the past five decades, is a system of war finance. By this we mean that it originated to respond to the needs of war, i.e. to serve not economic but political purposes, not trade and investment but military expenditure – the Cold War and specifically the Vietnam War.

However, unlike other, more explicit forms of war finance, such as those described by Cappella Zielinski (2016), it does not entail a direct or perceptible extraction of resources. Unlike taxation, it does not reduce the current income or wealth of the population. Unlike debt, it does not reduce future income or wealth either. The reason is that this debt is irredeemable, precisely because it is liquid. It works like the English financial revolution, but on a global scale. Hence, there is no need to terminate it – like the Bank of England, whose charter was continuously renewed because its expiration always coincided with times of war (Bowen 1995: 5–6).

This form of war finance does not finish with the war. Because it serves equally well the purposes of peace: welfare as well as warfare. More generally, it serves the purpose of the mobilization of political consent, the exercise of soft power – i.e. the form of mobilization and power that are peculiar to the Cold War. The continuation of war with different means.

Indeed, the liberalization of capital markets, starting from the 1970s, opened broader funding opportunities to all states – and for all purposes. At the same time, however, it allowed the United States to run persistent and increasing balance-of-payments deficits without suffering an excessive depreciation of its currency that would have jeopardised its monetary hegemony (Helleiner 1994).

Thus even the war does not finish. The Korean War ended in 1953 with an armistice. A proper peace treaty has never been signed: North and South Korea are technically still at war today. The United States has been constantly at war since World War II, from the military escalation and atomic confrontation that characterized the Cold War to the ongoing War on Terror (see Table 4.1). Until recently, US military expenditure exceeded that of all other countries put together.

Within this context, military expenditure is sometimes seen as a crucial, counter-cyclical, component of aggregate demand for economic systems structurally exposed to periodical crises of overproduction. In macroeconomic terms, it may be thought to contribute bridging the gap between savings and investments, supply and demand, by boosting investments, particularly in research, and hence output (see e.g. Baran and Sweezy 1966, and more recently Atesoglu 2004). This view has been increasingly challenged by recent research, in particular in relation to the cost-effectiveness and macroeconomic sensibleness of US military operations after the end of the Cold War (Hossein-zadeh 2006).

In any case, the truly distinctive feature of US military expenditure, regardless of its macroeconomic effects, is that it is financed by fiat

Table 4.1 *Wars involving the United States since World War II.*

1950–1953	Korean War
1958	Lebanon Crisis
1961	Bay of Pigs Invasion
1964	Simba Rebellion
1965–1966	Dominican Civil War
1965–1975	Vietnam War
1982–1984	Multinational Force in Lebanon
1983	Invasion of Grenada
1987–1988	Tanker War
1989–1990	Invasion of Panama
1990–1991	Gulf War
1992–1995	Somali Civil War
1994–1995	Intervention in Haiti
1994–1995	Bosnian War
1998–1999	Kosovo War
2001–2014	War in Afghanistan
2003–2011	Iraq War
2011	Libyan Crisis
2014-present	War against ISIS

Sources: Barbara Salazar Torreon, 'U.S. Periods of War and Dates of Recent Conflicts', Congressional Research Service, RS21405, September 29, 2016; retrieved from Federation of American Scientists; https://fas.org/sgp/crs/natsec/RS21405.pdf, accessed on June 19, 2017
Menadue, J. 2017 'The question Leigh Sales didn't ask Senator John McCain'. *Pearls and Irritations*, johnmenadue.com. Posted 6 June 2017. accessed June 21, 2017.

money and by irredeemable debt. This finance without end serves the purpose of a war without end:

U.S. forces [are] more or less permanently engaged in ongoing hostilities. In one theater after another, fighting erupts, ebbs, flows, and eventually meanders toward some ambiguous conclusion, only to erupt anew or be eclipsed by a new round of fighting elsewhere. Nothing really ends. [...] During the Cold War, peace never seemed anything but a distant prospect. Even so, presidents from Harry Truman to Ronald Reagan cited peace as the ultimate objective of U.S. policy. Today, the term 'peace' itself has all but vanished from political discourse. War has become a normal condition. (Bacevich 2016: 37)

The new world order consists in a continuous state of latent belligerence, a 'piecemeal world war' as it has been called by the Pope

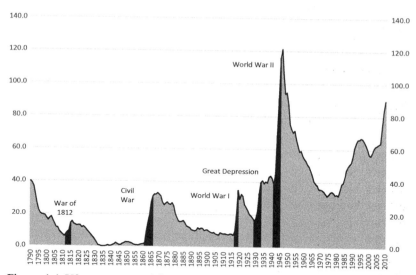

Figure 4.4 US government debt (percent of GDP) and wars.
Source: www.treasurydirect.gov/

(Bergoglio 2017). A war on peace itself, on the very conditions for peace, and particularly on the financial conditions.

Peace is not the end of this war as payment is not the end of its finance. No payments, no peace. This war does not finish with a peace in the traditional sense: demobilization, repayment of public debt, reduction of public expenditure. Since the beginning of the nineteenth century, US government debt has always increased in the wake of war, only to be paid out, or at least drastically reduced thereafter; even after World War II, US government debt was again reduced from over 100 per cent to roughly 30 per cent of GDP by 1980, but it then started to climb back up towards 100 per cent of GDP in the following decades (see Figure 4.4).

What has followed World War II is not a peace, but a truce. The indistinction between war and peace that has characterized the world over the past seven decades is indeed fostered by a peculiar form of war finance. At the cost of an increasing fragility of the financial position of the United States, measured not only by its mounting net foreign debts, but by its increasing inability to exercise a global hegemony and to promote any kind of international order.

Global Financial Markets as a Factor of International Friction

Without liberalized financial markets, it would hardly be conceivable to finance global imbalances on such a massive scale as recent decades have witnessed. When debts are so large and persistent, they can only be financed if they are liquid, i.e. if the creditor is given at least the benefit of being able to convert the credit promptly into cash. In turn, global imbalances, together with the global capital movements which are required to finance them, are a source of continuous social and political tension.

Over the past four decades, financial liberalization has implied the accumulation of debts that are not intended to be paid out, but indefinitely floated on international capital markets, producing an ever-widening gap between creditor and debtor countries. Such global imbalances are the dark side of financial globalization. On the one hand, mobile capital appears to unify the world, providing opportunities of investment for advanced economies and sources of funding to sustain the growth of emerging countries. On the other hand, the build-up of global imbalances between creditor and debtor countries is a permanent source of political tensions and wars. The relations between China and the United States are an obvious case in point. But so are the relations between the core and the periphery within the Eurozone.

Persistent global imbalances and global capital flows restrict the autonomy of domestic economic policies and produce chronic contrasts between national interests. In the concluding notes to the *General Theory*, Keynes observed that '[n]ever in history was there a method devised of such efficacy for setting each country's advantage at variance with its neighbours' as the international gold (or, formerly, silver) standard' (Keynes 1936 [2013]: 349). Today, we could possibly extend the remark to the current international regime of floating exchange rates and free capital flows. This might seem paradoxical, if we think that 'the end of systemwide fixed exchange rates during the early 1970s was often portrayed as an opportunity for governments to liberalize capital movements without giving up autonomy over their monetary policies' (Abdelal 2007: x). However, as recently shown by Rey (2015), the trilemma is, in fact, a dilemma: regardless of the exchange rate regime, free capital movements are at odds with autonomous monetary policies targeted at defending the interests of domestic economies. The mobility of international capital is at odds with the prosperity of national economies.

Persistent global imbalances, therefore, are a permanent threat to the preservation of peace: the constant subjugation of national economies to the vagaries of international finance foster the indigence and frustration, which are the seedbed of populism, nationalism and xenophobia. On the other hand, traditional social democracies appear incapable of providing an adequate response to the legitimate requests of their populations as long as restrictions on capital flows remain taboo.

International Money and Finance for Peace

Having denounced war debts and reparations as a major source of economic depression and political instability in the interwar period, Keynes proposed the International Clearing Union as a measure of 'financial disarmament' in view of a new economic order after World War II. The establishment of a truly international money, distinct from all national currencies, was intended as a means to establish a level playing field for economic and financial relations among nations. The introduction of symmetric adjustment mechanisms for creditors and debtors was conceived as a fair rule to encourage the reabsorption of global imbalances, to facilitate the payment of international debts, and to preserve peaceful relationships among nations (Fantacci 2013). In fact, the principles underlying Keynes's plan, embodied in the European Payments Union in the 1950s, proved effective in promoting peace and prosperity.

The inherent fragility of international monetary sovereignty under the post-Bretton Woods non-system has fostered a debate on the need to reform global money. Worthy of particular notice is the proposal by the governor of the People's Bank of China to draw inspiration from Keynes's plan and establish a truly international currency (Zhou Xiao Chuan 2009). Interestingly the proposal comes, this time, from a major creditor country.

A new international monetary and financial system is essential to achieving world peace. Mobile capital should not be part of it. The 'doux commerce' is only doux when it is restricted to real commodities. Free trade is beneficial when it does not extend its reach to money and finance. As Keynes remarked in his proposals for a postwar economic order:

So far from currency laissez-faire having promoted the international division of labour, which is the avowed goal of laissez-faire, it has been a fruitful source of all those clumsy hindrances to trade which suffering communities have devised in their perplexity as being better than nothing in protecting them from the intolerable burdens flowing from currency disorders. (Keynes 1941a: 22)

Financial markets that are deregulated and integrated on a global scale are a major factor of geopolitical, and not just macroeconomic, instability: they provide an unlimited and undiscriminating source of funding for military expenditure, they accommodate the build-up of balance-of-payments disequilibria, they foster the growth of shadow banking and non-transparent transactions. They encourage various forms of detrimental antagonism – regulatory arbitrage, currency manipulation, tariff wars – as opposed to peaceful competition in terms of comparative advantage in production. Ultimately, mobile capital is a system of war finance: its contribution to productivity is questionable, its support to destructivity is undisputable.

References

Abdelal, R. (2007) *Capital Rules: The Construction of Global Finance*, Harvard University Press, Cambridge MA and London UK

Amato, M. and Fantacci, L. (2012) *The End of Finance*, Polity, Cambridge

Arrighi, G. (2010) *The Long Twentieth Century: Money, Power and the Origins of Our Time*, 2nd ed., Verso, London and New York

Atesoglu, S. H. (2004) 'Defence Spending and Investment', *Journal of Post-Keynesian Economics*, Vol. 27, N. 1, pp. 163–169

Bacevich, A. J. (2016) 'Ending Endless War: A Pragmatic Military Strategy', *Foreign Affairs*, Vol. 95, N. 5, pp. 36–44

Baran, P. A. and Sweezy, P. M. (1966) *Monopoly Capital*, Monthly Review Press, New York and London

Bergoglio, J. (2017) 'Nonviolence: A Style of Politics for Peace', Message of His Holiness Pope Francis for the Celebration of the Fiftieth World Day of Peace, 1 January 2017

Bhagwati, J. N. (1998) 'The Capital Myth: The Difference between Trade in Widgets and Dollars', *Foreign Affairs*, Vol. 77, N. 3, pp. 7–12

Blachard, O. (2016) 'Currency Wars, Coordination, and Capital Controls', *Peterson Institute for International Economics Working Paper*, 16–9, July

Bowen, H. V. (1995) 'The Bank of England during the Long Eighteenth Century, 1694–1820', in R. Roberts and D. Kynaston (eds), *The Bank of England: Money, Power and Influence 1694–1994*, Clarendon Press, Oxford

De Cecco, M. (1974) *Money and Empire: The International Gold Standard, 1890–1914*, B. Blackwell, Oxford

Dickson, P. G. M. (1967) *The Financial Revolution in England: A Study in the Development of Public Credit, 1688–1756*, St Martin's Press, New York

Dudley, L. and Passell, P. (1968) 'The War in Vietnam and the United States Balance of Payments', *The Review of Economics and Statistics*, Vol. 50, N. 4, pp. 437–442

Economist (2016) 'The Mundell-Fleming Trilemma. Two Out of Three Ain't Bad', August 27

Eichengreen, B. J. (2012) *Exorbitant Privilege: The Rise and Fall of the Dollar and the Future of the International Monetary System*, Oxford University Press, Oxford; New York.

Fantacci, L. (2013) 'Why Not Bancor? Keynes's Currency Plan As a Solution to Global Imbalances', in M. C. Marcuzzo, P. Mehrling and T. Hirai (eds.) *Keynesian Reflections: Effective Demand, Money, Finance and Policies*, Oxford University Press, Oxford

(2014) 'From the Great Depression to the Current Crisis: More Than Analogy, Genealogy', *History of Economic Ideas*, XXII, 3, 2014, pp. 23–46

Federal Reserve Bank of St. Louis (1961) 'The United States Balance of Payments, 1946–1960', *Monthly Review*, Vol. 43, N. 3, March

Friedman, M. (1977) 'Nobel Lecture: Inflation and Unemployment', *Journal of Political Economy*, 85: 451–472.

Garfinkel, M. R. and Skaperdas, S. (2012) *The Oxford Handbook of the Economics of Peace and Conflict*, Oxford University Press, Oxford

Ghosh, A. R. and Qureshi, M. S. (2016) 'What's In a Name? That Which We Call Capital Controls', *IMF Working Paper*, 16/25, February

Harvey, D. (2007) *A Brief History of Neoliberalism*, Oxford University Press, Oxford

Helleiner, E. (1994) *States and the Reemergence of Global Finance: From Bretton Woods to the 1990s*, Cornell University Press, Ithaca, NY

Hossein-zadeh, I. (2006) *The Political Economy of U.S. Militarism*, Palgrave Macmillan, New York and Basingstoke

Høst-Madsen, P. (1963) 'The Changing Role of International Capital Flows', *The Journal of Finance*, Vol. 18, N. 2, pp. 187–210

Keynes, J. M. (1936) *The General Theory of Employment, Interest, and Money*, in D. Moggridge (ed.), *The Collected Writings of John Maynard Keynes*, Vol. 7, Macmillan, London, 2013

(1941a) 'Post-War Currency Policy', 8 September 1941, in D. Moggridge (ed.), *The Collected Writings of John Maynard Keynes*, Vol. 25, Macmillan, London, 1980, pp. 21–33

(1941b) 'Proposals for an International Currency Union', 18 November 1941, in D. Moggridge (ed.), *The Collected Writings of John Maynard Keynes*, Vol. 25, Macmillan, London, 1980, pp. 34–68

Kindleberger, C. P. (1984) *A Financial History of Western Europe*, George Allen & Unwin, London

King, M. (2016) *The End of Alchemy: Money, Banking and the Future of the Global Economy*, Little, Brown, London

Mundell, R. A. (1963) 'Capital Mobility and Stabilization Policy under Fixed and Flexible Exchange Rates', *The Canadian Journal of Economics and Political Science / Revue canadienne d'Economique et de Science politique*, Vol. 29, No. 4 (Nov.), pp. 475–485

Phelps, E. S. (1967) 'Phillips Curves, Expectations of Inflation and Optimal Unemployment over Time', *Economica*, 34 (August): 254–281.

Polanyi, K. (1944) *The Great Transformation: The Political and Economic Origins of Our Time*, Beacon Press, Boston, 2001

Rey, H. (2015) 'Dilemma Not Trilemma: The Global Financial Cycle and Monetary Policy Independence', *NBER Working Paper* No. 21162, May

Ricardo, D. (1821) *The Principles of Political Economy and Taxation*, 3rd ed., in *The Works and Correspondence of David Ricardo*, ed. by Piero Sraffa with the collaboration of M. H. Dobb, Vol. 1, Liberty Fund, Indianapolis, 2005

Rueff, J. (1971) *The Monetary Sin of the West*, Macmillan, New York

Triffin, R. (1957) *Europe and the Money Muddle: From Bilateralism to Near-Convertibility, 1947–1956*, Yale University Press, New Haven

United Nations (1948) *Proceedings and Documents of the United Nations Monetary and Financial Conference*, Bretton Woods, New Hampshire, July 1–22, 1944, United States Government Printing Office, Washington

Wriston, W. (1988) 'Technology and Sovereignty', *Foreign Affairs*, Vol. 67, pp. 63–75

Zhou, X. (2009) 'Reform the International Monetary System', *BIS Review*, 41. Available online at www.bis.org/review/r090402c.pdf (accessed 26 December 2016)

5 | Capital Moves Financially

Securitisation, Value and the Emergent Social Relations of Labour

DICK BRYAN AND MICHAEL RAFFERTY

In 1995 John Holloway wrote a short but powerful essay in *Capital and Class* called 'Capital Moves'. It was published before the two authors of this paper started their shared research. In the midst of an emerging literature on the newly-invented category of 'globalisation', depicting how capital was discovering new freedoms in the spaces-beyond-nation, Holloway issued a decisive challenge. It is part of what drew us, as Marxists investigating the global expansion of capital, to a shared research project.

In essence, Holloway said that if we want to understand capital as a thing – a fund of assets or as a corporation – then the meaning of its movement is not too difficult to understand. Indeed the subsequent 20 years has seen increasing analysis of the spatial movement of capital, covering issues from liquid capital and off-shore financial markets to multinational firms and globally outsourced production systems and supply chains. There are of course debates here, but there is also a widely held basic set of propositions.

But, contended Holloway, if we want to understand capital so as to challenge and subvert it, then we have to go to Marx's proposition that capital is not so much a thing, but a social relation: a social relation of value in movement (for example, 1885: 185). What does it mean to say that a social relation 'moves'? For Holloway in 1995, the answer was framed in terms of a contrast with feudalism, and the immobility of both lord and serf. The serf's transition to a working class became a flight from subordination, and hence a flight to insubordination; the lord's, a flight from insubordination, to a new regime of control we call capitalism. Critical here is that under capitalism capital has to move to escape falling profits and in search of higher ones: that is part of what capitalist competition implies. Capital is inherently mobile.

Perhaps people were inclined to just read part of Holloway's essay and then disengage, in the belief that there is mainly just a rhetorical point here. It seemed that Holloway was describing capitalism in relation to feudalism, but hadn't engaged capitalism at its late twentieth century frontier. If so, they would have missed the point that Holloway proposed, so astutely, that: "Value, in the form of money, is the new liquidity of the class relation."

Accordingly, the liquidity of finance is capital's new contemporary form of movement:

> It is the fact that the lord-turned-capitalist can convert his wealth into money that makes it possible for him to abandon one group of workers and move to another, and to participate in the global exploitation of labour... [Money] transforms the antagonistic relation of subordination/insubordination into a relation of money, transforms the flight of-and-from subordination which defines the capital-labour relation into the movement of money, the movement of capital (understood as an economic phenomenon).

This did indeed turn out to be the frontier of capital's movement. The danger, Holloway contended, is that in the conventional Marxist literature on globalisation, labour appears either not at all, or as a distributional victim. But in bringing labour to the centre of the question, capital's innate need to move can be framed differently: as a "manifestation of capital's incapacity to subordinate labour."

This reframing was an empowering perspective, for it opened up the issue that perhaps labour has power in its immobility: that capital's need to move is also its weakness. But was Holloway just involved in a linguistic reframing to inspire the defeated: a word play to make the victims look powerful, but without a real material basis to this reframing? What is there in the case that labour is powerful in capital's movement?

Before we get there, we must first present the position Holloway refutes, and then follow it with a material explanation as to why the powerless labour thesis might be based on a limited understanding of 'capital' in the twenty-first century. We are then in a position to frame the power in the contemporary immobility of labour.

Immobility Makes Labour Powerless Thesis

This labour powerlessness thesis is simple to recount, for it is the conventional wisdom of the left. It is the proposition that labour is the victim in the mobility of capital, albeit that the movement of capital is not simply reducible to the victimisation of labour. Indeed, that conventional wisdom would have it that much of the movement of capital is directed precisely to avoid the domain of labour, characterised as disengagement with the 'real', 'productive' economy and the flight to financial 'speculation', with off-shore financial markets its quintessential expression.

Issues of speculation aside, when it comes to relations within 'production', labour is cast by the conventional wisdom as victim of capital's mobility in any number of ways. It started historically with propositions of 'deindustrialization' of the centres of advanced capitalism. This process involved 'old', heavy industry abandoning the places of secure jobs, high labour costs and environmental and other state regulations that had built up in the post-war period. Capitalists left these places in search of cheap, docile labour, low environmental standards and low taxation rates. The resultant 'rustbelt' locations had been, the argument goes, the heart of the working class organisation and secure employment – people (overwhelmingly men) in permanent jobs that paid a living wage and with good conditions of sick leave, annual leave, health insurance and pension payments.

So as capitalists exited, the message for the working class in the advanced capitalist economics was clear. The only thing, supposedly, that would save jobs was a decline in the conditions of employment, away from permanent, full-time jobs with good conditions towards work compliant with technological innovations like 'just-in-time' and global sourcing via 'supply chains' and 'networking', and wages consistent with globally competitive norms of profitability.

Concurrently, a focus on finance and its global mobility gave rise to the proposition of 'shareholder value': that any public company, in any location, was under pressure from concentrated voting blocs of investors to deliver high returns. Capitalists presented these momentums as an inexorable and binding imperative that transferred pressure directly to labour: if jobs are to stay where they are, labour costs must fall and productivity must grow.

This all meant permanent jobs being replaced by increasingly casualised and part time work,[1] and the continual negotiating away

---

[1] The argument here is clearly simplified, for not everyone has suddenly lost access to 'permanent employment'. But where the formal conditions of permanent employment have been retained it is clear that the 'benefits' of permanence have reduced and traded away against wages. It is the direction of change, not the binary categories of permanent/impermanent that concern us here.

of the costs (to employers) of various sorts of leave and restrictive work practices. Increasingly, too, we saw the shift of work to self-employment and one-off 'gigs', with none of the protections of wage work. In each case there was a conscious passing of risks – the contingencies of work – onto workers, as a way to boost corporate profitability.

In this framing, labour is indeed cast as innocent victim of capital's calculative momentum, albeit that Holloway would remind us that capital is no less a victim of its own 'shareholder' logic. It's just worse for labour because it is further down the food chain, and hence the recipient of offloading of more of capital's costs and risks.

Whilst labour may well be a victim, there is also a distinct politics in this depiction, for it invokes a particular antidote. We see it in the popular belief on the left (but not just the left) that the advanced capitalist countries should be restricting the movement of capital to stop the offloading of jobs, costs and risks onto workers. For some, the aspiration is that, if this is done, permanent, full-time jobs might again become the norm. The state, the argument goes, should be containing capital and it should be defending the rights of labour. The election of Trump in the US (along with the support for Democrat candidate Bernie Sanders) and the 'Brexit' vote in Britain can be explained significantly in terms of the perceptions of powerlessness amongst voters who lost out from post-1970s changes in the labour market and the belief that a new policy regime will return us a long way to the former days of prosperity and security.

It is surely a fanciful proposition, for there is nothing yet apparent in current states in advanced countries that looks likely to implement such policies. Whilst President Trump talks of bringing back 'old' industries, he says nothing of bringing back old unions and the permanent labour contracts they secured. The position is certainly in danger of idealising working conditions of the 1960s which were anything but ideal for women, subordinate races and migrants, and negligent in terms of occupational health and safety.

But so long as changes over the last 40 years are framed in terms of 'permanence lost', it is perhaps not surprising that the alluring antidote is to create the vision of 'permanence regained'. When states do not deliver such change, we have seen recourse to critiques of 'neo-liberalism', to explain why nation states became diverted from this potentially redemptive policy agenda.

Holloway had no interest in this politics; indeed, he stands strongly for a non-statist politics (2002; 2010). We could debate some of the Autonomist dimensions of Holloway's politics at this point, but that is not our agenda here.

Reframing the Analysis I: Why Labour's Relative Immobility Matters for Value

If, following Holloway, we frame the changes in the labour market not in terms of loss, but in terms of 'becoming', a different politics emerges. This framing of becoming focusses on the emergent social relations of labour, and the requirement not just that capital must move but that it must also move through labour. This perspective directs us to the political potential that lies within labour as the recipient of mobile capital's offloading of risks and other costs. It also frames the new (emergent) ways in which labour is becoming critical to capital's twenty-first century agenda. But before we get to the social power and political potency that comes from contemporary (relative) immobility, we have to focus on the way in which immobility is critical theoretically.

In conventional Marxist theory, labour's immobility is the premise of the idea that labour power has a national value, and hence that surplus value – the 'spread' (to use the financial term) between the value of labour power (the cost of reproducing the worker) and the value created by labour – is in practice a nation-specific relation.

Marx's analysis focussed on the value of labour power being a social subsistence (and often more than a biological one) and that value of labour power is country-specific. The value of labour power depends, he contended, (1867:275):

... to a great extent on the level of civilization attained by a country. [It] contains a historical and moral element. Nevertheless, in a given country at a given period, the average amount of means of subsistence necessary for the worker is a known datum.

This always makes value difficult to conceptualise across different value of labour power spaces (broadly, nations). In Volume 1 of *Capital*, Marx contended that different values of labour power and working conditions in different countries result in output with "unequal international values" (1867: 702). For value theory, this difference was supposed to be offset by difference in the values of national currencies in reference to gold: a difficult proposition to hold to in the twenty-first century. Theoretically, though, this would be resolved in the transformation of labour values into 'prices of production': values adjusted for competitive norms, as explained in *Capital* Volume III. But, critically, Marx projected no formal competitive universalization of the value of labour power.

For Marx, the absence of a 'global average unit of universal labour', and his explicit desire to avoid such a measure (1867: ch. 22) needs explanation, and explanation beyond simply identifying Marx's historical context. Whilst commodities could have a (transformed) global value, and hence the bundle of commodities consumed by labour could have a global value, it is essential to Marx's theory of value that the value of labour power can be based only partly on the value of commodities consumed by labour. If it were entirely this that determined the value of labour power, that concept would be purely circular in definition: we can't know the value of commodities until we know the value of labour power and we can't know the value of labour power until we know the value of the commodities consumed by labour! It is the location-(and time-) specific social and moral norms in the determination of the value of labour power that breaks the logical circularity, and gives labour power a value determined differently from other commodities.

This is the sense that labour anchors value not just in terms of being the source of surplus value, but also in providing the absolute measure on which values are built.

When capital is recognised as mobile, 'globalisation' can be cast as capital playing off differences in this surplus spread in different locations. Location matters because in different locations the spreads can be different and sustained. This all depends on the acceptance of national differences in the value of labour power.

But what if globalisation is indeed breaking down international differences in the value of labour power, not in the sense that wages everywhere become equal, but that the value of labour power in any site and activity are increasingly found to be proportional to the profitability of capital in those sites and activities?

When labour becomes incorporated into global calculation and working conditions restructured in the way we have described it (and that description is not particularly controversial) the value of labour power, defined by reference to a bundle of consumption, loses its integrity as a <u>national</u> measure. When people are working in multiple jobs in a wide range of contractual conditions, with conjuncturally-contingent clauses, there is no longer an enforceable notion of a country's social minimum or even norm of living standards secured via wage labour. There is then no recognisable national or even regional value of labour power. In a critical sense, global competitive pressure has freed capital from being responsible for providing a living wage – incomes sufficient to reproduce the working class. Labour bargaining is less and less conditioned around the contest over what is a living wage, but instead increasingly determined by the needs of enterprise global competitiveness – measured in terms of corporate profitability. Capital's mobility becomes labour's contingent and variable 'value', and that expresses the ambiguity of value itself: increasingly, there is nothing outside of globally competitive calculus to anchor value.

For many, following David Harvey, this challenge to labour's subsistence created the pressure for working class households to access lines of (increasingly available) credit in an attempt to maintain living standards. The argument goes that, via this credit, the numeraire of a value of labour power was preserved in certain dimensions (the idea of basic consumption for the reproduction of the working class), though not as the basis of a measure of the value of labour time. For Harvey, this was a process that led to a debt-driven global financial crisis (GFC). That specific and widely held proposition is not the concern of the current paper, although it is critical to note that when the analysis of labour and class moves to issues of credit and speculation as the source of crisis, a materiality – the changing social relations of capital – can become lost inside a critique of overproduction/under-consumption.

Reframing the Analysis II: Emerging Social Relations of Labour

Our proposition shifts the focus. We argue that, in this debt-driven process, the critical class issue is not found in the dangers of increasing indebtedness for households; it is that capital has sabotaged its own unit of measure. Socially necessary labour time can no longer be expressed in a universal (national, leave aside international) unit of measure because the value of labour power becomes incoherent as the basis of the commensurability of value. Labour hours could not be converted into a universal monetary measure of abstract labour.

Analysis reverts to Ricardian units of measure – 'actual' labour time and 'actual' working conditions that diversified with the 'loss' of permanent employment, without a conversion to a commensurable measure of socially necessary time. Little wonder that Harvey finishes up with a Ricardian conception of crisis: that the owners of surplus invested it unproductively ('speculatively'), leading to a crash in the rate of 'real' accumulation. Ricardo wrote about unproductive landlords appropriating and 'wasting' ground rent; Harvey about unproductive hedge funds appropriating and wasting economic rent. It's essentially the same theory of crisis.

But what if the loss of a socially coherent value of labour power is itself the (or at least a) crisis?

For capital, the loss of labour power as an anchor unit of measure was associated from the 1970s with volatile and unpredictable exchange rates, interest rates and commodity prices. Marx's idea in *Capital* that national differences in the value of labour power would be reconciled via national differences in the value of money is now seen as simply wrong: there is no need to recount that currencies and exchange rates move in response to many other forces. We have argued elsewhere (Bryan and Rafferty 2006; 2007) that this volatility called forth the rise in the 1980s of derivative contracts; invented at this time to hedge volatility and simulate a stable, albeit temporary and private, store of value. Of course derivatives extend beyond simply hedging an increasingly ambiguous value of labour power and hence of output produced by labour. This is an issue we will return to shortly.

Even if the latter point about derivatives and stability is contested, and we appreciate that it is, the general point is that value needs an anchoring unit of measure, and that this role was historically being played by a value of labour power based in moral and social norms that are country-specific. If that country specificity is disappearing, what is being built by capital to replace it? How do we re-think value, in the era of globalisation and financialization, in relation to an immobile anchor unit of measure?

Re-Discovering the Social Relation of Capital in Finance by Finding 'Safe' Assets in Labour

If, in the tradition of Marxism, this unit of measure has to have a materiality in the class relations of capitalist accumulation, then the question becomes: can we identify an emerging social relation of capital, conceived differently from the conventional identity of labour's role in 'production'?

We contend that capital's current project is to re-insert the class of labour as the anchor measure of value, but in ways very different from the nineteenth and twentieth century. In this era of globalised finance, we see that the anchoring role of labour is being played out not so much in valuing *commodity* output, and the spread between the commodities required to reproduce the worker and the commodities produced by the worker, but rather as providing a measure of *financial* value, and the spread between the (financial) risks being absorbed by workers' and the risks implied in the value of output by workers: a risk spread.

This changing valuation role is, we believe, only emergent, and indeed it may not evolve in the way we project below. We do not claim a capacity to see the future; our goal is simply to open up new ways of thinking about the social relations of capital that build on current trends in capital accumulation. Uncertain possibilities in the future seem to us to provide more fertile ground for political thinking than the clearest, most precise depictions of losses in the past.

Our proposition opens up a large and complex set of issues, so in the current context we will simply present some stylised propositions. The objective here is to make a credible case; we are not providing a formal, testable hypothesis. The proposition, put simply, is that we are seeing labour, not so much just as workers providing reliable streams of paid work for employers, but reframed as household financial entities providing reliable streams of contractual payments. These payments are increasingly being looked to to provide a secure, stable finance in the form of securities backed by payments on a range of household contracts.

In developing this proposition, we start with a number of simple assertions, none of which is, in isolation, particularly controversial.

1 Treasury Bonds Are No Longer the Pre-eminent Safe Anchor of Financial Value

The standard 'risk-free' financial unit is treasury bonds, to be held as a 'safe' asset. Like state money, they are backed by the state, and hence (nominally) face no default risk. But things are changing. No doubt

there will for the foreseeable future be a large demand for treasury
bonds, especially US Treasury bonds. Central banks are large financial institutions with major financial assets and asset backing. Any
portfolio would want exposure to this asset class. But it is a different
matter to depict treasury bonds as 'safe'. In the wake of the GFC,
many states bailed out their banking systems and in so doing made
state default risk a possibility. Moreover, with quantitative easing
(QE) in many countries opening up as a domain of post GFC national
monetary policy, treasury bonds and their quantities, prices and
yields have been used as key tools of government policy. Indeed as
part of QE in some leading industrial countries, Treasury bonds have
been generating negative yields. This is hardly the profile of an anchor
unit of measure. But is there an alternative?

As explained by He et al. (2016) in the synopsis of their NBER
working paper:

US government bonds are widely considered to be the world's safe store of
value. US government bonds are a large fraction of safe asset portfolios,
such as the portfolios of many central banks. The world demand for safe
assets leads to low yields on US Treasury bonds. During periods of economic turmoil, such as the events of 2008, these yields fall even further.
Moreover, despite the fact that US government debt has risen substantially
relative to US GDP over the last decade, US government bond yields have
not risen. What makes US government bonds "safe assets"? Our answer in
short is that safe asset investors have nowhere else to go but invest in US
government bonds.[2]

This proposition that there is nowhere else to go just loads risk into the
concept of 'safety' and hence lacks credibility as an explanation of safe
assets. Or, to put the issue differently, when existing financial assets
lose their safety, we must surely be looking to financial market innovation, and state innovation too, to invent new safe assets (their capacity
to invent is beyond question) and also to state innovation in ways to
add safety to (reduce risk in) a suite of potentially safe assets. What is
interesting here is that safe assets are most likely to attach to the nation

[2] Helleiner (2014: 64) cites a Chinese official in 2009 making essentially the same
point in explaining why China kept buying US Treasury bonds during the crisis:
"Except for US Treasuries, what can you hold? ... US Treasuries are the safe
haven."

state – for states can guarantee against default risk in a way no private organisations can – but the form of that guarantee can change.[3] States can use their leverage to guarantee against default risk (create safety in assets) without themselves issuing the 'safe' asset.

2 New Sorts of Assets Are Emerging to Fill the 'Safe' End of Asset Portfolios

The premise here is that safety is not innate to an asset: the conditions of safety can be created (or withdrawn) by nation state policy. So whilst QE saw the state effectively withdraw certain conditions of safety associated with Treasury bonds, states have sought to create new forms of 'safety' in certain asset classes.

Critical here has been the process (and contractual terms) of privatisation of once-state-owned assets. All sorts of infrastructure, with a range of state underwriting of revenue streams attached (such as inflation-adjusted price approvals), have been released into private ownership. But what is significant here is that the state's underwriting of revenue streams on privatised assets creates possibilities for AAA rated securitisation: to sell the secure income streams on those assets without selling the assets themselves. Indeed, new sorts of assets, like infrastructure bonds, are emerging (and being called forth) in importance in meeting market needs for 'safe', liquid assets. So these bonds have many of the financial attributes of treasury bonds, and with guarantees of inflation-linked revenue for example, they may have more stable prices and positive yields than treasury bonds.[4]

---

[3] Robert Merton (2013), famous for the Black-Scholes-Merton options pricing model, contended in a back-of-the-envelope calculation that in 2013 the US state has explicitly and implicitly underwritten the value of financial assets totaling about $17 trillion. His agenda was to treat this underwriting as a put option, and thus create the technique for pricing that option, thereby explicitly pricing the state's underwriting. When its price is explicit it is possible to discuss its merits in public policy. But currently it is hidden. Of course, the price of that option (the value of underwriting) is relatively low when things are stable, but will rapidly grow as instability arises.

[4] For example, the British state has been toying with the possibility of issuing 'infrastructure bonds' rather than treasury bonds, essentially because the former are seen to be backed by 'real' assets; the latter just by state reputation. See, for example, Thorpe (2016).

3 Securities Backed by Household Contractual Payments Are an Emerging Category of Financial Assets

There is always likely to be a limited supply of safe infrastructure bonds, at least those associated with physical infrastructure like roads, ports and airports. The search for safe assets is seeing a more imaginative approach to the question of what assets can be made safe, and household-based assets clearly have potential to mimic the financial attributes of infrastructure. We need to break this proposition down into two: the first is the growth of financial assets backed by household payments; the second is how these assets are being made safe by nation states.

The impact of the 'financialisation of daily life' (Martin 2002) has seen an increasing proportion of household expenditures made on contracts (we might call it the 'contractualisation' of households): utilities payments are increasingly on contract, loan repayments, contracted fees for childcare, education and gyms, and growing household expenditure on pension funds and insurance are all evidence of contractualisation. The largest of these, by value, is mortgage repayments. Critically, the income streams that follow from these contracts (household mortgage payments) are themselves treated and traded as financial assets: as mortgage- and asset-backed securities (MBS and ABS).

There is good reason for this emergence. Nobel Prize-winning economist Robert Shiller reminds us that, in the era of finance and the financialisation of daily life:

Far more important to the world's economies than the stock markets are wage and salary incomes and other non-financial sources of livelihood such as the economic value of our homes and apartments. That is where the bulk of our wealth is found. (2003, 9)

But houses are illiquid assets: places to live. What makes them liquid 'capital' is not the house per se as a 'productive asset' but the monthly mortgage contract payments attached to household purchases of houses. The same is true of education or health insurance or electricity provision: they are illiquid and do not appear as 'financial capital'. To replicate the attributes of liquid financial assets, financial innovation creates derivative exposures to this large asset class, in the form of bonds or securities backed by household university fee or loan payments, health insurance payments and electricity bill payments (asset-backed securities).

4 Assets Backed by Household Payments Are Being Made (Relatively) Safe by Nation State Regulations to Ensure Households Stay on Contract

Why would we depict assets based in household payments as 'safe' assets? Indeed, given the fact that defaults on sub-prime mortgage payments crashed the MBS market and triggered the GFC, it may seem strange to identify households' payments as a safe asset and an anchor unit measure. But, since the crisis, things are changing; indeed perhaps the most significant consequence of post-crisis financial regulation does not pertain to controls over financial institutions, but over households: the secure foundations of MBS and ABS are being systematically rebuilt by state management (Bryan, Rafferty and Tinel, 2016). A number of changes combine to create this outcome.

First, household contract payments are being more carefully credit rated. Each mortgage within an MBS is now being individually rated for default risk, and these individual ratings are themselves the focus of enormous evaluation. What has become called 'big data' – the combination of data from a wide range of service providers, retailers and financial institutions – is all about assembling profiles on individuals and their households in order to accurately predict the risk of default on different contracts.

Second, because the contractual payments that go into MBS and ABS are payments for subsistence goods (housing, health, electricity etc.) and locked in by contract, households do not want to default, or they lose their subsistence. (Note here, this is one reason why sub-prime mortgage-lending was an aberration for long-term capital stability, for these were loans going to people who never anticipated buying a house, and the default risk they carried was tolerable for all immediate parties to the loans: the lenders passed on the default risk to unknowing securities buyers, and the borrowers were prepared to gamble on house prices as their one chance of home ownership.) The effect is that households will absorb risks for capital markets, for they keep up the contractual payments (provide the income streams for safe assets) even though their household income is itself increasingly precarious. This is the risk spread version of surplus we referred to earlier.

Third, the state is playing a critical role in standardizing household default risk. Financial literacy education and bankruptcy laws which bind people to contract repayments even when they are, in corporate terms, trading whilst insolvent (e.g. negative equity, income less that student debt repayments) are the clearest symptoms of this management. We believe that current initiatives in the US to increase minimum wages and in Europe and Canada to trial guaranteed minimum incomes, in combination with bankruptcy laws, provides increasing certainty that the mass of households will be held accountable for meeting their contractual obligations (Beggs, Bryan and Rafferty 2014). Increasingly, then, securities backed by household contractual payments, in combination with state policies of household financial risk management, are starting to look like 'safe' assets.

In combination, these four elements point to an emerging role of households as the providers of the payment streams on which safe assets are being built under the auspices of the state.

By way of illustrating this proposition, we point to the US state's response to the GFC. In response to a crisis that had been triggered by mortgage defaults causing crashes in MBS and in the credit default swaps that insured them, the US Federal Reserve did a remarkable thing. It didn't pursue the conventional tool of monetary policy, where the Treasury issues bonds and the Fed purchases them to release spending power to Treasury. It did some of this, but it pursued also an entirely unexpected agenda: it started buying MBS as the central pillar of its QE policy. So by the end of QE3 (round three of QE, ending in 2015) the Federal Reserve had tripled its asset holding compared with early 2007, and half those assets are now MBS. There are now more MBS on the books of the Federal Reserve than there were total assets before the crisis, and this holding is permanent – as Fed-held MBS naturally expire they are to be replaced by new purchases (Bryan and Rafferty 2017). Our proposition is that the Fed wanted to hold assets that had a material foundation in the payments of ordinary people – 'labour', albeit now appearing financially as 'households'.[5]

So what is the social relation of capital being invoked here? Mortgages immediately suggest debt, and the path to Harvey's framing of crisis.

---

[5] There was a credible initial argument, in QE1, that the state bought MBS because this was the part of the market that crashed and it needed support. But by the time of QE3, and especially the decision to permanently hold MBS, that support argument is no longer credible. The Fed holds MBS because of some intrinsic desirability of that asset class (Bryan and Rafferty 2017).

But the issue we address is not debt per se, for securitisation relates also to household contracts like electricity and health insurance that are not about debt (Bryan, Rafferty and Jefferis 2015). But to the extent that securitised debt is prevalent, it is the securitisation process, not the usury process that warrants focus.

Indeed the critical issue is not debt, but the regular (contractualised) payments for household subsistence – the same domain that defines the value of labour power, but now framed as a portfolio of financial contracts rather than a bundle of commodities.

Conclusion: Holloway Financialized

So we come back to the core unit of value found in conventional Marxian value theory: the value of labour power. We can now re-define it not as a simple bundle of commodities, but (also), in a financialized era, as a set of payments on the contracts by which many of these commodities are now purchased. We need to pursue this parallel.

In the conventional labour theory of value, labour could provide an anchor to value because it exists partly inside and partly outside market-driven processes of valuation: inside via the purchase of commodities but, critically, outside because the households in which workers are reproduced are not simply driven by a profit calculus. They are anchored in a social world beyond capital, and one defined by attachment; not mobility.

The same applies in the financialized version. Households are 'inside' the market-driven process, via the purchase of commodities (now on contract) and the selling into financial markets of those contractual payments as financial assets (ABS and MBS). But households are also 'outside' the profit-driven process in the sense that households will keep absorbing risk and meeting contractual payments when companies would not. Indeed, for companies it is formally illegal to trade whilst insolvent, but for households it is quite different: a failure to meet contracts, even when walking away from the contract would be more financially 'rational', remains illegal, and anyway it means a loss of subsistence goods and services.

If our proposition is credible, and we wish to reiterate that, as a projection of the future, it can be no more than a 'credible' proposition, we are framing a new way in which labour, now in the form of households, is coming to anchor value. In Marx's depiction in *Capital* this anchoring occurs in Volume I, via an explanation of (formal but asymmetrical) equivalence in exchange based on socially necessary labour time, and where labour's role in commensurating value is tied directly to its capacity to produce surplus value. That is what makes labour the centre of measurement and the source of profit. In our depiction of the twenty-first century, with a focus on finance, the issue shifts from a focus on equivalence in exchange to a store of value.

So in the context of growing mobility of capital, it is the immobility of labour not just as wage worker, but as sites of payment streams for consumption and household risk management – its fixity in the provision of its subsistence – that capital is seeking to re-subordinate via the securitisation of household subsistence payments. This is the new social relation of value in movement: that in search of exposure to labour and of 'safety', capital's flight takes it to the class of workers, now as households. Holloway, cited above, contended in 1995 that:

[Money] transforms the antagonistic relation of subordination/insubordination into a relation of money, transforms the flight of-and-from subordination which defines the capital-labour relation into the movement of money.

Our proposition is that in the contemporary movement of money, the historical destiny of capital as a social relation of value in movement is being drawn back to the need to 'pass through' labour (households) to reproduce its value and to capture a surplus in the process. This, we believe, is capital's emerging class vision – its innovation in its social relation with labour. It is also the site of potential resistance to capital, and the challenge here is that labour finds ways of refusing to play its allocated role in underwriting the store of value.

Holloway argued that capital was moving to free itself from labour's insubordination at work. The last twenty years has shown that this was indeed a credible proposition about the social relations of capital. We are also arguing that that over time capital's flight of-and-from subordination has also opened up a new dimension to labour's engagement with capital – as providers of a regular stream of payments on which safe financial assets are being built.

But in having to pass through labour's households this is requiring an even more intimate association of capital with labour, and one in which the state must support the viability of households at the same time as it seeks to crush the viability of organised labour.[6] In this emerging frontier of the capital-labour relation, new possibilities open up for labour to challenge the social relations of capital, and to lay claims to the wealth and possibilities that have been appropriated and in so doing to challenge the socially subordinate relations that defines capitalism as a social mode of organisation.

References

Beggs, M., D. Bryan and M. Rafferty 2014 'Shoplifters of the world unite! Law and culture in financialized times', *Cultural Studies* 26(5–6): 976–996.

Bryan, D. and M. Rafferty 2006 *Capitalism with Derivatives: A Political Economy of Financial Derivatives, Capital and Class.* Hampshire and New York: Palgrave Macmillan.

2007 'Financial derivatives and the theory of money', *Economy and Society* 36(1):134–58.

2017 'Reframing austerity: Financial morality, savings and securitization', *Journal of Cultural Economy* (currently on-line).

Bryan, D., M. Rafferty and C. Jefferis 2015 'Risk and value: Finance, labor and production', *South Atlantic Quarterly* 114(2): 307–329.

Bryan, D., M. Rafferty and B. Tinel 2016 'Households at the frontier of monetary development', *Behemoth: A Journal of Civilization*, 9(2): 46–58.

Harvey, D. 2011 *The Enigma of Capital and the Crisis of Capitalism.* London: Profile Books.

Helleiner, E. 2014 *The Status Quo Crisis: Global Financial Governance After the 2008 Meltdown.* Oxford: Oxford University Press.

Holloway, J. 1995 'Capital moves' *Capital &Class* 19(3): 137–144.

2002 *Change the World without Taking Power.* London: Pluto Press.

2010 *Crack Capitalism.* London: Pluto Press.

Martin, R. 2002 *The Financialization of Daily Life.* Philadelphia: Temple University Press.

Marx, K. 1867 *Capital, Volume I.* Harmondsworth: Penguin 1976.

1885 *Capital, Volume II.* Harmondsworth: Penguin 1978.

Merton, R. et al. 2013 'On a new approach for analysing and managing macrofinancial risks', *Financial Analysts Journal* 69(2): 22–33.

Thorpe, D. 2016 'Government infrastructure bonds can be "excellent investments"', *WhatInvestment*, November 17. Downloaded from www .whatinvestment.co.uk/uk-government-infrastructure-bonds-excellent-investment.

---

[6] We believe that this essential point is missed in most critiques of 'neo-liberalism'.

130 *Dick Bryan and Michael Rafferty*

Shiller, R (2003) *The New Financial Order: Risk in the 21st Century*. Princeton: Princeton University Press.

Zhiguo He, Arvind Krishnamurthy, Konstantin Milbradt 2016 What Makes US Government Bonds Safe Assets? NBER Working Paper No. 22017 February http://www.nber.org/papers/w22017.

6 | *International Money after the Crisis*
What Do We Know?

HERMAN MARK SCHWARTZ

International Money after the Crisis: What Do We Know?

Does the 2007–08 Global Financial Crisis (GFC) crisis signal the end of the US Dollar as the dominant International Reserve Currency (IRC)? Recent books by two prominent North American political economists offer typical, albeit competing assessments. Eric Helleiner (2014) expresses some surprise that so little has changed with respect to global financial governance and in particular the centrality of the US dollar; his title, *The Status Quo Crisis*, reveals his assessment. By contrast, Jonathan Kirshner (2014) sees the crisis as beginning the unravelling of US dollar centrality and US macro-economic policy autonomy. For him, the crisis dealt a mortal blow to US dominance by delegitimizing the market fundamentalist ideology justifying financialization of the global economy, free capital flows, and de-regulation of finance. Both books are right and wrong for the wrong reasons.[1] Both skate on the surface of what it is that makes the US dollar central because neither asks what it is that makes money money, and what

Acknowledgements: This paper emerged from three joint papers with Randall Germain and useful conversations with Anush Kapadia, with additional helpful comments from Ronen Palan and Jocelyn Pixley. Errors remain mine.
[1] Both books are also "early," despite publication dates six years after Lehman Brothers bankruptcy in September 2008, and four years after the official end of the acute crisis in 2010. In some ways, even though we are now almost a decade away from Lehman, it is still too early to tell. Historical memory compresses the relatively slow unfolding of the Great Depression, which occurred against a backdrop of unsettled geo-economic and geo-political questions from World War I, and in which immediate government reactions to the crisis were either incorrect or incoherent. The famous American stock market crash in October 1929 did not immediately provoke a massive downturn. Rather, the crisis percolated another 19 months until the collapse of the Austrian bank Credit-Anstalt. Moreover, the majority of US banks failed after the Credit-Anstalt crisis, and world trade did not complete its two-thirds nominal contraction until mid-1933. The political and economic effects of the US crisis still seem to be rippling outwards towards the global economic periphery, and especially China, as of 2017.

distinguishes international money from domestic money. Legitimacy matters; but why? International institutions and governance matter; but why?

In this respect, neither book is unusually superficial. Each addresses the key questions about international money in the usual way. Is an International Monetary System (IMS) based on a national currency inherently unstable? Does US economic and political power logically precede the use of the US dollar as the preeminent IRC, or is it the use of the US dollar that creates global economic power for the United States (Eichengreen 2011)? The usual answers to this question combine one-sided explanations from economics and international relations.[2] But both sorts of explanations assume the separation of the political and economic realms. Combining them in an additive or ad hoc manner replicates the inadequacies of each. In this case both books share a set of implicit assumptions deriving from Weber: that capital is different from the state; that capital is intrinsically mobile; that capital is fundamentally without nationality.

Other chapters in this book address these assumptions with respect to capital mobility and state policy. Chapter 5, in particular, sees mobility as state policy. In this chapter I analyse the likely trajectory of the IMS starting from an explicitly political economy point of view that assumes the unity of the political and economic spheres. This modified chartalist theory of money (see section 2 and briefly below) explains the operation of and tensions accruing to the IMS by using a different but less imperfect analogy to the operation of a domestic monetary system than that used in the usual explanations. The precise points of non-congruence in the analogy reveal why the IMS is inherently unstable and enable us to make coherent sense of the existing partial arguments and also to combine them coherently.

Put as simply as possible, monetary systems generally are composed of both inside money and outside money. Private actors create inside money, that is, credit to other private actors. In doing so, banks simultaneously create both assets and liabilities. The extension of credit creates a loan, which shows up as an asset; the deposit of loan funds into the borrower's account creates a liability for the bank.

---

[2] Some exceptions are Strange (1971) generally on the IMS, Otero-Iglesias and Vermeiren (2015) and Germain and Schwartz (2017) specifically on the Chinese RMB, and Germain and Schwartz (2014) specifically on the euro.

New loans simultaneously create assets and liabilities, and thus in principle balance sheets that net out across the whole economy. But this private credit creation is inherently unstable. First, absent some mechanism for collective discipline, private financial firms have an incentive to expand their balance sheets by creating excessive amounts of inside money. In principle, this behaviour nets out, but in practice an asymmetry plagues this accounting balance. While asset values can – and do – change in response to behaviour by market actors, liabilities in the form of debt have values that remain stable in nominal terms until a formal bankruptcy. If asset values fall (as they do in when a panic or crisis starts), then banks can fail as their liabilities (deposits) remain unchanged while the collateral behind their assets collapses. Second, as the other papers in this volume attest, credit money can flow across borders, destabilizing other monetary systems.

If private actors were disciplined, this asymmetry between assets and liabilities on banks' balance sheets would matter less. Indeed, Schumpeter's (1934) entire analysis of creative destruction is built on the assumption that credit creation to entrepreneurs is self-liquidating (or self-validating) because new production comes on stream that generates sufficient income to service this new debt. But Minsky (1977; see also Harvey 1982), by contrast, sees endogenous dynamics in the financial system leading banks to extend credit to borrowers with no present or future capacity to service that debt. Minsky (1977) argues that under almost all conditions private financial actors have incentives to expand their balance sheets beyond an economically sustainable level. By creating additional assets for themselves they necessarily create debt liabilities for others. In doing so, private actors create the possibility for a "Minsky moment," an endogenous economic shock that reduces the value of assets across the economic system. This shock creates an overhang of liabilities on private balance sheets, bankrupting the financial system. Only an authoritative, legitimate actor can constrain private actors from this excess credit creation (in normal times) and rescue them from the overhang of liabilities (in moments of crisis): the state.

The state creates outside money. Unlike inside money, state created outside money does not simultaneously create an explicit financial liability, and thus outside money can be used to absorb the overhang of private liabilities revealed in a financial crash. *Vide* the US Federal Reserve Bank (FED) and, less so, the European Central Bank (ECB)

in 2008–2010. Each used their outside money to buy up devalued
assets at par and thus re-establish balance in the financial system
(Schwartz 2009). The state's ability to create outside credit money,
and thus assets unburdened by formal liabilities aside from money
itself, rests on its ability to tax the territorial economy it controls. The
ability to tax in turn rests on the state's legitimacy. The central problems in the IMS arise from the absence of a superordinate authority
capable of extracting the resources that back its outside money, and
from a potential lack of legitimacy for the issuer of the dominant
IRC. Theoretically a legitimate global central bank capable of issuing
acceptable outside money is possible – this was the essence of Keynes'
proposed International Clearing Union and *Bancor* (see Chapter 4, this
volume). But Keynes' failure shows the political limits to this kind of
proposal.

Explanations of problems in the IMS that are one-sidedly economic, and look only at the efficiency of transactions or the size of a
state's economic zone, miss the importance of legitimate extraction of
resources in normal times; in a crisis they miss the importance of
a sovereign's legitimate claim to "enact a state of exception," in Carl
Schmitt's sense. Explanations that are one-sidedly power political,
and look only at blunt control over internal or external resources
and the threat to withhold or grant those resources, miss the importance of having a domestic or imperial economic zone with enough
productive resources to credibly sustain outside money. This plays
out as Triffin's dilemma in normal times, and as a run on a reserve
currency in abnormal times. In other words, both logics of consequence and logics of appropriateness matter. An IMS in which a single
national currency dominates thus faces a higher order version of
Triffin's dilemma: not confidence versus liquidity but capacity versus
legitimate authority.

This article thus takes four steps to make its case. First, it briefly
surveys the literature on the IMS to make the case for incompleteness
and one-sidedness in the current literature. Second, it explains how
all monetary systems are built on a combination of outside money
and inside money, and the state's role in generating, controlling and
rescuing the monetary system. Third, it applies this quasi-chartalist
view to provide a different understanding of what the GFC that began
in 2008 means for the US dollar as the IRC. It concludes with some
recommendations for both policy and the literature on the IMS.

With respect to the literature, a quasi-chartalist view both accommodates and logically orders the contributions of the core arguments about the IMS. With respect to policy, a quasi-chartalist view suggests that a more transparent and democratic body should supplement or supplant the informal congeries of swap agreements central banks have constructed if we want a more stable IMS. Given that this body minimally and necessarily will resemble Keynes' original proposal for an International Clearing Union, I doubt this will happen.

Section 1: The Usual Suspects

The existing literature on the IMS and IRCs is both incomplete and one-sided. The economic literature suffers from three major flaws. It makes an incorrect analogy to domestic money. It suffers from methodological nationalism. Combined, these two flaws mean that it can generate only necessary but not sufficient causes to explain the IMS. The political science literature suffers from its focus on coercive monetary diplomacy, and by unquestioningly accepting the economic analyses, imports methodological nationalism and a focus on transaction costs.

Much as in the tale of the blind men and the elephant, most single analyses capture a part of the whole. Equally, so, disciplinary perspectives and concerns tend to rigidly separate the political and economic spheres. Economists tend to focus too narrowly on the costs of adjustment, on the assumption that disequilibria by definition should be transitory. They advance policy recommendations aiming at constructing systems that avoid disequilibria (akin to Minsky's "lack of tranquillity"). At its best, as with Triffin (1960), this literature is attentive to an inherent tendency towards disequilibrium, and the essential indeterminacy of the choice of currency for an IMS. At its worst, as in many discussions of the reasons for European monetary union and the promulgation of the euro, the literature focuses on narrow technical issues, elevating lower transaction costs into the only and ultimate goal of policy (for criticisms, see the contributions in Matthijs and Blyth 2015). In this respect, nothing much has changed since Fred Bergsten (1975: 3) wrote in 1975 that his analysis of the US dollar's international role was venturing forth into new waters[3]

---

[3] He had perhaps not quite assimilated either Cohen (1971) or Strange (1971).

by combining political and economic factors, even if he immediately turned to adjustment costs as the main issue.

International relations (IR) scholars focus too much on the ways in which the issuer of the IRC exploits consumers of that IRC, and in which money in general can be a weapon of power politics. This relationship is sometimes reversed, as when control over oil, for example, becomes the basis for the maintenance of a given IRC. IR scholars thus also focus on the essentially political choice of an IMS (e.g. Helleiner 1996, 2003a), and (excessively so) on seigniorage as a motivation for compelling others to use one's currency as the IRC.[4] At its best (Strange, 1971; Cohen, 1998), this literature explores the hierarchy of monies in the global economy. Strange, for example, captures the different economic and political understandings of money in her typology of top, negotiated, and master currencies, which Cohen further subdivides and amends. In more narrow analyses – however good they might be on their own terms – it devolves into studies in the use of relational monetary power for narrow policy ends (see e.g. Kirshner 1997 or the studies in Andrews 2006). These studies successfully illuminate the instrumental use of relational power but do not allow us to draw conclusions about the normal (mis-)functioning of the IMS, or how that power translates into power in times of crisis.

Despite these problems, the existing literature raises issues that touch on the first principles informing any study of the IMS. Those first principles are the existence of a hierarchy among monies, the global (in-)adequacy of macro-economic demand, political legitimacy, and the ability to extract resources. Before surveying those issues, it is important to acknowledge a point Cohen (1971) made long ago: a functionally useful currency necessarily is issued by an economy that is large relative to the global economy, that has deep and liquid markets both for the currency itself and for the kind of assets that back that currency, and that has an infrastructure for supporting trading in that currency. These however, do not explain the dynamics of the IRC. They are necessary but not sufficient conditions.

---

[4] Seigniorage is the additional revenue a state obtained by coining money with a facial value of X, yet which contained less than 100 percent of X in terms of actual specie. In a fiat money system, foreign holdings of paper currency create seigniorage because holders are in effect offering an interest free loan to the sovereign issuing the paper. Cash generates no interest. But seigniorage amounts to very little in economic terms (Schwartz 2009).

Cohen's pioneering study on international money set much of the terms of the economic debate, working off an analogy to domestic money. Cohen (1971) argued that a fully developed IRC had to perform six critical economic functions similar to that of domestic money, acting as a unit of exchange, a store of value, and a unit of account, and at both the private and official levels. He further argued that possessing an IRC conferred several admittedly not overwhelming advantages on the country emitting the IRC. To the extent that foreign entities held currency in their reserves, the emitter benefited from seigniorage. Most analyses of seigniorage suggest that this is a trivial benefit relative to the size of the emitter's economy. More substantially, the ability to generate an IRC allowed the emitter to delay balance of payments adjustment in a world of fixed-exchange rates (as under Bretton Woods), or indeed avoid it entirely in a world of true fiat currencies. Cohen sees this autonomy or delay as the essence of global monetary power.

In *The Geography of Money*, Cohen (1998) generated a hierarchical typology of international and domestic monies. At the top of his currency pyramid were two historically unique currencies, the pound sterling in the nineteenth century and the US dollar in the twentieth. Like Strange (1971), Cohen identified these as *Top* currencies. Below those came *Patrician* currencies with some regional force, like the old Deutschemark and Yen – had the book been written later, one presumes he would have slotted the euro and the renminbi here, as he did in later work. These currencies circulated outside the territorial limits of the issuing country, but not as universally as the top currency. Moreover, though Cohen did not note this, the presence of multiple patrician currencies constitutes a kind of protection for the top currency, by limiting the network externalities of any given patrician currency. Below that were *elite* currencies, largely the currencies of former global empires, like sterling or the Dutch guilder, or the currencies of economic significant and stable countries like Australia or Switzerland. Four increasingly fragile currency types largely confined to domestic use or disuse constituted the bottom of Cohen's monetary pyramid. As with Strange (1971), Cohen (1998) points towards the importance of outside money without making the distinction.

While Cohen can justifiably be considered a grandfather of international political economy as a field, his causal explanation for differentiation of currencies is fundamentally economic. He (1998:2) posited "a kind of darwinian process of natural selection, driven by the force of demand" in which (1998:13) "transaction networks define the functional domains of individual currencies." This is explicitly and implicitly a model based on competition, efficiency and transaction costs. Natural selection operates blindly, after all, selecting on the basis of fitness for a given environment. By contrast, politics is about positive selection, the construction and use of power. Efficiency models are at best partial. Cohen (1998) describes the benefits of and uses that flow from currencies positioned farther up in the monetary hierarchy, but otherwise does not have a political explanation for why a hierarchy might exist. This is curious given that Cohen (1998:11) first dismisses Knapp's state theory of money but then puts forward an explanation that uneasily mixes essentially statist reasons for the imposition of a uniform currency in a defined territory with fundamentally market based rationales for "acceptability." By making a strong argument for monetary hierarchy, Cohen provides one piece of the monetary puzzle, but he leaves unclear where money comes from. Furthermore, he focuses overmuch on seigniorage and domestic macro-economic management to the exclusion of global macro-economic management.

By contrast Robert Triffin (1960) did elucidate the contradictions involved in global macro-economic management. The Triffin Dilemma highlighted the growing contradiction between the US dollar's global macro-economic role in the early Bretton Woods period and its fixed link to gold. The dollar supplied the world economy with the liquidity it needed to grow by facilitating the growth of other countries' reserves and thus their ability to sustain uninterrupted economic growth in an era of fixed-exchange rates. Yet, precisely this accumulation of dollar balances abroad risked undermining future confidence in the dollar's value in relation to gold, and thus its utility as an IRC. Given the Bretton Woods fixed-exchange rate system, Triffin (1960: 63) argued, "further increases in dollar balances cannot be relied upon to contribute substantially and indefinitely to the solution of the world illiquidity problem." Triffin saw that relying on outflows of a single dominant national currency to supply world liquidity was illogical and problematic. Much better to internationalize the provision of world liquidity.[5]

---

[5] Here Triffin agreed with Keynes about the need for a banking union, but not with Keynes' preference for the *Bancor*. Triffin instead proposed what became the Special Drawing Right (SDR) at the IMF (Triffin 1960: 90–93).

The critical takeaway from Triffin's analysis is the recognition that an international currency must expand the global monetary stock in sync with the growth of world trade. In this sense, Triffin's macro-economic counterpart to Cohen's micro-economic analysis is still tied to a conventional economic view of money as a useful commodity, as an efficient way of expressing claims, rather than also being a fundamental source of credit. On this view, money is a reflection of the real economy. Thus, for Triffin, money supply growth has to be synchronized to prior growth in the real economy in order to prevent either inflation or deflation, rather than money being a demi-urge for growth in the "real" economy by providing the financial counterpart to Schumpeter's productive entrepreneurs.[6] Nonetheless, Triffin's dilemma opens one pathway to endogenous crises.

Triffin's focus on liquidity derived from the scarring experience of competitive devaluations and deflation in the Great Depression. In this context, fixed rates and a generous supply of liquidity matter. In today's world of floating rates, the issue is whether or not the global economy has an output gap (Schwartz 2014). But in either context, liquidity provision is about expanding global aggregate demand by expanding either public or private credit. Not only are increases in liquidity and demand necessary for global economic expansion to occur, but the form which this growth takes is necessarily political in inception and operation. The need for growth in aggregate demand has been an enduring feature of the global political economy throughout the post-1945 period, despite changes in the precise mechanisms through which the US dollar as the dominant IRC helped expand demand. Yet Triffin correctly pinpointed what was in effect the potential gap between the assets the global hegemon possessed and the liabilities it incurred in its efforts to manage the global economy. For Triffin this over-extension took the form of a fear of inflation, and thus a loss of confidence. But we would see it rather as a fear of relative decline for the hegemon as the exorbitant burden ate into the hegemon's economy, reducing its relative economic pre-eminence (Nitzan 1998; Schwartz 2009). Generically, Triffin's dilemma at an economic level is a lack of current state income and/or assets (i.e. future income)

---

[6] Chapter 5 makes the same assumptions about money from a Marxist point of view, seeking to anchor money in a labor theory of value. Nitzan and Bichler (2009) provide a thorough critique of this view.

to validate overseas liabilities denominated in the dominant IRC. This is similar to but not isomorphic to what Bryan and Rafferty (this volume) see as the problem of money becoming an unstable store of value.

Both Cohen and Triffin deliberately analogize international money to the standard neo-classical economic understanding of money, where money arises spontaneously. Money, for economists, is simply a convenient way to denominate commodities, store value, and facilitate exchange. This analogy informs the pre-requisites for an IRC, namely transaction costs and liquid markets, and the problems each sees for a dominant IRC, namely issues of inflation or deflation. In this approach money is not explicitly political. Rather, both adapt economics' methodological individualism to a methodological nationalism (Wimmer & Glick Schiller 2002; but the term seems to have originated with Gore 1996). In methodological nationalism, states or nations are taken as the unit of analysis, and, like individuals in micro-economics, ascribed rationality, preferences, and the ability to act on those preferences. One of those choices is which IRC to use. Thus for Triffin, defection from the dollar is a calculation around differences in inflation rates, productivity growth, and the potential that US gold reserves might be exhausted through speculation.

Cohen (1998, 2016) understands the limits to a purely transaction cost based analysis – thus his hierarchy in *New Geography of Money* – but generates a political analysis that is marked by the same methodological nationalism. Where Triffin examined defection from the dollar, Cohen understood the politics of the IRC as revolving around the ability to obtain and exploit autonomy, which he defined as the ability to defer adjustment to a deteriorating balance of payments. But politics is not reducible to economics, and countries are enmeshed in a global structure of power. Kindleberger (1981), who added the issue of legitimacy, and even more so Strange (see the essays in Germain 2016), who added the issue of hegemony, went farthest in breaking away from this economistic approach to politics. Both of the analyses of the post-crisis IMS noted at the beginning pick up these themes. In a reversal of Kirshner (1997), which looked at the instrumental use of control over a dominant IRC to coerce target countries, Kirshner (2014) stresses the overriding importance of ideas about proper macro-economic management. In Triffin's world, the Europeans lacked confidence in the US economy; in Kirshner's world, the Chinese lack confidence in US economic ideas and policy.

Helleiner (2014), for his part, is surprised how little international institutions matter. Instead, the centrality of American financial and state institutions in the global financial architecture anchor the IMS on the US dollar.

Charles Kindleberger (1981) had already considered legitimacy in relation to Triffin's confidence problem. Where Triffin stressed the question of how to meet the demand for additional world liquidity, Kindleberger emphasized the channels through which that demand flowed. During the 1960s, New York financial institutions provided global intermediation by borrowing short domestically and lending long globally. Global demand, in other words, was not simply a function of the volume of imports a leading economy consumed, but also its mediation through the creation and distribution of financial assets (cf Schwartz 2009). Kindleberger thus explicitly connected the IRC to the creation of and distribution of assets globally, but in line with traditional views saw this as a natural outcome of transaction cost considerations. The dollar functioned as a kind of universal language for Kindleberger. Kindleberger, like Triffin, saw the central problem as one of balancing inflation against growth. Where Triffin sought a technical solution, Kindleberger proposed an explicitly political solution to this problem. Rather than pooling currencies into some apparently neutral or apolitical currency like a Special Drawing Right (SDR) or *Bancor*, Kindleberger suggested putting foreigners onto the US Federal Reserve Bank Open Market Committee as a way to legitimate decisions about expanding or contracting the global monetary supply. Europeans who feared that the United States might prove a malign hegemon might then see it instead as a benevolent supplier of public goods. Or at least be implicated in any harsh decisions. By emphasizing legitimacy, Kindleberger took a giant step, albeit only a half-step, towards seeing money as a political creature. But his analogy that the United States functioned like a bank stopped at the possibility that banks might endogenously create money.

Susan Strange also noticed the political nature of money. She (1996: 14) feared that global financial instability arose from financial markets having outgrown states, with "The diffusion of authority away from national governments [leaving] a yawning hole of non-authority, ungovernance it might be called." Here Strange seems akin to Kindleberger, Cohen and Triffin, in that she appears anchored in a world in which states are discrete entities opting to use (or not) a particular IRC.

This methodological nationalism marked her early work (1971, 1976) and obviously even some of the later work (1996). But by the 1980s she began tentatively moving in a different direction. The two most important departures concerned the nature of money, and the degree to which hierarchy and empire characterized the international system rather than independent units.

Strange pooh-poohed (1994: 30) the traditional neo-classical economics and Marxist idea that credit had its roots in the accumulation of profits: "Many [marxists] still entertain the old fashioned notion that before you invest you must accumulate capital by piling up this year's profits on last year's, that capitalism somehow depends on the accumulation of capital. What they do not understand is that what is invested in an advanced economy is not money but credit, and that credit can be created. It does not have to be accumulated." Credit creation was the province of the banking system. But what kind of credit did banks create? Strange similarly began to attack the liberal institutionalist idea that independent, individual states rationally chose various modes of participation and cooperation and thereby constituted the international system we observe. Instead, Strange (1989) makes a straightforward argument for hierarchy, coercion and structural power. The international system was an empire, rather than academic realism's anarchic collection of paranoid billiard balls or liberal internationalism's collection of states seeking to cooperatively reduce transaction costs around trade.

The gaps in Cohen, Triffin and Kindleberger, and Strange's half steps towards filling those gaps all point us towards the ineluctably intertwined economic and political character of international money. Money in the form of an IRC is more than simply a payments system. Rather, the IRC is also a system for creating and extending credit. As both money and credit, an IRC cannot be detached from the political system that underwrites that money. To see why, we need to look at state theories of money.

Section 2: States and Outside Money; Banks and Inside Money

Suppose we analogize to state theories of money rather than the usual neo-classical economics analogy to domestic money. Two things differ in this analogy. First, money does not arise spontaneously in order to resolve the problem of a double coincidence of wants, even though money does in fact help solve that problem. Instead, both the state and the financial system create money. Second, while both the state and financial system can create money, there is a profound difference between state created money – labelled "outside money" because it arises outside the financial system – and financial system money – labelled "inside money" because it originates inside the financial system. This difference boils down to the state's legitimate ability to coerce payments from the entire economy via taxation. Unlike inside money and assets denominated in inside money, the state's outside money is backed by the entire future stream of income generated inside the economy the state governs. This drastically reduces the probability of default. As with the usual analogy, the analogy between an IRC and state created money is imperfect. In particular, even in the kind of hierarchical system that both Cohen (1998) and Strange (1989) observe, the hegemonic IRC lacks both the full legitimacy that domestic outside money possesses, as well as the state's ability to extract resources at will. These problems drive the problems that Triffin and Kindleberger observed. Nonetheless, the IRC can function as a kind of global outside money – as the US dollar did spectacularly in the acute phase of the 2009–2010 GFC, as well as in other, lesser global financial crises.

As Knapp argued back in the nineteenth century, states create money by putting tokens into circulation when they claim resources, and accepting those tokens as payment for taxes (Maclachlan 2003; Wray 1998, 2004).[7] Americans will be familiar with "legal tender for all debts public and private"; Britons with the Bank of England's and the Bank of Scotland's eventual monopoly on note issue after 1844. A note is a token. The state's tokens can and do circulate in the private economy, because all actors can anticipate having some future tax liability. Moreover, the state historically had an interest in monetizing the economy in order to expand its claims on locally produced but often immobile resources. The state's token money is a liability for the state, but the greater its ability to draw on the output of the entire economy long into the future, the greater the implicit asset corresponding to this liability. As a gross generalization, the state thus rarely finds itself in a situation of bankruptcy.

---

[7] See Fox (1971) for a description of this process in late medieval France; the problem is generic to all societies with states, however.

The reader will immediately object: "yet we see bankrupt states." The obvious limits to the gross generalization above derive from varying degrees of state-ness and state power (Mann 1984, 1986). Money as a unit of account and a store of value is ultimately an enumerated claim on the future behaviour of individuals located inside a legally defined territory within which a given state currency circulates. In the absence of sufficient social power, sufficient "caging," to compel or induce those future behaviours, state promises to redeem tokens are weak (Mann 1986, but of course also: Bourdieu 1977; Foucault 1977; Nitzan and Bichler 2009 – all provide different flavours of the same argument, as does Bryan this volume). The limiting case illuminating a "bankrupt" state is a failed state, that is, a state with no social power.

Secondarily, states that accrue liabilities in currencies they cannot produce, that cannot borrow in their own currency, that are marked by Ricardo Hausmann's (1999) "original sin," can go bankrupt, insofar as they cannot automatically generate a claim on future resources that might satisfy liabilities denominated in foreign currencies. But these states by definition cannot generate an IRC. By contrast, domestic political legitimacy and a robust economy are obvious pre-requisites for supplying money to the global economy (Seabrooke 2006; Germain and Schwartz 2014, 2017). The deep and liquid capital markets in the standard economic view of an IRC are the product of prior state social power. This state power validates outside money. Indeed, it can make an IRC powerful enough that it circulates inside the domestic economies of fragile states emitting equally fragile currencies (Helleiner 2003a, 2003b).

By contrast, money created *inside* the domestic financial system is much more fragile than state money. But a clarifying note is necessary before explaining why. Historically, state money and bank money were different things, that is to say, different tokens. Banks used to issue their own notes, and these were not acceptable as payment for tax liabilities. The parallel circulation of private money was pervasive, as Helleiner (2003a, 3; see also Forsyth and Verdier 2003) noted:

Before the nineteenth century, monetary structures in all parts of the world, including Europe, diverged from the territorial model in three ways: foreign currencies frequently circulated alongside domestic currencies, low-denomination forms of money were not well integrated into the official monetary system, and the official domestically issued currency was far from homogenous and standardized.

The internal standardization of what Helleiner calls territorial currencies occurred as states generated infrastructural power by imposing
capitalist markets on predominantly agrarian societies. This blurred
the distinction between "low-denomination forms of money" – often
local tokens – and "official money." The broad standardization and
homogenization of private money with state money occurred when
states permanently severed the link between specie and money in the
Great Depression (although this process had started in Britain with
the Bank Charter Act 1844, which gave the Banks of England and
Scotland a de facto monopoly on note issue). From roughly 1930
forward, identical notes circulated as outside and inside money in most
countries. But inside money, money created by banks, is intrinsically
weak in the absence of state backing. Why?

Banks can create (inside) money. In the standard economics story,
savings and money arise outside the banking system, and allow loans
to occur when savers deposit this money into banks. Banks are mere
pipelines in this transformation of savings into investment. But there
is increasing recognition that this story is wrong. Rather, banks create
money when they extend a loan, because in the act of extending a
loan banks simultaneously create a deposit in the borrower's account.
Both sides of the bank's balance sheet are enlarged simultaneously –
the deposit constitutes a liability and the loan an asset (Schumpeter
1934; Wray 2004).[8] Even central banks have acknowledged this
conclusion in their official publications (see McLeay, Radia and
Thomas 2014).

Yet banks face a collective action dilemma around credit creation.
As Minsky (1977; see also Pettis 2001 and Polillo 2013) argued,
credit creation has a public good aspect in that new loans stimulate
the economy by increasing aggregate demand. By increasing aggregate demand, they validate earlier credit creation and raise the value
of collateral. Each new extension of credit thus encourages more
lending. But banks' greater tolerance for risk in an expanding economy, and the inevitable exhaustion of reasonable investment opportunities, means that lending shifts from what Minsky called *hedge*

---

[8] Obviously this simplifies a bit. In a multibank system an initial deposit might be
immediately siphoned off into a different bank. But aggregating balance sheets
across banks, the effect is the same, with clearing houses facilitating net flows to/
from banks and the repo market or central bank accommodating temporary
imbalances.

finance, in which prudent borrowers create new productive assets
whose cash flow can cover their principal and interest payments (note
the similarity to Schumpeter 1934), to *ponzi finance*, in which borrowers buy existing assets at prices too high for cash flow to cover
either principal or interest payments. Ponzi borrowers inevitably
must capitalize their interest payments into their loans, which means
they need large capital gains in order to emerge with a profit. Yet
anyone buying an asset at a price sufficient to award profits to the first
ponzi buyer by definition finds themselves in an even worse position.
With no new borrowers to validate asset prices, forced sales ensue as
banks perceive the abyss and begin limiting credit to the weakest
borrowers.[9] At that point the collateral behind banks' assets (loans)
collapses, and with it the market value of those loans. But banks'
liabilities (deposits) remain at the same nominal level, at least until
depositors begin running on the bank. The collapse of bank asset
values, but not their liabilities, bankrupts banks and causes the financial system to collapse.

Private banks can sometimes organize a rescue for individual banks.
Historically private British banks have occasionally bailed out what
regulators would today call systemically important financial institutions (SIFIs), as with Barings in 1890 (though there is considerable
evidence that the Bank of England orchestrated the bailout). Similarly,
the House of Morgan (again, perhaps helped by the US state) resolved
the Panic of 1907 (Chernow 2010; Bruner and Carr 2008). But generally panics cannot be resolved by creating new inside money. Because
new inside money increases both the asset and liability side of a bank,
it simply increases the volume of potentially bad assets and the volume
of crippling liabilities.

The state's regulatory role, and the role of outside money should
now be clear. On the one hand, an effective state will try to regulate
and limit credit creation by banks in order to prevent a financial
crisis. Indeed, the first Basel accord emerged after the debt/financial
crisis of 1982 threatened to bring down the US financial system after
banks created excessive credit for Latin American and other emerging

[9] The 2006–2008 housing bust in the United States is a clear example, with the
house price-to-income ratio and the house cost-to-rental-cost ratio both rising to
160 percent of the historic average. House prices stopped rising in 2006 as the
marginal home buyer returned to the rental market either voluntarily or by force
of circumstance.

markets.[10] Basel 1 aimed to slow credit creation by imposing capital requirements on internationalized banks. The Basel 2 accord theoretically strengthened capital requirements and expanded regulatory supervision, yet enabled banks to game those requirements and evade supervision by acquiring mortgage assets, which were considered risk free.

Section 3: From State Money in Theory to Crisis Response in Practice

Efforts at regulation will inevitably fail. As Minsky (1977) argues, the longer a period of state enforced stability, like the Great Moderation of the 1990s, the greater the incentives for banks to pursue various forms of regulatory arbitrage in order to create what they perceive as relatively riskless credits. On the other hand, the state's ability to create outside money allows it to buy up impaired assets (or loan cash against impaired collateral) in order to repair the asset side of banks' balance sheets. During and after the 2009 US financial crisis, for example, the US FED bought up (among other assets) $1.7 trillion in mortgage backed securities (MBS) at face value, permitting Fannie Mae and Freddie Mac to continue functioning. The Troubled Asset Relief Program similarly bought up billions of dollars of MBS outside the FED's remit. This helped prevent the entire $8 trillion in notional US home equity that banks had created during the bubble from completely collapsing. In effect, the FED created cash and handed it to the banks in exchange for MBS whose value, if marked to market in 2009, was dubious at best and near zero at worst.[11]

Does the IRC play an analogous role in the IMS? Yes. But as with the analogy from standard economic accounts, with limits. First, recall Kindleberger's argument that the United States acted as a global bank, borrowing short term from the world and lending long term

---

[10] While the first committee aiming at global regulation was formed after the 1973 Bank Herstatt collapse, nothing much was done until 9 of 10 major US banks found themselves technically insolvent if Latin American debtors were allowed to default in 1982. See Mayntz, this volume, for a history of failed efforts at global regulation.

[11] See Chapter 5 for a different argument about MBS that seems to imply that the FED somehow gains from holding MBS to maturity. To be sure, dumping MBS into the market would bankrupt the FED. But it would also bankrupt various SIFIs also, as MBS are a big part of their capital reserves.

(see also Germain 1997). Kindleberger understood that this situation gave the United States discretion over global interest rates, prompting his recommendation that the FED be opened up to foreign representation in order to create legitimacy for decisions about that interest rate. But he missed the possibility that the United States was in fact creating credit via expanded inside money and thus increasing aggregate demand for the world via its perpetual trade deficits (Schwartz 2009, 2014).

The US housing market was central to the creation of excess inside money in the 1990s and even more so the 2000s (Seabrooke 2006; Gotham 2006; Schwartz 2009). Excess here means: $8 trillion over a period of four or five years, or in other words, roughly ten times the Obama stimulus program (the American Recovery and Reinvestment Act, 2009, was $841 billion over two years). This credit creation drove economic growth that validated massive investment in productive capacity in China and a massive increase in housing supply in the United States. In both cases lending set off the kind of positive feedback loops described in Minsky (1977) and Pettis (2001). These loops produced a massive overhang in capacity and passive assets that eventually triggered a Minsky moment in US housing in 2008, and seem to be triggering a slow-motion Minsky moment in a China currently plagued by excess industrial capacity, falling profit rates and a rising share of non-performing loans in the banking sector. Finally, European banks were doing much the same in the 2000s, lending to private borrowers in Europe's periphery for housing and automobile purchases. European banks inserted themselves into the US housing bubble, intermediating US derived credit back into the US market. By 2008 European banks held roughly $1.1 trillion in US dollar denominated assets, with both a maturity and a currency mismatch (McGuire and von Peter 2009; Borio and Disyatat 2011).

So the US dollar, as the IRC, facilitated a global expansion of credit in the form of rising exports of US dollar denominated and often US sourced financial assets. These assets naturally were matched by liabilities: for US investment banks, to the commercial money market in the form of asset backed commercial paper (ABCP); for northern European banks the same, but denominated in dollars; for southern European banks, to northern European banks; for Chinese firms, to the giant state owned banks and the new wealth management trusts that constitute the Chinese shadow banking system.

When the Minsky moment came, only the US FED could step in and orchestrate the creation of outside money. This obviously had a domestic component. But the FED also created global outside money to rescue European and other banks in 2009 (McGuire and von Peter 2009). The FED provided roughly $600 billion in dollars to the ECB, Bank of England, and Bank of Switzerland for distribution to beleaguered European banks between March and October 2008. Altogether roughly $10 trillion in claims flowed through the swap channels from 2007 to 2010 (Tooze 2016). In this instance, not only was the ECB legally unable to bail out member banks, but it also was practically unable, given that their liabilities were US dollar denominated. The legitimacy of this intervention went unquestioned for two pragmatic reasons. First, the ECB had no wish to see the European financial system collapse along with the US financial system. Second, probably more importantly, the US and European, and in particular the US and British banking systems were inextricably intertwined (Fichtner 2014, 2016). It was impossible to rescue one without also saving the other. But the asymmetry here is clear: the US FED could bail out Europe, but Europe could not bail out the United States.

Understanding international money through the lens of state money helps resolve the conflicting assessments in Helleiner (2014) and Kirshner (2014) noted at the start of this paper, while also highlighting the inherent instability of the IMS. Put simply, the United States supplies outside money to the entire global financial system. No other currency can currently replace it. Given that banks and especially the large internationalized banks will tend to overproduce inside money (of various sorts), no one can afford to remove the US dollar and the US state from their central position. Thus Helleiner's stability. A supra-national entity as fragile as the G20 cannot replace this US role.

On the other hand, the US government does not possess the kind of legitimacy that a well-developed national state has within its own borders. Legitimacy is mechanical rather than organic. Equity cross holdings, repo arrangements, counterparty positions and other links bind global banks together. Given the centrality of US banks (Fichtner 2016), no major bank can avoid some US dollar position, and thus no major bank has an interest in displacing the US state as the source of outside money. But this narrow interest is not matched by identity or organic legitimacy, which is why Kirshner (2014) is correct that the delegitimation of the US economic and financial model in the 2008 crisis is analogous to the Triffin's crisis of confidence in the 1960s.

Here both material and ideational factors fuse. Part of what makes outside money outside money is the state's ability to capture revenues from an extensive economic territory, and over a longer time horizon than any single economic entity. From 1990 forward, the US economy largely captured revenue from the rest of the world through its control over finance and its firms' control over various intellectual property rights. Both channels show up in the enormous gap between US payments to foreign multinational firms and foreign earnings by US-headquartered multinationals. The delegitimation of finance weakens the first channel. Slower economic growth subsequent to the 2008 crisis lowers the probability that trade deals reinforcing intellectual property rights will be signed. This is the modern version of Triffin's confidence problem: can the US economy generate enough US dollar denominated claims, services and goods to make other economies need those dollars?

Section 4: Conclusion

This paper started by asking whether an IMS based on a national currency was inherently unstable. The IMS is inherently unstable if it relies on a single IRC. Behind Triffin's deceptively simply confidence-liquidity dilemma lies a fundamental problem in finance: banks will expand inside money to the breaking point. Only the state can coerce cooperation among banks in limiting inside money. Even this, by creating financial stability, risks inducing regulatory arbitrage in pursuit of what seem like easy profits (Minsky 1977). When the inevitable crash comes, only the state can put things right by substituting outside money for devalued inside assets. But the international system lacks a state with the legitimate authority to create outside money, and any regular system of taxation that might validate that money.

The supplier of the IRC thus confronts a Janus-faced exorbitant privilege and exorbitant burden. Putting demand and money out into the international economy requires a trade deficit; running a trade deficit slows domestic growth (Triffin's confidence problem). Slower growth can be offset by monetary expansion (the inflation that so troubled Triffin), but monetary expansion risks financial instability. What Cohen sees as the structural power that flows from the ability to delay adjustment is also a requirement to supply global demand. What Kindleberger sees as a need for cooperation is actually a need for some form of legitimation for the creation of outside money in a crisis. What Strange sees as uncontrolled finance is largely the United States generating bigger and bigger piles of assets to cover a trade deficit that has been the source of a good bit of world growth.

Is it possible to design an IMS that does not suffer from destabilizing flows of excess inside money from the IRC issuer, and from limited legitimacy on the part of that issuing country? Keynes was right with respect to his preferences for structuring both the domestic and the IMS. Given unequal incomes, a high marginal propensity to save among the rich, and any degree of fear on the part of business, growth rates would be suboptimal. Given the lack of an international currency, the IMS was inherently unstable, as the 1920s and 1930s showed. Keynes' prescription was domestic financial repression to induce higher rates of investment and growth, and an artificial international currency, the *Bancor*, that would obviate the need for global financial flows.

While Keynes' comprehensive socialization of investment did not imply state ownership of the financial system, it did imply euthanasia of the rentier, so as to increase the marginal propensity to consume, and state direction of savings into productive investment, so as to overcome fear. Minsky of course thought that Keynes was pollyannish about how stable this might be. Still, the post-war record of rapid growth fell apart more because of endogenous social dynamics – strikes by semi-skilled male labor, bored housewives, and excluded immigrants/minorities – than it did because of financial instability. At the same time, Keynes' *Bancor* was intended to limit the possibility that one country's inside money might spread to the rest of the world. The *Bancor* was designed to force trade surplus countries to absorb output from trade deficit countries, validating investment in those deficit countries. Countries with trade deficits would have been able to borrow *Bancor* from the International Clearing Union and use those *Bancor* to cover their deficits. Countries with accumulations of *Bancor* from trade surpluses could only use those *Bancor* to buy goods from deficit countries, allowing deficit countries to extinguish their debts to the ICU. In this way, destabilizing international capital flows could not arise as quickly as with private finance of trade deficits. Moreover, the *Bancor* assured that one country's inside money could not flow overseas, bloating balance sheets everywhere.

But the euro and RMB are not plausible rivals to the US dollar's position as the dominant IRC, and something like the *Bancor* is flatly impossible. The very fact that two apparent rivals exist (or three, with the Yen), means that a capital market rivalling that of the United States is unlikely to emerge. Europe and China will not cede first place to the other, fragmenting alternatives to the US dollar. But more pointedly, the euro and ECB currently lack even domestic legitimacy. The RMB has barely enough domestic legitimacy to keep massive capital flight at bay; the People's Bank of China shed nearly $1 trillion of its reserve holdings in 2015 and 2016 as capital moved off-shore. Neither economy can generate sufficient inside money to sustain global demand (Germain and Schwartz 2014, 2017), and neither currency is entangled enough with all branches of global finance to be able to supply outside money in a crisis. Thus the tension between Helleiner (2014) and Kirshner (2014) cannot be resolved in favour of one or the other. It rests on the necessarily incomplete revenue capacity of the US state, which cannot openly tax the entire world economy, and the necessarily fragile legitimacy of the FED with respect to either limiting inside money or creating outside money for the world. Short of the kind of political suicide that a Trump Presidency seems to constitute, the medium-term position of the US dollar as the IRC seems assured. This also means that instability in the IMS is a certainty, as the FED has abetted rather than deterred excess creation of inside money for the past three decades and the Trump administration seems dead set on destroying the legitimacy of the US state and of global governance institutions.

References

Andrews, David M., ed. (2006). *International Monetary Power*. Ithaca, NY: Cornell University Press.

Bergsten, C. Fred. (1975). *The Dilemmas of the Dollar*. New York, NY: New York University Press.

Borio, Claudio, and Piti Disyatat. (2011). *Global Imbalances and the Financial Crisis: Link or no Link?* No. 346. Geneva: Bank for International Settlements.

Bourdieu, Pierre. (1977). *Outline of a Theory of Practice* (Vol. 16). Cambridge University Press.

Bruner, Robert, & S. D. Carr, (2008). *The Panic of 1907: Lessons Learned from the Market's Perfect Storm*. New York, NY: John Wiley & Sons.

Chernow, Ron. (2010). *The House of Morgan: An American Banking Dynasty and the Rise of Modern Finance*. New York, NY: Grove/Atlantic, Inc.

Cohen, Benjamin J. (1971). *Future of Sterling as an International Currency*. London: MacMillan.

(1998) *The Geography of Money*. Ithaca, NY: Cornell University Press.

(2016) in Germain, Randall (ed), (2016) *Susan Strange and the Future of Global Political Economy: Power, Control and Transformation*. London: Routledge.

Eichengreen, Barry. (2011). *Exorbitant Privilege: The Rise and Fall of the Dollar and the Future of the International Monetary System*. New York: Oxford University Press.

Fichtner, Jan. (2014). Privateers of the Caribbean: The hedge funds–US–UK–offshore nexus. *Competition & Change*. 18(1), 37–53.

(2016). Perpetual decline or persistent dominance? Uncovering Anglo-America's true structural power in global finance. *Review of International Studies* 43(1), 3–26.

Forsyth, D. J., & Daniel Verdier. (Eds.). (2003). *The Origins of National Financial Systems: Alexander Gerschenkron Reconsidered*. Routledge.

Foucault, Michel. (1977). *Discipline and Punish: The Birth of the Prison*. Vintage.

Fox, Edward Whiting. (1971). *History in Geographic Perspective: The Other France*. New York, NY: Norton.

Germain, Randall. (1997). *The International Organization of Credit*. Cambridge: Cambridge University Press.

Germain, Randall, & Herman Schwartz. (2014). The political economy of failure: The euro as an international currency. *Review of International Political Economy*, 21(5), 1095–1122.

(2015) Political Limits to Renminbi Internalization, ch 17 (pp. 133–160) in Domenico Lombardi and Hongying Wang (eds), *Enter the Dragon: China in the International Financial System*, Waterloo, Canada: CIGI.

Germain, Randall & Herman Mark Schwartz. (2017). The Political Economy of Currency Internationalization: The Case of the RMB. *Review of International Studies*, 43(4), 765-787.

(ed). (2016) *Susan Strange and the Future of Global Political Economy: Power, Control and Transformation*, London: Routledge.

Gore, C. (1996). Methodological Nationalism and the Misunderstanding of East Asian Industrialisation. *The European Journal of Development Research*, 8(1), 77–122.

Gotham, Kevin. F. (2006). The Secondary Circuit of Capital Reconsidered: Globalization and the US Real Estate Sector. *American Journal of Sociology*, 112(1), 231–275.

Harvey, David. (1982). *The Limits to Capital*. London: Blackwell.

Hausmann, Ricardo. (1999). "Should There Be Five Currencies or One Hundred and Five?" *Foreign Policy* Fall, pp. 65–72.

Helleiner, Eric. (1996). *States and the Reemergence of Global Finance: From Bretton Woods to the 1990s.* Ithaca, NY: Cornell University Press.

(2003a). *The Making of National Money: Territorial Currencies in Historical Perspective.* Ithaca, NY: Cornell University Press.

(2003b). Dollarization Diplomacy: US Policy towards Latin America Coming Full Circle? *Review of International Political Economy,* 10(3), 406–429.

(2014). *The Status Quo Crisis: Global Financial Governance after the 2008 Meltdown.* New York, NY: Oxford University Press.

Kirshner, Jonathan. (1997). *Currency and Coercion: The Political Economy of International Monetary Power.* Princeton: Princeton University Press.

Kindleberger, Charles. (1981). *International Money: A Collection of Essays.* Boston, MA: George Allen & Unwin.

(2014). *American Power after the Financial Crisis.* Ithaca, NY: Cornell University Press.

McCauley, Robert, and Goetz von Peter. (2009). The US dollar shortage in global banking. *BIS Quarterly Review.*

McGuire, Patrick & Goetz von Peter. (2009). The US dollar shortage in global banking and the international policy response. Bank for International Settlements Working Paper: No 291. http://www.bis.org/publ/work291.htm. Geneva.

Maclachlan, Fiona. (2003). Max Weber and the State Theory of Money. Manhattan College: Unpublished paper. Available at *http://home.manhattan.edu/~fiona.maclachlan/maclachlan26july03.htm.*

McLeay, Michael, Amar Radia, & Ryland Thomas. (2014). Money creation in the modern economy. *Bank of England Quarterly Bulletin.*

Mann, Michael. (1984). The autonomous power of the state: its origins, mechanisms and results. *European Journal of Sociology,* 25(2), 185–213.

(1986). *The Sources of Social Power, vol. 1, A History of Power from the Beginning to AD 1760.* Cambridge: Cambridge University Press.

Matthijs, Mathias, and Mark Blyth, eds. (2015). *The Future of the Euro.* New York, NY: Oxford University Press.

Minsky, Hyman. P. (1977). The financial instability hypothesis: an interpretation of Keynes and an alternative to "standard" theory. *Challenge,* 20(1), 20–27.

Nitzan, Jonathan. (1998). Differential accumulation: towards a new political economy of capital. *Review of International Political Economy,* 5(2), 169–216.

Nitzan, Jonathan, & Shimshon Bichler. (2009). *Capital as Power: A Study of Order and Creorder.* New York: Routledge.

Otero-Iglesias, Miguel & Mattias Vermeiren. 2015. China's state-permeated market economy and its constraints to the internationalization of the renminbi. *International Politics* 52(6): 684–703.

Pettis, Michael. (2001). *The Volatility Machine: Emerging Economies and the Threat of Financial Collapse.* New York: Oxford University Press.

Polillo, Simone. (2013). *Conservatives versus Wildcats: A Sociology of Financial Conflict.* Stanford University Press.

Schumpeter, Joseph. (1934). *The Theory of Economic Development: An Inquiry into Profits, Capital, Credit, Interest, and the Business Cycle.* New Brunswick, NJ: Transaction Publishers.

Schwartz, Herman. (2009). *Subprime Nation: American Power, Global Capital, and the Housing Bubble.* Cornell University Press.

—— (2014). Imbalances and the International Monetary System, ch. 5 in *Handbook of the International Political Economy of Monetary Relations.* Thomas Oatley and W. Kindred Winecoff (eds). Cheltenham: Edward Elgar.

Seabrooke, Leonard. (2006). *The Social Sources of Financial Power: Domestic Legitimacy and International Financial Orders.* Cornell University Press.

Strange, Susan. (1971). *Sterling and British Policy: A Political Study of an International Currency in Decline.* Oxford University Press.

—— (1994). *States and Markets.* London: Continuum International Publishing Group.

—— (1976). *International Economic Relations of the Western World: 1959–1971.* A. Shonfield (Ed.). Royal Institute of International Affairs.

—— (1989). "Towards a Theory of Transnational Empire." Pp. 161–176 in Ernst Czempial and James Rosenau (eds), *Global Changes and Theoretical Challenges,* Lexington: Rowman & Littlefield.

—— (1996). *The Retreat of the State: The Diffusion of Power in the World Economy.* London: Cambridge University Press.

Tooze, Adam. (2016). Just another Panic? *New Left Review* 97: 129–138.

Triffin, Robert. (1960). *Gold and the Dollar Crisis.* New Haven: Yale University Press.

Weber, Max (G. Roth & C. Wittich, eds). (1978). *Economy and Society: An Outline of Interpretive Sociology.* Berkeley: University of California Press.

Wimmer, A., & Glick Schiller, N. (2002). Methodological nationalism and beyond: nation–state building, migration and the social sciences. *Global Networks,* 2(4), 301–334.

Wray, L. Randall. (1998). Modern money. *The Jerome Levy Economics Institute Working Paper 252,* Annandale, NY: Bard College.

—— (ed). (2004). *Credit and State Theories of Money: The Contributions of A. Mitchell Innes.* Cheltenham: Edward Elgar.

7 | Beware of Financialization!
Emerging Markets and Mobile Capital

ANDREAS NÖLKE

1 Introduction

The increasing importance of mobile capital is part of a broader process of financialization.[1] Financialization comprises of two major components, on the one hand the internal transformation of the financial sector (from "boring banking" to all kinds of securitized financial products) and on the other hand the increasing importance of financial markets, motives, institutions and elites outside of the financial sector (Epstein, 2005; Palley, 2013; Heires and Nölke, 2014a, 2014b; van der Zwan, 2014). Here, the financial sector has broadened its reach. It has developed a strong grasp on other economic sectors, e.g. by focusing corporate governance in industry on shareholder value. It also has extended its reach to various sectors of society, such as the provision of education, health services and old age provisions, through student loans, private house insurances, or defined contribution pension schemes. Most recently, finally, financialization has even extended its reach to natural resources, for example based on climate certificates and large scale investments in land resources (Ouma, 2014).

The notion of "financialization" is not only an analytical term, but also has a normative component, usually a negative one. Why is financialization considered to be a problem? First, financialization leads to rising inequality (Kus, 2012; Lin and Tomaskovic-Devey, 2013; Dünhaupt, 2014; Nölke forthcoming a). Company strategies that focus on shareholder value frequently depress wages. At the same time, only the well-off are able to invest at financial markets and, thus, profit from rising share prices and other financial investments.

---

[1] Most helpful research assistance by Brigitte Holden, Christian May and Johannes Petry is gratefully acknowledged. The chapter has also very much benefitted from comments by Jocelyn Pixley, Hanseok Suh, Marcel Zeitinger and an anonymous reviewer.

Furthermore, rising inequality tends to depress demand, given that the rich have a much higher savings rate. Many workers, in contrast, tend to spend most of their income. Depressed demand, however, is not the only macroeconomic problem caused by financialization. Another factor leading to low growth rates is the wide-spread practice to invest company profits in stock buy-backs, instead of using these profits for productive investments. Together, these factors lead to a reduced rate of economic growth in the long run, in particular in the non-finance sector (Hein and Van Treeck, 2010; Tomaskovic-Devey et al. 2015). In the short run, in contrast, financialization may stimulate growth, making credit more easily available to social strata that usually do not have credit access. Thus, for a couple of years, financialization often leads to a boom before consumers are unable to raise additional credit and have to start decreasing their indebtedness, thereby depressing demand even further.

A second major problem of a high level of financialization are the typical cycles of boom and bust that go hand in hand with a strong role for the financial sector (Aalbers, 2008; Foster, 2008; Lapavitsas, 2009; Nölke, 2009; Heires and Nölke, 2011; Stockhammer, 2012). In contrast to other types of markets, financial markets tend to have a higher degree of fluctuations. They tend to build up higher and higher valuations over an extended period of time, before these valuations decrease in a very short period of time. Various cycles of boom and bust have been typical for the financial sector for centuries. Financialization has both increased the size of the financial sector as well as its interconnectedness. Thus, the cycle of the financial sector has much more severe repercussions on the rest of the economy than cycles in other economic sectors. Furthermore, financial booms and busts do not remain limited to one economy, but also affect other economies that are linked for example via inter-bank lending.

Until quite recently, the discussion of financialization and its dangers described above had been limited to the OECD economies. The globalization of financial markets and the corresponding rise of mobile capital do not only affect the established economies, but also emerging markets. Correspondingly, we now see the emergence of a discussion on financialization in emerging economies (Correa et al., 2013; Tyson and McKinley, 2014; Isaacs, 2016; Kaltenbrunner and Painceira, 2016; Karwowski and Stockhammer, 2016; Lechevalier et al., 2016; McKinley, 2016; Reither, 2016; for an early predecessor see Grabel, 2003). In order to further this debate, my contribution will concentrate on the cross-border dimension of financialization – the issue of mobile capital – instead of following the usual focus on domestic financial deepening (financial sector, households) and its consequences with regard to increasing inequality. Arguably, at least with regard to emerging markets, "domestic financialization" is subordinated to "international financialization" (Kaltenbrunner and Painceira, 2016) and a strong focus on the non-financial company sector is warranted because of the desire for catch-up industrialization.

While the degree of financialization in emerging markets usually is much lower than in the advanced economies, a strong role of mobile capital carries more dangers in the former. Emerging markets try to organize a catch-up process of industrialization. This process requires massive industrial investments based on long-term economic stability. Without stability, companies will be reluctant to undertake major investments. Mobile capital can inhibit these investments in multiple ways, be it through banking crises, currency volatility or through a company focus on short-term financial results. Many emerging markets try to protect their sovereignty against mobile capital through a variety of means, including a small role for global financial markets in corporate governance and investment finance, capital controls and through the accumulation of huge foreign currency reserves. However, we can find strong diversity between emerging markets with regard to these measures, with particularly strong differences between the protective large emerging markets of China and India on the one side, and the more liberal emerging markets of Central Eastern Europe/CEE on the other.

In order to support these arguments, I will first define financialization and provide some data on its historical development (section 2). Second, I will highlight the special challenges posed by international financialization to emerging markets in the light of mobile capital (section 3). Third, I will highlight how emerging markets can protect themselves against some of these challenges. Fourth, drawing on an emerging market comparative capitalism perspective I will demonstrate how the large emerging markets China and India differ from the CEE economies with regard to international financialization (section 4). Given that the weight of the large emerging economies within the world economy has increased tremendously during the last decades, the conclusion highlights how the establishment of this protective model also affects the institutions of global capitalism (section 5).

2 Financialization: Definition and Historical Development

Given the broad nature of the phenomenon of financialization, it is important to pinpoint empirical developments with specific data. Otherwise the notion of financialization risks becoming a catch-all term similar to "neoliberalism" (Christophers, 2015). Although a generally accepted measure of financialization does not yet exist, several attempts have been made in order to document the development of financialization over long historical periods. Otherwise it would be difficult to decide whether, e.g., the degree of financialization has decreased after the 2008 crisis. Crucially, this documentation relies on a precise measurement of financialization (Nölke, 2014a). Based on the definition mentioned above, financialization – for the time being – can best be measured via the localization of profits (Krippner, 2011). On the one hand financialization leads to an increasing profit share of the financial sector in comparison to other sectors of the economy. On the other hand, non-financial sectors of the economy derive a larger part of its profits from financial services and financial speculation (e.g., share buy-backs), in comparison to traditional manufacturing and services.

Based on this definition, the most precise measure of financialization available is the share of financial profits as a share of total profits. Again, this is not a complete measurement of financialization because it does not take into account the financial profits made in the non-financial sector. Moreover, comprehensive data for this measure of financialization is only available for the United States, based on the National Income and Product Accounts (NIPA). Still, a historical overview (Figure 7.1) demonstrates that the high level of financialization of the 1920s decreased until the Second World War, remained on a fairly low historical level throughout the 1950s and 1960s and then significantly increased between about 1980 and the year 2000. In 2008 the global financial crisis caused a strong reduction of the profit share of the financial sector but this sector has been recovering since and we are still living in a period of very high financialization when compared to historical data.[2]

---

[2] Not all economies show a similar extent of financialization. In most cases this will be lower than in the United States, but in some cases, such as the United Kingdom, even higher, given the importance of the financial sector for the UK economy.

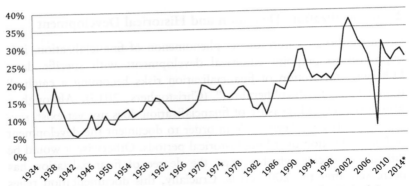

Figure 7.1 Financial profit as a share of total domestic profit, United States, 1934–2016.
Source: Bureau of Economic Analysis (bea.gov), Table 6.16 Corporate Profits by Industry, Profits are with IVA and CCAdj
Variables: domestic industries, financial
* 2014 only based on first three quarters

Since the 2008 financial crisis, many governments have decided regulating banks and other major financial sector actors more comprehensively. However, this re-regulation of the financial sector was not able to substantially decrease the level of financialization. First, many banks still are too big and too important to fail, thereby inclining governments to take a soft look on the financial situation of these institutions. Second, post-2008 regulation strongly focused on the banking sector, given that the last financial crisis took off from this sector. More severe regulation of the banking sector, however, leads to increasing activities in the so-called shadow banking sector that undertakes similar activities to banks, thereby evading standard banking regulation. Correspondingly, it is very difficult to drastically reduce the level of financialization in a short period of time, unless one opts for a completely different economic system as was the case during the Second World War.

The account of the historical development of financialization depicted above is confirmed by alternative measures of the phenomenon. The first of these measurement attempts is based on a study for the US Bureau of Economic Research (Philippon, 2011). Here, the income share of finance within the overall income of non-farm civilian incomes is measured on various historical data sources. Although not all data sources are completely comparable in their measurement of this income share, the overall development becomes abundantly clear. The survey demonstrates a significantly increased share of income in the financial sector (including insurance and real estate) until the 1929 financial crisis, followed by a steep decline of these incomes until the mid-1940s. The income share of finance remained moderate until about 1980, and then increased tremendously, recently overtaking the record shares of the late 1920s.

Another method to measure the long-term degree of financialization is to record the amount of cross-border capital mobility. Capital mobility is a crucial component of financialization as defined above, together with the domestic liberalization of the financial sector. A high degree of capital mobility typically very much contributes to the profits made in the financial sector. A study by Reinhart and Rogoff (2008) depicts the long-term development of capital mobility. It becomes clear that capital mobility strongly increased until the outbreak of the First World War and recovered substantially until the late 1920s, before falling to its lowest amount in the late 1940s. After a period of fairly low capital mobility it strongly increased since about 1980. The study also covers the number of countries that are in a banking crisis. It becomes obvious that a high degree of capital mobility goes hand in hand with a high degree of countries in banking crises, whereas a low degree of capital mobility goes hand in hand with a low number of countries in showing this type of crisis. This is obviously the case during the period of particularly low financialization between the late-1940s and the mid-1970s. Here, the data set composed by Reinhart and Rogoff shows no banking crisis at all for extended periods.

In sum, the various measures indicate that the world has seen two major phases of financialization, one until the 1920s and one starting in the 1980s and reaching its maximum around the millennium. Of course the exact features of financialization during these two phases have been different. In both cases, however, a high degree of financialization has led to massive financial crises. Between these two phases of financialization, the post–World War II economic order had put strong limits on the freedom of capital markets, both domestically and internationally. During the 1970s, however, the erosion of the system of Bretton Woods eliminated these limits internationally, while financial market deregulation did the same on the domestic level. Both crises mentioned above had their origin from the high degree of financialization in the center of the world economy. However, financialization also poses a major problem for emerging markets.

3 Challenges of Financialization for Emerging Markets

In emerging markets, financialization poses specific challenges, in particular with regard to external financial openness or "international financialization." These countries try to organize a long-term catch-up process of industrialization. Financialization – in our case cross-border capital mobility – potentially inserts a high degree of volatility into these economies. Volatility is a core ingredient of financial globalization – or, as the IMF has put it: "Capital flows are fickle: anytime, anywhere" (Bluedorn et al., 2013). Volatility, however, is a major problem for long-term investments. The latter are very important for successful industrialization. Moreover, in order to prosper, emerging economies want to nurture their domestic industries. Global capital markets that play a major role with regard to the ownership and conduct of these industries have different short-term priorities that sometimes are difficult to reconcile with long-term industrialization. Mobile capital may quickly withdraw in a situation of low or lacking profits – leading to lack of investment, plant closures and unemployment. Let us look at these two major challenges – macroeconomic volatility caused by cross-border capital mobility and microeconomic short-term perspectives caused by a strong role of global capital markets – in turn.

From a macroeconomic perspective, global capital flows can be a major challenge for the economic sovereignty of emerging markets. In particular the 1997/1998 crisis in South-East Asia has made this abundantly clear (Stiglitz, 2002). When Thailand had depleted its currency reserves after months of speculative attacks, its currency devaluation was the start to similar processes across the region, followed by capital flight and banking crises. The crisis also heavily impacted the non-financial economy, with strongly decreasing investment and a massive recession. While the crisis had multiple origins, strong credit growth and heavy foreign borrowing were among the most prominent ones. In order to assist the countries in crisis, the international financial institutions mobilized substantial aid packages, but these loans came with conditions with regard of domestic economic reforms that deeply affected the sovereignty of the countries in the region. These conditions have led towards resentments against mobile capital and the Western institutions promoting the latter that has become very influential for policy discussions in emerging markets (Higgott, 1998).

In more general terms, a high degree of cross-border capital mobility can lead to domestic financial crises in emerging economies. Particularly dangerous is the sudden stop of capital inflows if transnational investors become concerned about the economic situation of an emerging economy (Calvo, 1998). Given the strong interconnectedness of global capital market participants – the well-known "herd effect" – these concerns quickly become a self-fulfilling prophecy, particularly if the country carries a lot of debt with short-term maturities. This can lead to a steep devaluation of the emerging market currency, followed by rising inflation (particularly with a high degree of imported goods) and a rise of the central bank rate (in order to combat inflation) that can be very negative to further investments. Banks are confronted with an increased amount of non-performing loans and become cautious regarding further credit allocation. Indebted companies may go bankrupt, thereby destroying precious human capital and affecting other companies via inter-enterprise credits.

However, not only sudden capital outflows can be a challenge for the industrialization process of emerging markets, but also strong inflows over an extended period of time. These inflows can lead to a strong appreciation of the emerging market currency. This appreciation has very negative consequences for the domestic industries in these economies, because it hampers their competitiveness against imports and on global markets. A part of the large flows towards emerging markets has been caused by the low interest rate policy of the Western central banks that has led financial investors to seek higher interest rates in emerging economies (carry-trades). A case in point is Brazil, where the currency became massively overvalued against, for example, the US Dollar, before plunging very deeply in the mid-2010s crisis (Bresser-Pereira, 2015; Kaltenbrunner and Painceira, 2016). In sum, both strong (short-term) currency devaluations and strong currency appreciations have negative effects for catch-up industrialization in emerging markets. The latter process primarily requires long-term stability of currency relations.

Next to these macro-level phenomena, financialization in terms of trans-border mobile capital also carries major challenges for emerging markets on the micro- or company level. Here the focus is on the financialization of the productive economy, predominantly via foreign direct investments and the expansion of stock markets as markets for corporate control, in our case also for cross-border capital. These forms of mobile capital usually have a much better reputation than the very short-term speculative flows that previously were discussed in the context of the macro level. In contrast to conventional views about the benefits of financial deepening for financing corporate growth, however, this form of financialization may also become a restriction for company development (Singh, 1996; Singh and Weisse, 1998). The short-term focus of financial investors on quarterly profit figures is very difficult to reconcile with the long-term company strategies that are necessary for a major industrialization strategy. If foreign investors dominate in the corporate governance system of emerging market companies, they may prefer financial investments over industrial investments. Moreover, these investors also show a more limited interest into the long-term evolution of the institutional economic context in emerging economies, for example for investments with regard to the further strengthening of the education system (Schneider, 2013).

4 Emerging Markets' Strategies for Protection against Financialization

Against the challenges highlighted above, emerging markets have developed a number of instruments in order to limit the degree of financialization in their economies. Again we can distinguish between instruments that focus on the macro level and instruments that focus on the micro level. Not all of these instruments are being used by all emerging economies, since they can have side effects and may also witness political opposition, domestically and internationally. As will be argued in sections 5 and 6, their utilization often depends on the degree of institutional complementarity within the economic model of the specific emerging economy.

On the macro level, measures to control the volatility of financial in- and outflows have to be mentioned. Classical instruments for this purpose are capital controls that come in various forms, such as financial transaction taxes, limits for buying and selling currencies or the mandatory approval of cross-border financial transactions

(Grabel, 2001, 2016). Capital controls were an integral part of the Bretton Woods system, but have been abolished by most industrialized countries since the 1970s, before making a comeback in the Iceland financial crisis and (involuntarily) in the Cyprus and Greek Eurozone crises.

Next to capital controls, emerging markets – particularly after the 1997/98 Asian Financial Crisis – have chosen to accumulate substantial foreign currency reserves with their central banks, in order to be able to intervene in a situation where financial outflows threaten to lead to a massive short-term devaluation of the currency. The alternative option, reducing short-term foreign liabilities, is much less prevalent (Rodrik, 2006), although it might even be more effective with regard to the prevention of financial crises caused by currency fluctuations.

On the micro level, many emerging markets limit the influence of global financial investors in the corporate governance and corporate finance of domestic companies. The focus here is, e.g., on the regulation of foreign direct investment. With regard to corporate governance, state ownership – often as a minority shareholder with special voting rights (Musachio and Lazzarini, 2014) – or the dominance by founding families limit the influence of transnational financial investors in exchange-listed companies. Moreover, instead of using the volatile stock markets for the financing of investments, the latter rather are financed via credits by domestic banks or funds that have been internally generated within the company.

Another important instrument with regard to the financing of major investments – without necessarily to global financial markets – are public development banks that allocate credit according to the state's industrialization strategy. Whereas the German Kreditanstalt für Wiederaufbau/KfW is the largest national development bank in industrialized countries, the most important emerging markets development banks is the Brazilian BNDES (May and Nölke, 2016).

5 Financialization and Catch-Up Strategies: A "Varieties of Emerging Capitalism" Perspective

Not all emerging economies use these instruments for protection against financialization. As will be documented below, we can find strong differences between the countries of Central and Eastern

Europe that are very open to global capital flows and the large
emerging economies of China and India. Other emerging markets
range in between. In order to make sense of this divergence, we
can turn to institutionalist research in the comparative capitalism
tradition. While the early comparative capitalism literature focused
on the strict comparison of country cases, recent scholarship pays a
lot of attention to interactions between different national types of
capitalism and to cross-border financial flows (Kalinowski, 2013;
Nölke, 2016).

Scholarship in comparative capitalism has alerted us to the fact that
economies differ a lot based on their institutional setup. This type
of research has been pioneered by the "Varieties of Capitalism"
approach, developed by Peter Hall and David Soskice (2001). Their
epochal study distinguished between "liberal market economies"/LME
(in particular in the United States and the United Kingdom on the
one hand) and "coordinated market economies"/CME (in particular
Germany and Japan) on the other hand. Later research has extended
this approach to additional types of economies. The Visegrad economies in Central and Eastern Europe, the Czech Republic, Slovakia,
Poland and Hungary, form a third distinct type that has been called
"dependent market economies"/DME because of their high degree
of dependence on foreign direct investment from Western Europe
(Nölke and Vliegenthart, 2009). More recently, scholarship has moved
on to study the specific capitalism that has evolved in large emerging
markets such as China, India, Brazil and South Africa. The specific
type of capitalism emerging in these economies has been called "state-
permeated market economy"/SME because of the significant role of
the state, but the absence of powerful central state direction, as in the
East Asian developmental states (Nölke et al., 2015). The different
types of capitalism are not permanent features of these economies,
but rather "snapshots" at a specific point of time. The US and UK
economies, for example, have been much less liberal during earlier
phases of development (Nölke, 2012).

The DME and LME types of emerging market capitalism differ
considerably with regard to their strategy towards financialization.
Whereas the DMEs embrace financialization wholeheartedly – particularly
with regard to foreign direct investments (FDI) – the SMEs are highly
reluctant with regard to mobile capital. Arguably, the openness of the
DMEs had to do with the specific historical situation after the end of

communism. Free markets were very much welcomed by the population, whereas multinational corporations were happy to invest in economies with a very qualified population and great proximity to European markets. Under these circumstances, we have witnessed the emergence of a coherent economic model that is strongly focused on the attraction of FDI – but of course is also highly dependent on the continuity of these investment flows (Nölke and Vliegenthart, 2009). The 2008 global financial crisis has highlighted the risks of this economic model and the new Polish government, for example, has indicated that it wants to turn to a different, less externally dependent model (Morawiecki, 2016).

In contrast to the DMEs – and many other developing and emerging economies – large state-permeated emerging economies such as China and India are not dependent on the continuous mobilization of large amounts of foreign direct investments, due to their large domestic markets. These SMEs cannot be forced to open up their economies towards the demands of transnational (financial) investors. They can avoid a "sell-out" and are able to impose their conditions upon investors who want to access their large domestic markets. Smaller emerging markets and developing countries cannot afford such luxury. Correspondingly, SMEs tend to undergo a much lower degree of financialization than DMEs, at least with regard to trans-border mobile capital.

6 Protection against Financialization in Large Emerging markets: A Comparison of Economic Models

In order to illustrate how large emerging markets put limits on financialization, I will subsequently compare some features of the Chinese and Indian state-permeated market economies, in contrast to the liberal market economies of the United States and the United Kingdom, the coordinated market economies of Germany and Japan and the dependent market economies of the Czech Republic and Slovakia. I will start with the micro level of corporate governance and company finance, before turning to the macro level of capital controls and currency reserves. Given that most of the discussion on the role of mobile capital with regard to emerging markets is on the macro level, I will discuss the micro level in somewhat more detail. Given space constraints, the focus will be on a rough juxtaposition based on

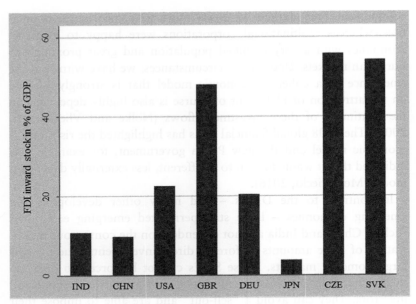

Figure 7.2 Levels of foreign ownership, FDI Inward Stock as percent of GDP, 2011.
Source: UNCTAD, World Investment Report[3]

statistical data, whereas I have to neglect a more detailed discussion on the various institutional processes involved.[4]

With regard to issues of corporate governance, protection against the negative aspects of financialization in the large SMEs takes the shape of a low degree of foreign ownership. Figure 7.2 compares a number of economies with regard to the foreign direct investment inward stock as a percentage of gross domestic product/GDP. Against current wisdom that in particular China is strongly permeated by foreign direct investment, it becomes obvious that India and China, together with Japan, are the economies where foreign owners comparatively play a rather minor role. The Chinese and the Indian

---

[3] The abbreviations follow the three-letter country codes as established by ISO. IND=India, CHN=China, GBR=United Kingdom, JPN=Japan, CZE=Czechia and SVK=Slovakia.

[4] See Nölke and Vliegenthart, 2009 and Nölke et al., 2015, for a more detailed discussion of the different types of capitalism; the figures were originally compiled for the latter publication.

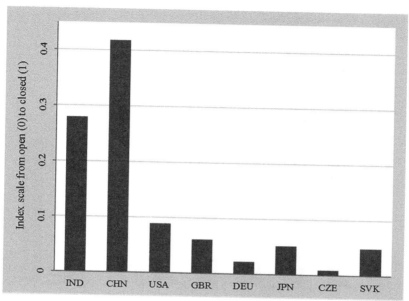

Figure 7.3 Barriers to incoming FDI, FDI Regulatory Restrictiveness Index, 2012.

Source: OCED, FDI Regulatory Restrictiveness Database

economy are strongly dominated by national capital, either by family capitalist or by the state. The dependent market economies of Slovakia and the Czech Republic, in contrast, show a very high degree of foreign ownership. The latter also is very high in the United Kingdom – particularly since the Thatcher period (privatizations and the 1984 "Big Bang" in the financial sector) – but also in the German CME, where most of the shares of the large companies ("DAX 30") today are in foreign hands, inter alia triggered by the liberalization reforms undertaken by the Schröder governments.

These differences are not by coincidence, nor a simple reflection of the state of economic development. In spite of its importance as a destination of foreign direct investments, China is the most restrictive of all fifty-five countries that a have been surveyed by the OECD. Figure 7.3 contains the data on the OECD index for the countries of our comparison. It demonstrates the much larger openness of the East European DMEs towards mobile capital, being similar to the established economies in this respect.

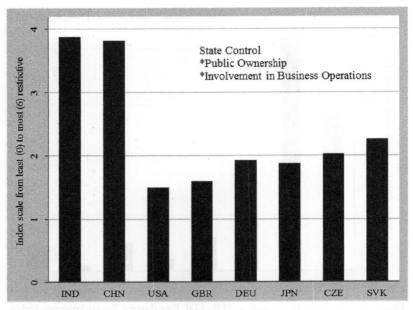

Figure 7.4 Levels of state control, 2008–2013.
Source: OECD, Product Market Regulation Database

Whereas national control is a core feature of large emerging markets, a more specific form of protection against financialization via cross-border mobile capital is the strong role of the state in business operations. Another index compiled by the OECD is highly instructive in this regard (Figure 7.4). This index gives an idea of the degree of state control in the economies of our comparison. It is based on two sub-indicators, public ownership of companies and state involvement in business operations (both based on several sub-indicators). Again, China stands out, followed by India.[5]

The comparatively low degree of financialization of large emerging markets also becomes obvious when we are taking a closer look at the sources of corporate finance. Figure 7.5 gives the shares of bank

---

[5] Interestingly, the level of state control during the 2008–2013 period is not particularly low in the United States and the United Kingdom. This partially reflects the consequences of the Lehman collapse, after which the state took over a number of major banks. See also Figure 7.6.

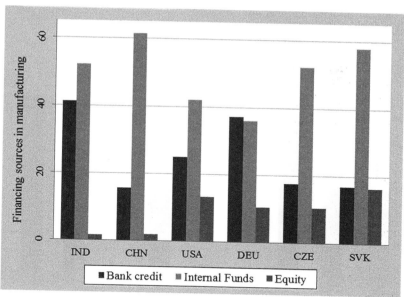

Figure 7.5 Sources for financing investments in manufacturing in percent, 2007–2011.
Source: World Bank Enterprise Surveys, China National Bureau of Statistics, US Census (no comprehensive data for Great Britain and Japan available)[6]

credits, internal funds and equity as a source of investment finance for companies. It clearly demonstrates that equity finance is playing a much lower role in the large emerging economies than in other types of capitalism, including liberal, coordinated and dependent market economies. The most important sources of finance in China and India are internal funds, followed by bank credit, whereas stock markets are marginalized. While a strong reliance on bank credit may create risks of its own (and borrowing in foreign currencies ranges among the most dangerous strategies for emerging market companies), this funding structure is not only supposed to minimize the volatility that may be induced by a strong role of equity finance (for example focus on quarterly reports), but also to reduce the incentives for

---

[6] "Internal funds" is a category within the World Bank Enterprise Surveys. It contains several categories, such as retained earnings or support by other companies within a business group. All categories share their independence from external sources such as equity markets or banks.

172   *Andreas Nölke*

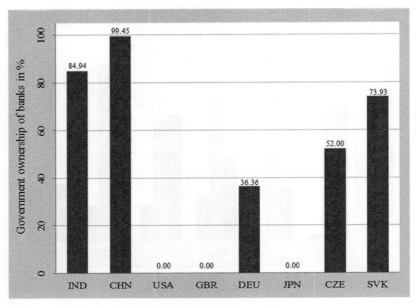

Figure 7.6 State ownership of the largest banks, 2002, in percent.
Source: La Porta, Lopez-De-Silanes and Shleifer 2002

non-financial corporations to focus their activities on financial activities
(for example, share buy-backs) instead of investments in production.

The importance of national control and of protection against the
volatility of global financial markets on the micro level also becomes
clear by taking a closer look at the type of banks that are dominating
large emerging markets. Here, national private banks and public development banks usually dominate the mobilization of domestic savings
for investments in catch-up industrialization. Figure 7.6 demonstrates
that the largest banks in China and in India are owned by the state.
State ownership of large banks, in contrast, was completely absent in
the United Kingdom, the United States and Japan before the financial
crisis, with the "Kreditanstalt für Wiederaufbau" in Germany being
the major exception in the industrialized economies.[7]

---

[7] This situation has somewhat changed during the financial crisis, when, for
   example, the United Kingdom took over most of the ownership of the Royal Bank
   of Scotland.

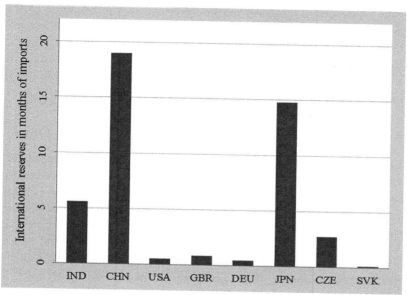

Figure 7.7 International reserves minus gold in months of imports (2011).
Source: World Bank Database, all values for the year 2011, except for India (2010)

Turning finally to the macro level, we have to note that both China and India have imposed fairly comprehensive capital controls (Dierckx, 2015). This is in marked contrast to all advanced economies, but also to the DME countries in Central Eastern Europe. Moreover, China and India have invested huge sums in international reserves, in order to fend off speculative attacks on their currencies (Figure 7.7). Although the latter – somewhat ironically – may have problematic consequences for the intensified financialization of households and of the financial sector such as a switch from lending for productive investments to lending for consumption and housing (Kaltenbrunner and Painceira, 2016: 15–19), it assists the non-financial sector against sudden stops and financial outflows.

In sum, the large emerging markets have built up several measures of protection against the global process of financialization, in order to safeguard their nationally organized process of catch-up industrialization. These measures can both be found on the micro level of corporate governance and finance, as well as on the macro level of capital controls and the accumulation of international reserves.

This observation stands in marked contrast to the behavior of the dependent market economies in East Central Europe that do not use most of these measures. Only time will tell which strategy is more successful. However, recent tendencies in the CEE region towards a more protectionist, state-dominated economy (Morawiecki, 2016) indicate that the SME strategy may become more dominant.

7 Conclusion and Perspectives for the Global Financial Order

In conclusion, there are considerable differences between the two basic types of emerging markets with regard to the openness to trans-border mobile capital. Whereas the dependent market economies of Central Eastern Europe embrace this type of capital, the state-permeated market economies of China and India are far more reluctant in this regard. Other important emerging markets, such as Brazil, Mexico and South Korea, range in between (Correa et al., 2013; Isaacs, 2016; Kaltenbrunner and Painceira, 2016; Lechevalier et al., 2016; Reither, 2016). However, we should acknowledge that the focus of this article is on international financialization, in particular with regard to the interruption of industrial catch-up processes via globally mobile capital. Domestic financialization, however, is also a major issue in China, including the related issue of inequality (Luo and Zhu, 2014; Kotarski, 2015).

Returning to the issue of international financialization, the large emerging markets China and India have built up several measures of protection against the global process of financialization, in order to safeguard their control over the process of catch-up industrialization. On the micro level, they have erected barriers against foreign ownership of domestic companies and have limited the use of volatile stock markets for the financing of long-term investments. On the macro level, they have erected capital controls and have accumulated large amounts of foreign currency reserves, in order to be able to intervene in a situation of a sudden devaluation. Thus, our comparative capitalism-based study supports recent findings in the comparative assessment of the degree of financialization between countries, where China and India systematically stand out with regard to a low degree of financial deregulation and capital account liberalization/foreign financial inflows (Karwowski and Stockhammer, 2016: 20–23).

Given the very different perspectives of the large emerging markets on capital mobility and global processes of financialization, if compared to established industrialized countries, combined with the growing political importance of countries such as China and India, we may ask whether these differences could be the nucleus of future conflicts about the global financial order. Does the rise of large emerging markets potentially lead to a critical junction in the development of this global order? It is yet too early to comprehensively answer this question. However, we can undertake a thought experiment and juxtapose the type of global financial institutions that look desirable from a large emerging market perspective with the existing liberal institutions.[8] In order to do so, first the two cases of global institutions on the microeconomic level are singled out, namely those on corporate governance and those on company finance, before turning to the macroeconomic issue of capital controls (there is no global regulation on the amount of foreign currency reserves).

While there is no powerful regulation of corporate governance on the global level, the OECD governance standards usually serve as a benchmark for national regulation. With regard to emerging markets, these principles form the basis for IMF/World Bank assessments in the context of a Review of Observance of Standards and Codes/ROSC or as part of a Financial Sector Assessment Programme (OECD, 2007). The OECD standards typically focus on the protection of minority shareholders against block-holders that are dominating corporations. Although the notion of minority shareholders usually is carrying the image of an individual investor, de facto these guidelines are most important for the large institutional investors that are dominating the trade with equities. From the perspective of large emerging markets, however, the protection of individual investors or institutional investment houses (usually based in the advanced economies) is much less important than the long-term stability of companies that is guaranteed by the existence of a block-holder. Correspondingly, large emerging markets would not agree to an intensified enforcement of OECD standards globally and some of them have already refused to disclose information on ROSC (Mosley, 2010).

A second bone of contention between Western economies and large emerging markets with regard to corporate governance and ownership refers to the role of the state as shareholder. Here, Western governments would like to limit this role, in contrast to the preferences of

[8] For a detailed discussion of the latter see chapter 1 by Renate Mayntz.

large emerging markets that have developed a specific type of state capitalism (Nölke, 2014b). Recently, this conflict has led to several cases of contention, when Western governments did not allow the acquisition of companies by state-controlled companies from large emerging markets.

In the field of corporate finance, the most important global standards are set by the International Accounting Standards Board/IASB based in London. IASB standards take the perspective of an (financial) investor and therefore highly value most transparent company reports (Perry and Nölke, 2007; Nölke and Perry, 2008). Emerging markets frequently have reservations about these standards, because they permit investors to exercise considerable pressure with regard to their participation in the distribution of profits. For the long-term company perspective that is necessary for a catch-up industrialization, a focus on shareholder value and quarterly reports is not desirable. Correspondingly, large emerging markets may well officially sign up to IASB standards, but often do not implement these standards effectively (Nölke, 2013). More recently, large emerging markets also have insisted on a better presentation in the bodies of the International Accounting Standard Board in order to influence future standards. While this increased representation has been granted by the G20, the role of emerging market perspectives in the daily work of the IASB has remained very limited (Nölke, 2015).

Based on this short survey, we can highlight a number of fields where large emerging markets and Western economies (both CME and LME) have divergent preferences on the outlook of global economic institutions (see also Kalinowski, 2013). So far, these global institutions still follow Western – more specifically: LME – preferences. Emerging markets usually limit their opposition to these institutions to a weak implementation of the standards set by global Western-dominated institutions. Correspondingly, emerging markets sign up to IASB or OECD standards, but we cannot assume that these standards are thoroughly enforced on the ground. More recently, however, there are also small indications of a modification of the adherence of important global institutions to the liberal Western ideal of free capital mobility. Here, the International Monetary Fund stands out with regard to its reconsideration of the issue of capital controls. During the last couple of years, IMF economists have increasingly developed a more positive take on capital controls that have been rebranded from completely wrong interference to legitimate tool (Grabel, 2016). For the time being, however, it is much too early to judge whether this is the first indication of an alternative global economic order in the making or just a minor exception that still confirms the general rule.

Recent developments, including the Brexit vote and the election of US President Trump point towards an economic order that gives a higher priority to issues of national sovereignty, against the forces of globalization. The focus in these recent debates is on the globalization of trade and of labor migration, but a major setback in these fields could also have impacts on the globalization of financial markets, even if the current US and UK governments are rather in favour of liberal financial markets. Taken together with the rise of neo-populist parties in many Continental European countries, we may well be at a critical juncture towards a less liberal and more organized world economic order (Nölke forthcoming b).

Bibliography

Aalbers, Manuel (2008) The Financialization of home and the mortgage market crisis. *Competition & Change* 12 (2), 148–166.

Bluedorn, John, Duttagupta, Rupa, Guajardo, Jaime and Topalova, Petia (2013). *Capital Flows Are Fickle: Anytime, Anywhere* (IMF Working Paper 13/183). Washington, DC: International Monetary Fund.

Bresser-Pereira, Luiz Carlos (2015). *Brazil's 35 Year-Old Quasi-Stagnation: Facts and Theory* (Working Paper No. 399, Escola de Economia de São Paulo da Fundação Getulio Vargas). Sao Paulo.

Calvo, Guillermo A. (1998). Capital flows and capital-market crises: The simple economics of sudden stops. *Journal of Applied Economics* 1 (1), 35–54.

Christophers, Brett (2015). The limits to financialization. *Dialogues in Human Geography* 5 (2), 183–200.

Correa, Eugenia, Vidal, Gregorio and Marshall, Wesley (2013). Financialization in Mexico: Trajectory and limits. *Journal of Post Keynesian Economics* 35 (2), 255–275.

Dierckx, Sacha (2015). *Capital Controls in China, Brazil and India: Towards the End of the Free Movement of Capital as a Global Norm.* PhD Dissertation, Ghent University.

Dünhaupt, Petra (2014). *An Empirical Assessment of the Contribution of Financialization and Corporate Governance to the Rise of Income Inequality* (IPE Working Paper 41). Berlin: Institute for International Political Economy.

Epstein, Gerald (2005). *Financialization and the World Economy*. Cheltenham: Edward Elgar.

Foster, John Bellamy (2008). The financialization of capitalism and the crisis. *Monthly Review* 59 (11), 1–19.

Grabel, Ilene (2003). Averting crisis? Assessing measures to manage financial integration in emerging economies. *Cambridge Journal of Economics* 27 (3), 317–336.

(2016). *Capital Controls in a Time of Crisis* (PERI Working Paper Series). Amherst: University of Massachusetts.

Hall, Peter and Soskice, David eds. (2001). *Varieties of Capitalism: The Institutional Foundations of Comparative Advantage*. Oxford University Press.

Hein, Eckhard and van Treeck, Eckhard (2010). Financialisation and rising shareholder power in Kaleckian/post-Kaleckian models of distribution and growth. *Review of Political Economy* 22(2), 205–232.

Heires, Marcel and Nölke, Andreas (2011). Finanzkrise und Finanzialisierung. In Kessler, Oliver (ed.) *Die Internationale Politische Ökonomie der Weltfinanzkrise*, Wiesbaden: Springer VS, 37–52.

(2014a). Finanzialisierung. In Wullweber, Joscha, Graf, Antonia and Behrens, Maria eds. *Theorien der Internationalen Politischen Ökonomie*, Wiesbaden: Springer VS, 253–266.

eds. (2014b). *Politische Ökonomie der Finanzialisierung*. Wiesbaden: Springer VS.

Higgott, Richard (1998). The Asian economic crisis: A study in the politics of resentment. *New Political Economy* 3 (3), 333–356.

Isaacs, Gild (2016). *Financialisation and Development: The South African Case Study*. (FESSUD Working Paper Series No. 142). University of Leeds.

Kalinowski, Thomas (2013). Regulating international finance and the diversity of capitalism. *Socio-Economic Review* 11 (3), 471–496.

Kaltenbrunner, Annina and Painceira, Juan Pablo (2016). *International and Domestic Financialisation in Middle Income Countries* (FESSUD Working Paper No. 146). University of Leeds.

Karwowski, Ewa and Stockhammer, Engelbert (2016). *Financialisation in Emerging Economies: A Systematic Overview and Comparison with Anglo-Saxon Economies* (Post Keynesian Economics Study Group Working Paper 1616). Kingston University.

Kotarski, Kristijan (2015). Financial deepening and income inequality: Is there any financial Kuznets curve in China? *China Economic Journal* 8 (1), 18–39.

Krippner, Greta (2011). *Capitalizing on Finance: The Political Origins of the Rise of Finance*. Harvard University Press.

Kus, Basak (2012). Financialisation and income inequality in OECD Nations: 1995–2007. *The Economic and Social Review* 43 (4), 477–495.

La Porta, Rafel, Lopez-De-Silanes, Florencio and Shleifer, Andrei (2002). Government Ownership of Banks. *The Journal of Finance* 57 (1), 265–301.

Lapavitsas, Costas (2009). Financialised Capitalism: Crisis and Financial Expropriation. *Historical Materialism* 17 (1), 114–148.

Lechevalier, Sébastien, Debanes, Pauline and Shin, Wonkyu (2016). *Financialization and Industrial Policies in Japan and Korea: Evolving Complementarities and Loss of Institutional Capabilities* (CEAFJP Discussion Paper Series 16–06). Paris: Centre d'Etudes Avancées Franco-Japonais de Paris.

Lin, Ken-Hou and Tomaskovic-Devey, Donald (2013). Financialization and U.S. income inequality, 1970–2008. *American Journal of Sociology* 118 (5), 1284–1329.

Luo, Yu and Zhu, Frank (2014). Financialization of the economy and income inequality in China. *Economic and Political Studies* 2 (2), 46–66.

May, Christian and Nölke, Andreas (2016). Finance and industrial policy in state-permeated capitalism: The case of Brazil, paper presented to the workshop on "Finance for Growth and Development," Cambridge, 29th November.

Morawiecki, Mateusz (2016). The Polish Case for Less Economic Liberalism, Politico-EU-Online, 21 October, http://www.politico.eu/article/the-polish-case-for-economic-illiberalism-stability-development/.

McKinley, Terry (2016). *The Impact of Financialisation on Major Emerging Economies* (FESSUD Working Paper Series No. 162). University of Leeds.

Mosley Layna (2010). Regulating Globally, Implementing Locally: The Financial Codes and Standards Effort. *Review of International Political Economy* 17 (4), 724–761.

Musacchio, Aldo, and Lazzarini, Sergio (2014). *Leviathan in Business: Varieties of State Capitalism and Their Implications for Economic Performance*. Cambridge, MA: Harvard University Press.

Nölke, Andreas (2009). Finanzkrise, Finanzialisierung und Vergleichende Kapitalismusforschung. *Zeitschrift für Internationale Beziehungen* 16 (1), 123–139.

— (2012). The Rise of the B(R)IC Variety of Capitalism: Towards a New Phase of Organized Capitalism? In: H. Overbeek, and B. van Apeldoorn (eds.), *Neoliberalism in Crisis*. Houndmills: Palgrave, 117–133.

— (2013). A political economy explanation for country variation in IFRS adoption – a comment on "The international politics of IFRS harmonization" by K. Ramanna. *Accounting, Economics and Law* 3 (2), 69–76.

(2014a). Politik der Finanzialisierung: Zum Wohlfahrtsbeitrag des Finanzsektors in Rechnungslegungsstandards und volkswirtschaftlicher Gesamtrechnung. In Heires, Marcel and Nölke, Andreas eds, *Politische Ökonomie der Finanzialisierung*, Wiesbade: Springer VS, 79–94.

ed. (2014b). *Multinational Corporations from Emerging Markets: State Capitalism 3.0.* Houndmills: Palgrave MacMillan.

(2015). Rising powers and transnational private governance: The International Accounting Standards Board. In: Lesage, Dries and Van de Graaf, Thijs eds, *Rising Powers and International Institutions*. Houndmills: Palgrave MacMillan, 96–116.

(2016). Economic causes of the Eurozone crisis: The analytical contribution of comparative capitalism. *Socio-Economic Review* 14 (1), 141–161.

(forthcoming a). Financialisation as the core problem for a "Social Europe." *Revista de Economia Mundial (REM)/Journal of World Economy.*

(forthcoming b). Brexit: On the way to a new phase of organized capitalism. *Competition and Change.*

Nölke, Andreas and Perry, James (2008). The power of transnational private governance: financialization and the IASB. *Business and Politics* 7 (3), 1–27.

Nölke, Andreas and Vliegenthart Arjan (2009). Enlarging the varieties of capitalism: The emergence of Dependent Market Economies in East Central Europe. *World Politics* 61 (4), 670–702. ·

Nölke, Andreas, ten Brink, Tobias, Claar, Simone and May, Christian (2015) Domestic structures, foreign economic policies and global economic order: Implications from the rise of large emerging economies. *European Journal of International Relations* 21 (3), 538–567.

OECD (2007). *Methodology for Assessing the Implementation of the OECD Principles of Corporate Governance.* Paris: Organization for Economic Co-Operation and Development.

Ouma, Stefan (2014): The new enclosures: Zur Finanzialisierung von Land und Agrarwirtschaft. In Heires, Marcel and Nölke, Andreas eds. *Politische Ökonomie der Finanzialisierung*, Wiesbaden: Springer VS, 197–210.

Palley, Thomas I. (2013). *Financialization: The Economics of Finance Capital Domination.* Houndmills: Palgrave MacMillan.

Perry, James and Nölke, Andreas (2007). The political economy of international accounting standards. *Review of International Political Economy* 13 (4), 559–586.

Philippon, Thomas (2011). The Size of the US Finance Industry: A Puzzle? Mimeo. http://www.newyorkfed.org/research/conference/2011/NYAMP/Fed_Philippon_v1.pdf.

Reinhart, Carmen M. and Rogoff, Kenneth S. (2008). *Banking Crises: An Equal Opportunity Menace.* Mimeo http://scholar.harvard.edu/files/rogoff/files/banking_crises.pdf.

Reither, Susanne (2016). Finanzialisierung und Finanzmarktstabilität in Brasilien: Eine Perspektive der Regulationstheorie. *Momentum Quarterly 5* (3), 156–171.

Rodrik, Dani (2006). The social cost of foreign exchange reserves. *International Economic Journal* 20 (3), 253–266

Schneider Ben Ross (2013) *Hierarchical Capitalism: Business, Labour, and the Challenge of Equitable Development in Latin America.* Cambridge University Press.

Singh, Ajit (1996). *Financial Liberalisation, Stockmarkets and Economic* Development (MPRA Paper No. 53897). Munich.

Singh, Ajit and Weisse, Bruce A. (1998). Emerging stock markets, portfolio capital flows and long-term economic growth: Micro- and macroeconomic perspectives. *World Development* 26 (4), 607–622.

Stiglitz, Joseph E. (2002). *Globalization and Its Discontents.* New York: W.W. Norton.

Stockhammer, Engelbert (2012). Financialization, income distribution and the crisis. *Investigación Económica* 71 (279), 39–70.

Tomaskovic-Devey, Donald, Lin, Ken-Hou and Meyers, Nathan (2015). Did financialization reduce economic growth? *Socio-Economic Review* 13 (3), 528–548.

Tyson, Judith and McKinley, Terry (2014). *Financialization and the Developing World: Mapping the Issues* (FESSUD Working Paper Series No. 38). University of Leeds.

Van der Zwan, Natascha (2014). Making sense of financialization. *Socio-Economic Review* 12 (1), 99–129.

8 Lagoon Immobility

The Exceptional Case of Imperial Venice

SAM WHIMSTER

In considering the mobility of capital, historical case studies greatly expand our ability to conceptualize just what is involved when we use this term. I examine Venetian capitalism through the lens of three major figures: Fernand Braudel, Max Weber, and Carl Schmitt. The last named should make us feel uncomfortable. Schmitt attacked the democratic constitution of the Weimar Republic 1919–1933, placing the survival of the state as the paramount reality. This led him to support Hitler and the resurrection of a German Empire after its collapse in 1918. His expulsion from the National Socialist Party in 1937 does not count as political exoneration, but did allow a certain intellectual detachment. *Land and Sea*, published in 1942, is a rumination on geopolitics whose intellectual novelty, for me, is the way he thinks about relationality – most obviously in this book the different phases of the relationality of land and water (so including riverine civilizations).

I start and finish with Schmitt (1888–1985). Early on in his short book he brings up the case of Venice. 'With her, a new mythical name entered the grand stage of world history. For almost half a millennium, the Venetian Republic symbolized the domination of the seas, the wealth derived from maritime trade and that matchless feat which was the conciliation of the requisites of high politics with "oddest creation in the economic history of all times"'(Schmitt, 2001: 8). Venice's power came from the sea, symbolised and interpreted by all at the time, by the Assumption festivity when the *doge* put to sea and threw a ring into the water, so renewing Venice's 'marriage to the sea'. 'The glory of this fairy-tale like "queen of the seas" kept expanding from the year 1000 to the year 1500' (2001: 9).

The mobility of capital, which we might infer at this point, comes from its trade with Byzantium and the Levant. For Schmitt, however, this marks its smallness as a maritime power which was 'limited to the Adriatic and the Mediterranean basin alone, at a time when the huge expansion of the oceans of the world were cast open.' There is sea power and there is sea power; Venice's is closed in contrast to oceanic sea power. Venice was wedded to a coastal and 'lagoon civilization'. Venetians looked inwards not outwards to the oceans, its navigational abilities were limited and its ships were oared vessels. It fought its sea battles as if on land, attacking with archers and boarding enemy ships. Venice treated its seas in terms of rituals and not, to use Weberian language, though the unmagical attitude of world mastery of the Atlantic seafaring nations.

Schmitt was a jurist and he grasps the significance of oceanic power through the law of the sea and rules of warfare. War on land is typically conducted by territorial states, one against each other. There is no moral right or wrong and this is true of most continental landmasses until the nineteenth century. There is no culpability for war between states, each has a right to deploy its armies according to whatever *casus belli*. Schmitt termed this the non-discriminating concept of war.[1] Civilians are not subject to warfare and are victims only in respect to disruption. Oceanic sea power changes this, British, Dutch, Spanish and American navies are able to attack any country in the world. At the time of writing (April 2017) Exocet missiles are launched from US warships in the Eastern Mediterranean targetted at Syrian airbases. The Syrian regime of Bashir al-Assad protested vehemently that this was an infringement of their sovereignty. For Schmitt the protest would be legitimate and represented territorial state power. Steaming up to another country and attacking them was illegitimate, but also the new reality; equally questionable for him was claiming moral superiority for such an attack (which President Trump displayed with considerable moral sententiousness on 6 April) and the presumed culpability of the attacked state; a feature Schmitt attributed to the Entente powers at the Versailles Peace Treaty of 1919.

We can dismiss Schmitt's apologetics. He did not support the League of Nations, nor would he the United Nations and the accompanying commitment to international law. His was a pre-nineteenth century juristic landscape. Nevertheless, his juristic facility highlights the shift

---

[1] Joshua Derman (2011: 181–189) explains this concept more fully. He points out that Schmitt was not consistent in the use of these arguments, which reflected his political expediency during the Nazi period and the Second World War. Schmitt sought to delegitimize the British Empire and to find extra reasons to persecute the Jews.

in maritime power and its justification that is now simply taken for granted by the leading powers. In respect to the mobility of capital a Schmittian reading would not be amiss. In global-think there is a presumption that financial capital can and ought to be deployed without let or hindrance, irrespective of territorial boundaries. Schmitt is the resentful theorist who asks why maritime powers are so presumptuous and why this massive extension of power (by predominantly the Anglo-Saxon world) went unchallenged, both theoretically and juristically. I will return to this at the conclusion of this chapter.

Carl Schmitt's analysis of Venice, while acknowledging its wealth and culture, is an argument that trading in the Eastern Mediterranean was an historical cul-de-sac, unable to break out to the Atlantic and the infinite extension of the seas of the world. He omits any discussion of the dynamics and structuring of Venetian trade, which in contrast has been the major attraction for economic historians who see in Venice a crucial forerunner of modern capitalism. Schmitt sounds a negative, and critical, note which is worth retaining as we turn to the more exuberant accounts of Venetian 'mobile' capital.

For Braudel, Venice marked the start of capitalism as we moderns understand it. Venice stands out as the most successful of the Italian city-states. Income per head of population ranked far above any other European state. In turnover alone the Venetian state was the equal of France (Braudel, 1984: 119–124). Its fabulous wealth enabled it to build a city on water, cutting out a system of canals, embanking against the sea and driving oak piles into the sand and gradually replacing the original wooden structures of houses and bridges into stone and marble magnificence. 'The economic power of Renaissance Venice was founded on the experience of four centuries of almost uninterrupted commercial and colonial expansion', writes the economic historian John Day (1999: 28). It had established itself as a world power by the thirteenth century and it only succumbed to Napoleonic invasion at the end of the eighteenth century.

The city of Venice was a jurisdiction spread over sixty islands and islets. It looked outwards to the Adriatic and Mediterranean seas and was mostly cut off from the mainland where its initial territorial links were curtailed. It was a 'town reduced to bare essentials, stripped of everything not strictly urban, and condemned, in order to survive, to obtain everything from trade' (Braudel, 1984: 108). 'Venice was able to penetrate more successfully than any other power the huge, ineffectually defended market of Byzantium, rending many services to the empire and even contributing to its defence', writes Braudel (1984: 109). Venice controlled trade routes to Byzantium and the Levant and extended them into the Atlantic (*pace* Schmitt) to London and Antwerp. It also controlled trade routes inland through the eastern Alps to northwest Europe. Venice, therefore, had positioned itself at the crossroads of the profitable traffic in commodities. Venice, notes Braudel, 'had become a sort of universal warehouse of the world as Amsterdam was to be, on a larger scale, in a later century' (1984: 125). Venice also had its own artisanal industries of wool, silk, glass etc. whose standards of manufacture was tightly supervised by the *Collegio alle Arti*. Venice was the leading capitalist economy of early modernity.

By capitalism is simply meant that where property of any sort is an object of trade and is utilized by individuals for profit-making enterprise in a market economy, there we have capitalism. This is a paraphrase of a definition provided by Max Weber when writing on agrarian society in the ancient world (Weber 1976: 50–51). For Weber, it was land that was traded for profit in ancient Rome, in Venice it was predominantly commodities that were traded for profit.

Weber's definition of capitalism here is generic. We can specify this more closely for Venice and the other leading Italian cities states, as do all economic historians, as mercantile capitalism. The profits of invested capital derive from trade carried on by merchants. The Braudel school, which includes der Vries and der Woude's *The First Modern Economy. Success, Failure, and Perserverance of the Dutch Economy, 1500–1815*, is very much a bottom-up history responsive to the habits and working practices of the different strata of society. It does not shy away from the concept of class, though it does break with Karl Marx's dialectical progress of history. For Marx the urban bourgeoisie dissolves the previous feudal mode of production inaugurating the rise of industrial capitalism. For the Braudel school the principle linkage between an increasingly successful medieval economy and modern capitalism is the ascendancy of merchant capitalism. Merchant capital and its expertise with money and banking, which Geoffrey Ingham (2015: 160–191) has also foregrounded, is the decisive factor in western Europe in creating modern capitalism.

Still in a loose usage, terming this 'mobile capital' places the emphasis on inter-territorial trade routes, capital, banking and financial instruments. Venice's sophistication in these respects has been a focus of

economic historians. This was a distinctive business model that produced large profits from the use of capital. The economic and status
distinctions were marked. The rich families, with their palaces on the
Rialto, put up the capital for merchant ventures, the merchants who
oversaw and carried through the ventures were inferior partners, and
the bankers were subsidiary to both the former.

The exact character of the business venture attracted the attention of
a young Max Weber who studied it for his doctorate in 1890 (2003).[2]
While trade and traffic was continuous in and out of Venice, the capital
to pay for cargo space and the overseas purchase of goods in bulk was
raised separately for each venture. Ninety percent of the capital was
from investments made by consortia of wealthy families. The partnerships, known as a *colleganza*, included the active merchant travelling
with the ship and buying and selling commodities as a junior partner.
Venetians did not have access to deep pools of financial capital. Instead
they invested in a serial pattern, moving from one venture to another,
often involved in multiple ventures as they alighted in one port and
set out for another. In short capital markets did not exist, nor did fixed
investment in 'shipping lines', nor joint stock companies, since *colleganza* partnerships, though multiple, operated on a case by case basis.
The proceeds were shared out on a proportional basis and then the
venture was liquidated. The investors charged 20 per cent for the
loan of capital and an additional 20 per cent profit was realized after
the sale of commodities (Braudel 1984: 121). The distinction between
investor and active merchant changed over time. Some investors
started out as actively involved in the trading ventures and then settled
on the Rialto or Cyprus, and other capital poor merchants gradually
accumulated profits becoming investors in their own right.

This analysis is early Weber, years before his Protestant ethic thesis
and decades before his ideal typology of economic ethics and the world
religions. His mental space was formed by his supervisor Levin Goldschmidt (1829–1897), author of the legendary (for jurists) *Universal
History of Commercial Law*. Weber followed Goldschmidt in arguing

---

[2] Weber notes (2003: 77) the slow transformation from a family based unit
(*compagnia fraterna*) into a venture specific partnership. Venice stood apart from
the general development of Roman and canon law which made it distinctive
though not influential from the point of view of development of commercial law.
The commercial partnership of the *commenda* was more the focus of his study, in
Genoa particularly.

that commercial law was crafted piecemeal by the trading practices of the Italian city-states with Weber examining Venice, Genoa, Pisa and Florence. Weber devotes a chapter to family partnerships, a feature that eventually had to be changed from family communism to the separation of the household and business accounts as a pre-requisite for modern rational capitalism. This was law and working practices customised for merchants and it did not have the character of public state law. The later Weber saw modern capitalism emerging within a mature state and public law context (more on this below). The mercantile phase of capitalism was just that, and it implied no necessary 'evolution' to modern capitalism. In this sense, Weber anticipates Carl Schmitt (though in fact Schmitt attended Weber's lectures 1919–1920 on economic history). We should therefore probably exclude Weber's understanding of Venetian and Genoan venture expeditions as counting as 'mobile capital'. Capital was controlled by leading families, in a hierarchy that subordinated the merchants, sea captains, and relegated bankers to the bottom rung.

To this should be added the political economy of Venice, which while termed a republican commune, was in fact a ruthless authoritarian oligarchy comprised of the leading wealthy families. Venetian foreign policy was dedicated to asserting its ascendancy over the Adriatic and the Eastern Mediterranean seas. The Venetian state built ships, in the Arsenal, manned them and supplied soldiers to defend them. Trading expeditions were strictly timetabled by the Admiralty. Units of cargo space (*carats*) in the ship were auctioned by the state, and ships sailed in convoys on dates fixed by the Venetian Senate: mid-July to Romania, mid-August to Beirut, late August early September to Alexandria, March and April to Flanders (Mueller 1997: 306). The state also built and owned the warehouses (*dogone*) so crucial to Venice's entrepôt role.

The Venetian authorities insisted that all trade between merchants (both Venetian and foreign) be conducted in the market places of Venice. Trading profits were secured to Venice and measures were taken to constrain other financial market intermediaries from profiting from Venetian trade. For example, the government was 'hostile to innovations in this field' and it was illegal for the bill of exchange to be passed on through endorsement to anyone other than the merchant to whom it was made out (Day 1999: 31). This also meant that the discount rate would not be determined through the buying and selling of bills of exchange which would have turned them into negotiable credit instruments, a step that occurred later in the 'state-free' environment of Antwerp, and became a major tool of banks and state banks thereafter.

When we come to Weber's *Herrschaftssoziologie* and 'The City', which form the early drafts of *Economy and Society*, autonomous self-governing city-states are overtaken and incorporated by the growing territorial state, the patrimonial state as Weber called them. Venice flourished in an imperial, maritime system of its own making (along with the initial support of Byzantium). It was ill-adapted, indeed incapable, of adjusting to the new '*Binnenland*' territorial and proto-national state system that was gaining the upper hand from the sixteenth century onwards. When Venice fell to Napoleon in 1797 it was a hollowed-out relic. Weber's 'mobile capital' (see Introduction) only comes into its own in the context of landmass territorial states.

Venetian Banks and the State

Historians of central banks, almost to a man, refer to Venice (as well as Genoa) as innovating the first banks to the state and in general they laud the innovation of paper credit. These arguments must be qualified by the more detailed research, which points to the rackety nature of Venice's banks and state finances. In detail, the credit and fiscal mechanisms were extraordinary, and again suggest that the Venetian context was never going to be established as the basis of modern, rational capitalism.

Creating markets, maintaining them and protecting them from competitors involved considerable expenditure by the state. Venice was challenged by other Italian city-states, notably Genoa, leading to at least four wars. Other wars were fought against the cities of Padua, Verona, Brescia and Bergano from 1405–1427, and Ferrara in 1482/3. After Constantinople fell to the Turks in 1453, Venice had a new enemy, leading to initial wars 1463–1479 and only concluding a peace treaty with the Turks in 1718. And it fought the Candia war in 1649–1669 for control of Crete. The Venetian state also maintained an extensive diplomatic network of ambassadors across Italy, Europe and the Mediterranean that was able to intervene and influence the foreign policy and coalitions of larger European territorial states. These expenditures frequently exceeded the state budget, which was based on a system of first voluntary loans and then obligatory loans of those who fell within the taxation registry (*estimo*), and over the years was extended to purchase and excise taxes. When a war was not going in Venice's favour it bought more mercenaries, and it paid for these frequent spikes in expenditure by taxing more frequently and from enforced loans. Wars were an essential overhead of the Venetian trading empire, which included tribute from its colonies. They were not, however, the disastrously expensive wars – like the 100 Years War fought by feudal dynasts north of the Alps. The spikes in expenditure had to be met and this is where the close linkage between the private banks and the state came into its own. For Gino Luzzato (2nd ed. 1964), writing in the 1930s, this linkage demonstrated that the private banks were offering a public function to the state. Luzzatto argues that the state exercised the right to demand that bankers advance credit for state expenditures and that bankers confine themselves to giro activities. In short, if banks were going to lend it would be to the state alone and in this respect the banks were acting as public banks. This was happening in the thirteenth century onwards, a long time before actual public banks came into existence.

Frederic Lane and Reinhold Mueller (1997) through their comprehensive examination of the Venetian archival sources and the correspondence of European merchant bankers have altered this picture in major respects. Metallic money was as equally important for banks as the fabled credit money. When a large convoy left the lagoon for the Levant, it was as if Venice had been drained of gold and silver (Braudel 1984: 132). Reinhold Mueller is able to chart the resulting pricing of credit money against metallic money. Over-reliance on credit, when an expedition was underway, reduced its price against the scarce gold and silver. And when the merchants returned they deposited their profits in specie as well as booking a credit in a bank journal. At this point the price of gold and silver declined relative to credit bank money. In addition banks operated deposit accounts in specie for clients. Some of these were sealed and provided a return, for instance to a widow or orphan, other accounts were current and money was lent out on these.

Clearly Venice's banks were not confined solely to giro transactions. Mueller also points out that the Venetian authorities, despite their officials patrolling the *banchi* on the Rialto, had little control of the bill of exchange. This was a Florentine invention and the business was conducted by Florentine merchant bankers in Venice. It was profitable for two reasons. One currency was being exchanged for another, Venetian ducats for Byzantine coin (*hyperpers*) for example, and if the exchange rates were accurately reckoned the rates of exchange were written in the bank's favour. The merchant bank was also advancing credit and specie for a specific period of time: five days, ten days, one month, three months. Theological authorities allowed that the banker was involved in an unavoidable expense in lending out scarce money for a merchant venture, and this could legitimately be priced into the bill (Schumpeter 1954: 102–104). That price difference was termed *agio*, an Italian word that interestingly comes from *lazio*, meaning ease. It was recognized that profit was being earned without labour, and labour was considered the font of virtuous economic behaviour.

Many banks failed and this was not an infrequent occurrence. In 1584, the senator Tommaso Contarini wrote: 'In the 1,200 years during which this Republic exists by grace of God, one finds that 102 banks private banks were erected, of which 96 failed ... and 7 alone succeeded' (Mueller 1997: 122). It is not known what records he had access to and he is dating Venice from its mythical foundation in 420 C.E.; also, he was probably including the more transient money changers, who frequently expanded their activities into banking proper. Reinhold Mueller's research documents 50 bank failures between 1340 and 1500 – 'few banks avoided a bitter end', he notes (1997: 122). This raises the question of the institutional solidity of a bank. Banks had a moveable character, tables for counting money set up on the side of the Rialto, and requiring a journal for making credit and debit entries. Little capital was required, just the good name of the guarantors who provided sureties. Bankruptcy proceedings were routinised and oriented to the practical task of dividing up the remaining credit and sureties among creditors. By contrast, on mainland Italy, a bankrupt had to humiliate himself by hitting his naked buttocks against a post in the public square (Mueller 1997: 125). On the other hand, the principal Venetian banks handled large amounts of money, their journal entries had the force of law, and their accounts followed local bookkeeping conventions. It may make sense to perceive them, certainly not as banking houses on the grand Florentine model, but as more flimsy institutions.

This is especially so in their relations with the Senate. Luzzatto advanced a number of claims: the banks fulfilled a public role in lending money to the state especially at times of extreme need like famine and wars; the banks forwarded credit to the various offices of the state without any reserve deposit against which this credit was advanced. At this point, Luzzatto points out, the state was issuing fiduciary money through the private banks.[3] Fiduciary money here is bank credit money that is convertible back into specie on demand. At times, the state had little cash to cover their loans, neither did the banks. The specie money had all gone; for example, in a war ships had to be equipped, armaments bought and mercenaries paid. The *agio* on specie would increase and the merchant bankers would go in search of gold and silver to rectify the imbalance in Venice. But, in effect, the private banks and the state were operating a 'float' or a collective overdraft until such time when conditions normalised, which they invariably did.

The private banks were helping the state out, in its hour of need, by entering a credit on the current account of creditors to the state. The state had no money to pay them, so the private banks stepped in. As Mueller says, 'then the banker was creating money. He was substituting his promise to pay for that of the state, on the basis of the state's promise to repay him. The supplier of goods and services to the state could then draw on the account to make his own payments by bank transfer. The same was true even without an authorized loan, when the banker discounted a private party's credit due from the state. The result was the creation and the potential multiple expansion of fiduciary money' (Mueller 1997: 427).

The extent of the 'potential multiple expansion of fiduciary money' would depend on the number and types of state creditors being propped up by private bank transfers. Subscribers to the public debt – often special war loan subscriptions, such as the Monte Nuovo in 1482 and the Monte Nuovissimo in 1509 – were 'guaranteed' interest rate payments of around 5 per cent paid in twice yearly instalments. These funds, called *monte* were both a patriotic duty for rich citizens and had practical value as an annuity, for instance for widows.

---

[3] Luzzatto (1964: 57) attaches the fiduciary function to the actual establishment of a state bank, the *Banco del Giro* in the early seventeenth century: 'A côté de la Monnaie qui pourvoit à la circulation des espèces métalliques, la Banque crée une véritable circulation fiduciaire, qui acquiert quelquefois dans le commerce vénetien une importance plus grande que l'argent comptant (cash account).'

Periods of stress, however, raised the probability of bankruptcies.
Reinhold Mueller has assessed one such complaint by a leading banker.
In the spring of 1499 there was a run of bank failures as Venice
prepared for another war against the Turks. Two banks had gone
down, and two remained by May of that year. Alvise Pisani, of one
of the remaining banks, was fighting the loss of depositors withdrawing their money and he complained bitterly about the failed banks
causing a panic owing to the low level of surety that a bank had to
put up by law. 'When the banks are not trusted, the state has no credit',
he is reported as saying (Quoted in Mueller 1997: 425). This goes
to the heart of the relation between the state sovereignty and financial
power, and is underlined by a report of a discussion in the Papal
consistory, where the Pope drew the mistaken conclusion that in the
light of these bank failures, Venice had lost its lines of credit and would
be forced to withdraw from its treaty obligations and therefore was
finished as a major military power.

Reinhold Mueller accepts that in the fifteenth century the private
banks had indeed taken over the national debt. 'When the Grain
Office declined, the role of managers of the floating debt was taken
over in the Quattrocento by the private banks of the Rialto, which
assumed more than ever the nature of an institution in the public
interest' (1997: 360). But he finds little evidence that banks failed
because of their forced loans to the state. In exceptional circumstances the state would turn to the banks, so much so that supervising
officials often became organs of government compelling the private
banks to forward loans. In the case of the run on Alvise Pisani's bank,
the Signoria dispatched three officials to the bank with a guarantee
of 100,000 ducats (Mueller 1997: 244). The panic of withdrawals
subsided and the tide of money reversed. Also for their services,
private banks received certain privileges, such as tax immunity, from
the state. Besides, despite the emergency incidents and panics, the
banking sector overall and in terms of a longer continuity was rich,
and the annual turnover of the Venetian economy far exceeded any
emergency demands.

The line of determination, therefore, *pace il Papa*, did not run from
bottom to top, from loss of trust, to the absence of credit, and termin-
ating with the loss of state power and sovereignty. It went the other
way. Venetian state sovereignty was supreme, the tax payer and the
banks had to conform to the fiscal and monetary demands of the

state, and the institutional interfaces had a permeability and fluidity that allowed crises to be negotiated.

There is a seeming paradox here, in that the state debt, the consolidated debt of Venice, was the rock (the *monte* of debt) on which the overdraft provision by private banks was justified. A major debt was supporting minor debts. The explanation takes us to the issue of trust. The sovereignty and the legitimacy of the state were inviolable and could not be questioned. If the state had to fight wars to defend its trading interests, there was no choice, and if the state had to levy extraordinary taxes that was its prerogative. If the state could not cover its expenditures, then the banks would step up and provide bank money. The agio would move in favour of specie against credit money. This system continued until in 1584 the banking houses of Pisani and Tiepolo collapsed in 1584 with debts owing of half a million ducats. Mobile capital, it seems, leaked from the banks like a sieve and it was the state that stemmed the losses. What is described in the next paragraphs below is analogous to the setting up of the Bank of England in 1694 (covered in the Introduction to this volume). It is the extension of credit by a private bank to the state and the institutionalization of these arrangements that lead central bank historians to mark Venice as the important predecessor of the Bank of England. However, as Max Weber pointed out (1927: 350–351), the Court of the Bank of England rapidly got rid of its speculative founder, William Paterson, and replaced him with more reliable Puritan figures from the City of London. The Venetian situation was far more fantastical and continuously speculative. It was the relationship to the state that was so different in each case, as we shall see.

At a somewhat late stage the state stepped in and created the *Banco della Piazza di Rialto* in 1587. The intention was to return to the virtues of giro banking: deposits were to be held securely and not lent out, and the bank was to make transfers between accounts and these were to be reliably recorded. Clients were to be paid immediately when they wished to convert their credit in the bank into currency, and bills of exchange drawn in Venice had likewise to be redeemed on request; but they could not be assigned onwards to another debtor. These regulations strongly suggest that private bankers had acquired by the mid-sixteenth century considerable autonomy in the handling of merchants' money, or indeed that merchants had themselves gone into banking. Fraud, and failure to honour credit or bills of exchange point to the dangerous extension of liabilities without sufficient reserves in deposits or effective sureties.[4]

State Sovereignty Determines Credit

The Senate set up a new bank, *Banco del Giro*, in 1619, and this gradually took over the previous functions and users of the *Banco della Piazza di Rialto*. In spite of its name, the new bank was not a simple transfer bank operating for the security and needs of its depositors, and the circumstances of its establishment make this clear. The Republic was faced with paying a merchant (a Giovanni Vendramin) for a large consignment of silver and gold, for minting at the *Zecca* and it 'agreed to make him a large loan in bank credit. At the same time there were merchants, to whom the republic was indebted for goods and for bills of exchange, who had received assignments upon the mint and other public offices, the collections upon which were slow and embarrassed by official forms' (Dunbar 1892: 324). The Republic was making a large credit to one merchant and was failing to realize its revenue from state enterprises to pay other merchants. Both problems were solved in the establishment of the *Banco del Giro*. The unpaid group of merchants were given credit at the new bank, which they were then able to convert on demand into currency. The bank then required deposits to meet those creditors. At the same time Vendramin had to be paid, and he had agreed in his contract to supply the mint that payment be part in credit and part in currency. Vendramin's silver and gold was minted and 150,000 ducats placed in the reserves of the *Banco del Giro*. In addition, the Senate ordered the mint to pay 10,000 ducats per month – later increased to 30,000 – into the bank's reserves. The state stipulated the bank's debts could not exceed 500,000 ducats. Vendramin was paid and credited with the currency and bullion he himself had supplied and the other merchants were also satisfied.[5] At a legislative stroke the Republic

[4] Morosini writing c. 1623 in his *Historia Venetia* speaks of their 'fraude, avaritia, crebrisque decoctionibus ingentes jacturas damnaque patiebantur' - that the merchants were suffering from large losses because of the fraud, avarice and frequent skimming by the bankers; and that this was very detrimental to state finances. Quoted by Dunbar 1892: 320.
[5] The creditors would receive 'pronto e ispedita soddisfazione' – quick and expedient satisfaction, quoted Luzzatto 1934: 53.

had turned its debt obligations into credit money with currency reserves capable of meeting demands for payment in cash.[6]

The Venetian case provides almost an ideal-typical model of how state, bank and financial power are configured and interact. The territorial and marine power of the state is paramount and political power is organised within an authoritarian structure so that the decisions of the governing council, the Signoria, are put into effect by the magistrates and officials and disobedience is not tolerated. Economic power rests with the merchants who control investments and profits, and this power is maintained through the status of merchants, as the urban nobility, and through their representation on the Signoria. Banking is not an established institution and remains under the twin forces of the merchants, as holders of capital, and the state, which is both a legislative and executive power. Direct taxation is excluded by status group ideology, for property is a familial patrimony, an almost sacred idea that still reflects the cultures in the Western and Eastern Roman empires. Public debt is an established institution and is maintained through interest bearing loans. The state bank, Banco del Giro, is founded on an extension of state debt. Bankers and later (Florentine) merchant bankers play two crucial intermediating roles: they register the merchants' credit and debits in a journal, and they manage the fluctuations in agio resulting from the respective credit needs of the state and merchants. There are two units of account, bank credit money and the physical transactions of specie moneys (gold and silver). Both private banks and the state bank become through their operations banks of issue – not of fiat money in the form of banknotes but of fiduciary money, credit money which can be converted into specie. Within Venice the state mint has a monopoly on creating the coinage and demanding that merchants deposit other currencies within the mint for re-minting; the mint alone benefits from seigniorage.

[6] Luzzatto's prose (1934: 55) captures this turn-around very well: (in translation) 'While the Banque du Rialto is above all a deposit bank, an exchange bank and a transfer bank, created for the needs of commerce, the new institution, which should not properly be termed a "bank," is in reality only one of a number of financial expedients by which the treasury, ruined by wars, must have recourse to pacify the more demanding of its creditors, and to ensure for itself new sources of credit; in effect, through a deposit of 150,000 ducats and a simple promise of lodging 350,000 ducats with the bank over three years, it was obtaining an immediate credit of 500,000 ducats.'

The Venetian case elicits the kind of awe, among economic historians, in the same way that John Law does. Both offered a seeming
mastery of credit money and an escape from specie and shortage of
coin; not least, the perpetual insufficiency of taxes could be sidestepped in the bid for growth through colonial ventures. However,
despite the sophistication, bankruptcy was actual or near at hand, and
the sustainability of the economic model was precarious. Mercantile
capitalism itself was constrained but supported by the Venetian oligarchic state.

From City-State to Territorial State

The way in which Weber deploys the idea of mobile capital, demands
a different form of state. Braudel rescues the financial sophistication –
or rather blatant risk-taking with a state back-stop – of Venice with an
argument that sees the financial expertise relayed from one financial
centre to another. The expertise is handed on like a baton from the
Italian city-states, through the Champagne fairs to Antwerp, Amsterdam, London and New York. It is the changes in market conjunctures –
where the economic centre of gravity rests – that cause the geographical
move (Braudel 1983: 27–34).

Weber gets to Amsterdam and London by a different route, the
changing nature of the territorial state. In the *General Economic
History*, which is the translated title of a lecture course, the one Schmitt
attended, Weber introduces the concept of colonial capitalism (Weber
1927: 298–301). Under the Stuarts and Bourbons colonial adventures
were licensed as state monopolies. This was the first Atlantic state
form for oceanic ventures. The next step occurred in those European
countries which overthrew kingly state monopolies. This happened in
England with the alliance of mobile finance capital with the newly
ascendant Whig party in Parliament. This phase occurred earlier in
Amsterdam, which kept its distance from state monopolies, allowing
the Dutch East India company full reign according to the extravagant
greed and consumption needs of Dutch burghers. Colonial exploitation from this point onwards was driven by financial capital underwriting adventures and underwriting the protecting navies of the
Dutch and English.

The crucial point of the argument for Weber is that the European
states, in part dynastic in part territorial unities, were locked in conflict.

The Catholic Hapsburgs vied with the Protestant (Dutch) United Provinces, and Catholic France plotted with the British Stuarts for dominance in North West Europe and were opposed by William of Orange the Dutch Stadtholder, who effectively was invited to invade Britain by the Protestant party in the country, not least by the radical Puritans in the City of London. The financial centres of first Antwerp and then Amsterdam, heirs to the financial memes of Venetian financial finesse, pushed their advantage. Investors in the newly founded Bank of England came from Amsterdam, the final relay point in European financial centres. As examined elsewhere in this volume, Weber's mobile capital were the wealthy investors who saw good profits in financing the wars of the leading states.[7]

These wars, as emphasized by Norman Davies (1996: 625), should not be seen solely as fighting for territory and establishing of European national frontiers. These were wars fought for the first global expansion, proxy wars for which country would achieve advantage in the Americas and the East and West Indies, and Oceania. Venice at this juncture was lagooned, irrelevant. The prize money lay with the oceanic seas. For the possessor of mobile capital, the calculation was determined by risk and return. Overly indebted states could renege on their interest payments, famously Charles II's stopping of the Exchequer. States, from their side, could create institutional reliability on interest payments. This is exactly what the English state, in an alliance of the crown of Protestant William and Mary with Parliament, achieved. The foundation of the Bank of England followed this strategy. Return on capital was good, reliable and offered added opportunities for initial investors. A legislative Parliament guaranteed interest payments on the back of legitimate taxation. It was on this basis that Britain's rise to international dominance during the eighteenth century was secured.

Weber goes so far to opine that modern capitalism was born from the competition between the European states. This gave financial -mobile- capital its crucial breakthrough. 'The separate states had to compete for mobile capital, which dictated to them the conditions under which it would assist them to power. Out of this alliance of the state with capital, dictated by necessity, arose the national citizen

---

[7] For example, in the Introduction, Chapter 15, and cf. Chapter 6 on the contemporary United States.

class, the bourgeoisie in the modern sense of the word. Hence it is the closed national state which afforded to capitalism its chances for development – and as long as the national state does not give place to a world empire capitalism will also endure' (Weber 1927: 337).

This extraordinary bold set of statements takes capitalism out of the lagoon into the framing narrative of competing territorial states. Mobile capital – footloose capital put forward by investors exploiting the political and economic landscape for advantage – turns out to be a matter of relationality. Mobile capital is not the truism that wealth can be called up and placed with appropriate financial instruments into a perceived optimised situation. Rather, opportunity for profit is determined by sociological parameters. Venetian capital was precessed by the oligarchic control of imperial power. It was mobile capital but within the geographic limits of a coastal environment. Weber's 'true' mobile capital has its parameters set by the contingencies of inter-state competition and a fiscally supportive legislature – one that pointed, as Weber saw it, to a citizen-empowered modernity. Mobile capital without state parameters, which is one way of describing what Weber intends by 'world empire', is one that breaks down in terms of relationality. Relation to what? This is ominously like the flow of global financial capital, impatient of state boundaries and regulations, always looking for optimised returns but entirely negligent of the real sociological parameters – political, economic – through which trade and production generates a return. It is, as Schmitt complained, analogous to the stealthy and lethal emergence of sea power, infinite without boundaries, not order but anomie.

References

Braudel, Fernand. 1984. *Civilization and Capitalism 15th–18th Century. Volume III. The Perspective of the World*, trans. Siân Reynolds (London: Collins).

Davies, Norman. 1996. *Europe. A History* (Oxford: Oxford University Press)

Day, John. 1999. *Money and Finance in the Age of Merchant Capitalism* (Oxford: Blackwell).

Derman, Joshua. 2011. 'Carl Schmitt on Land and Sea', *History of European Ideas*, 37.

Dunbar, Charles. 1892. 'The Bank of Venice', *Journal of Economics*, 6.3.

Ingham, Geoffrey. 2015 '"The Great Divergence." Max Weber and China's Missing Link', *Max Weber Studies*, 15.2.

Luzzatto, Gino. 1964. 'Les Banques Publiques de Venise' in van Dillen ed., *History of the Principal Public Banks* (London, Frank Cass, 1964; 1st edition Martinus Nijhoff, 1934).

Mueller, Reinhold C. 1997. *Money and Banking in Medieval and Renaissance Venice. Vol II. The Venetian Money Market. Banks, Panics and the Public Debt. 1300–1500* (John Hopkins University Press).

Schmitt, Carl. 2001. *Land and Sea*, trans. Simona Draghici (Corvallis, OR: Plutarch Press).

Schumpeter, Joseph A. 1954. *History of Economic Analysis* (Oxford: Oxford University Press; reprint Allen & Unwin).

Soll, Jacob. 2014. *The Reckoning. Financial Accountability and the Making and Breaking of Nations* (London: Allen Lane).

Vries, Jan de and Woude, Ad van der. 1997. *The First Modern Economy. Success, Failure, and Perseverance of the Dutch Economy, 1500–1815* (Cambridge University Press).

Weber, Max. 1927. *General Economic History*, trans. Frank Knight (London: George Allen & Unwin).

1976. *The Agrarian Sociology of Ancient Civilisations*, translated R. I. Frank London: NLB.

2003. *The History of Commercial Partnerships in the Middle Ages*, trans. Lutz Kaelber (Lanham, Maryland: Rowan and Littlefield).

9 Impacts of Mobile Capital's 'Convenient Reverse Logic'

JOCELYN PIXLEY

John Kenneth Galbraith often warned 1980s students graduating in the social sciences that they'd find the opposite thought processes on leaving university. Logic taught them that social ills of poverty or unemployment must have causes, such as monetary policy that raises the jobless rates (Galbraith suggested). Fairer remedies were easily at hand. But 'Convenient Reverse Logic' proceeds not 'from diagnosis to remedy' such as increasing minimum wages and decent jobs, or providing competent social services. No, it starts at 'the preferred remedy back to the requisite cause'. That remedy should not 'involve a painful transfer of resources from the affluent'. To the wealthy, a 'cause of poverty is because the poor lack motivation ... [as] they are already unduly rewarded ... whereas the rich have not been working because they have too little'. Thus, President Reagan reduced taxes on the affluent, 'to enliven the economy' (Galbraith 1986: 35–8) and the situation became more enfeebled, disruptive and mean.

Galbraith's wit was disarming, except to apologists for ruling classes, urging greater poverty, more regressive taxes and bleak working lives. Since no justifications for this decades-long state of affairs exist logically or morally, today, august newspapers of record tend to hire journalists who can write with charm and logic, not jargon and mendacious statistics, instead, well-informed, plain talk. Galbraith and C. Wright Mills (1953) both saw Thorstein Veblen as 'the only comic writer' in the social sciences. Mills remarked that Veblen rigorously used the wildly acclaimed 'efficiency' to taunt American financiers: their 'insatiable straining for invidious distinctions' and for domination over rivals fighting to inflict or endure the most 'pecuniary damage' created *inefficiency*. Ownership was primary: Veblen analyzed the layers built on the earliest *property right* to own women (of 'husbands' and to sexual exploitation), to slaves, land and, by his day, 'capital as investment' in stock, absentee ownership, not as productive-creative capacities: a 'right' of sheer force.[1] Perhaps this subsided after Veblen, in more democratic times.

Yet, hopes for equality, efficiency and professionalism of postwar mixed economies seemed dashed as business-financiers, the exclusive disrupters (in sackings, mergers: Veblen 1904; Galbraith 1986), became costlier and arrogant *because* a growing majority was poorer and disrespected. Mobile capital and (willingly) captive states had large roles, as did managers, in creating anew the 1900s–20s distribution patterns in our day. Another dangerous twist, we've stressed, dragged entire OECD populations to endure usury to survive, and renewed work exploitation. In 1922, Veblen worried about a 'fearsome and foolish credulity' of many Americans to these 'predatory exploits'. Thomas Piketty in 2014, famous for research on poverty in *Capital*, warned that without a turnaround like a global wealth tax (his remedy), 'many may turn against globalization. If, one day, they found a common voice, it would speak the disremembered mantras of nationalism and economic isolation.' Perhaps he meant Marine Le Pen's demagoguery or gruesome eras in his historical studies, in which, as with all serious social scientists, his statistical work did not mistake correlations with causes. It contrasts with today's hectoring for austerity, as by Kenneth Rogoff or Alberto Alesina that omits significant counter cases. Even the IMF refuted their (infamous) reversal: high national debt is *not* related to low growth, instead, stagnation tends to generate high debt, enlarged by bank bail-outs and military expenditure.[2]

The task of this brief chapter is support for this volume by making direct links between the mésalliance between financial sectors and governments imposing convenient policies against populations, on which the extremes of wealth relies. It is argued today's edifice is

---

[1] Veblen 1904: 32; In 1899, he wrote 'The barbarian status of women', cited in Nitzan 1998: 181, who carefully distinguishes, like Mills (1953), Veblen's split between owners, from creators-professionals and engineers of 'fixed capital', unlike Schumpeter or Galbraith. The latter admired Veblen greatly; JAS respected him (1954), but loathed Veblen's stress on 'inefficiency' of financier-disrupters. To him, the banker was the 'magistrate' of 'creative destruction' and entrepreneurial dynamism, although Schumpeter 1931 [1911] warned of 'destruction without function' in bank money production.

[2] I include the *NYT*, *Spiegel* and *FT*, not Murdoch-Berlusconi 'moguls' of tabloid journalism. Wright Mills' Introduction to Veblen (1899) 1953; Piketty 2014. Blyth 2013: 205–216 on IMF; Herndon, Pollin et al. 2013 shows how Rogoff conveniently 'omitted' high deficit countries *with* vibrant economic activity.

indifferent and counterproductive. First a few distribution trends are laid out; second, trends in the direction of investment away from economically and socially useful ends; third the minimum wage question and *relation* between shares of capital and wages is discussed. The mantra of austerity, fourth, supports mobile capital, via how the metaphysical ups and downs of money's value boosts financier myths in the labour theory of value, negatively.

Correlation in Patterns of Distribution

The macabre story is that alarming graphical depictions of the rise of mobile capital in financial profits, wealth, etc. follow the exact same upward movement as rising rates of inequality and poverty from the late 1970s to present-day OECD countries. Thus, in Andreas Nölke's Figure 7.1 (see Chapter 7), US financial profit shares dropped in the 1940s (5 per cent cf. total domestic profits) to 1970–1, whereupon they steadily rose (Nixon onwards; one brief collapse from the GFC) by 2016 to about 35 per cent or more. Likewise, central banks show the rise of bank money (M3) and stagnation of state money (M1) from 1970; Reserve Bank of Australia and Bank of England statistics provide the same result of a ratio 97:3 of M3 to M1, even after the BoE's Quantitative Easing (QE). QE created a large quantity of state money intended to revive banks (not people), yet the 97 per cent bank money did not change. Before 1970, the ratio had been 50:50 for 100 years of records.

If we superimpose further variables onto these simple ones,[3] which only *suggest* or hint that the previous 50:50 ratio M1:M3 showed a *correlation* of bank money creation (or financial profits) in line with economic activity, the data is more convincing. As Table 9.1 sketches briefly, Palma (2009: 852–3) shows trends in financial assets *and* private investment in the United States from 1947 to 2007, dividing his long time line between the alleged financial 'repression' of 1947 to 1979, from the period of financial 'liberalization' of 1979 to 2007.

Where under 'repression' of forty years, financial assets (large) and private investment (modest) stayed *roughly* similar, after 1978, US investment collapsed. A sole peak of 18.5 per cent GDP dropped sharply and stagnated thereupon, and asset inflation-bubbles took off

---

[3] Pixley forthcoming; Ryan-Collins et al. 2011.

Table 9.1 *Assertions of social-economic benefits of 'light touch' in the United States.*

	Financial 'repression' 1947–1977 as % US GDP	Financial 'liberalization' 1978–2007 as % US GDP
Private Investment	15–17%	15%
Financial Assets	500%	600%–1100%

Source: Palma 2009: 852–3
Reworked using minimal detail of Palma's longer Figure.

to more dangerous heights (1100 per cent). Since the GFC, poverty-inducing trends have continued. Palma argues instead of the *convenient* benefits claimed from 'liberalization' – an alleged 'positive pulling effect on private investment' – asset inflation had a zero or negative impact on investment in productive capacities, and busts reduced economic activity. Iwan Azis in Chapter 2 shows the same effects in Southeast Asia.

Palma (2009: 852–3) cites many debates on the 'the damage that the disproportionate growth of the financial sector [and construction] was inflicting' and 'the crowding out of the non-financial tradable sector (both exports and import-competing sectors)'. That led, as many despair, to the situation of banks 'too large to save'. Meantime *also from* 1978, the income share of the US top 1 per cent from its lowest ever, shot up to the same level of rent-seeking as the 1929 US peak. Poverty increased also with utility privatizations raising consumer-business costs of electricity, water, transport. Figure 9.1 shows the Economic Policy Institute's calculations of various countries: the United Kingdom and the United States lead inequality. Other OECD countries resemble Japan's and France's trajectories.

This rise in the 1 per cent share grew while 'convenient reverse logic' insisted that only state spending and state money creation were 'rent-seeking' and 'inflationary'. As well, highly regressive tax cuts on top incomes (wealth and corporations too) are more evident in UK/US plot lines than other countries since the 1980s. And, since the GFC, long-term investment for productive, services and green economic activity is pitiful given continual arbitrage of financial assets (André Orléan 2014 makes clear). Financial market trading is information-free and it does not in itself create anything but profits and losses. With over

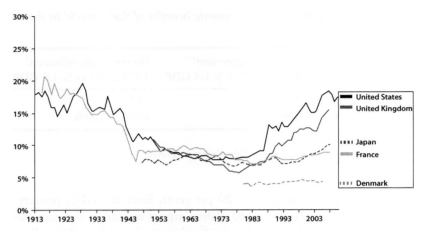

Figure 9.1 Share of income held by top 1 per cent in developed countries, 1913–2009.

Source: Economic Policy Institute's State of Working America Data Library. 2017.

SWA-Income I Figure 2AB I I State of Working America 17/3/17, 3'32 pm. *Updated June 18, 2012 Economic Policy Institute* Source: Authors' analysis of *The World Top Incomes* database (Alvaredo, Atkinson, Piketty, and Saez various years)

60 per cent of high frequency trading in the United States (on 2015 Fed data), computers are programmed to copy traders, to engage in what remains *de jure* legal front running against pension funds, the sainted savers (duped).

The sole datum the well-off world can highlight positively is *somewhat* reduced world starvation. World Bank data shows the incidence of 'extreme poverty' has declined across the world: In 1981, 42.15 per cent endured the lowest of $1.90 per day (PPP), whereas in 2013 that per cent declined to 10.68 of the world's population on $1.90 a day.[4] Against that (Table 9.2), the World Bank shows drastically regressive changes in *shares* of global income:

Famines and disruptions of wars worsen as climate change takes greater tolls. The impact on the world of a US Depression proper is hard to contemplate, we saw in chapters on Asia and Europe. A potential rise in the nuclear arms race in 2017 is at *best* useless economically since

---

[4] Purchasing Power Parity of 2011, per cent of the population starving ($1.90). one can also cite mortality rates etc. Data on poverty; income shares: worldbank.org

Table 9.2 *Changes in shares of global income.*

	1980	2014
Lowest 50%	20	10
Top 1%	12.5	20

Source: Income shares: worldbank.org
Reworked using minimal detail from the World Bank's longer Figure

unproductive. Regressive taxation and central bank policy to slash wages and jobs have been typical responses to war finance's far closer links to the financial sector since the postwar period, the United States notably. Fantacci and Gobbi in Chapter 4 explain war's never-ending debt. As well, Schwartz shows of offshore US firms (in Chapter 6) that if some profits stay in emerging market countries, most is brought back to the United States in intellectual property rights.

Investment Going Nowhere Useful for People

If we just dwell on the details of this *disproportionate* growth of Finance, Insurance and Real Estate (FIRE), useful theoretical detail explains how this occurred. To Keynesian scholars like Jörg Bibow, the convenient illogic that the well-off *might* invest in long-term enterprises has grave problems. Reagan and Thatcher started with the tax cuts that were said later 'to trickle down' – but as above data shows went up. Arthur Laffer's 'curve' is *again* revived, still unproven, entailing further cutbacks in social services. Proposed tax cuts in Australia and the United States enhance trends in competitive tax reductions across the world. Ironically, low tax countries are less enticing to financiers than a ruinous usury of a 20 per cent return, and energy and transport access. On top are offshore tax havens and bond vigilantes making state investment hard. Fewer state-owned enterprises (not for profit), mean less revenue.[5]

[5] No 'Laffing' matter, the Laffer Curve plots zero to 100 per cent tax, and sticks a pin somewhere: Seccombe 2016. Bibow 2009; Martin 2017 'Company tax', cites Australia's current Treasury Secretary, former UBS Global Assets head in London, boasting of predatory usury. UAE has zero tax: low corporate tax regime firms invest heavily in Australia to 97 per cent of all 'foreign investment'; Wall St buys up childcare centres for state subsidies, and raise prices and cut costs (etc.).

After the GFC, our chapters show, in many Asian, European and American countries private long-term investment remained flat, because the US Fed's QE programmes only saw asset inflation take off. QE increased countries' redistribution *up*. In the Keynesian literature, this failure to restart economic activity is from the Fed's QE's 'loanable funds' assumption. That is, in the Laffer curve and in QE, central banks assume, first, that banks collect puddles of so-called 'loanable funds' to make long-term investments *instantly*, and second ignore that *banks create money out of nothing in the deposited loan*. QE did not help those with mortgages for example, and, given loans could not be serviced when property prices collapsed, the result was business and households cutting back, not demanding new loans, and saving more if possible. What is saved, however, is not spent, so a negative multiplier effect went downwards, also impacted by business cutting wages and jobs. The fallacy of composition operates: what is 'rational' for one firm or saver is disastrous for all firms and savers.

QE policies *imagine* those with sufficient wealth do make long-term investments in economic activity, which may be job-creating. But this *inducement* does not impose any specific direction to financial decisions of the affluent and banks with 'loanable funds', which are *free to choose*! Also, it's cheaper and less *dangerous* (assuming the quick exit trick) to create more bank money (topped up with QE) to engage in trading financial assets (at 20 per cent return). The potential for specific asset classes to collapse, with loan defaults, do not affect state-saved Wall St but pension funds. QE's main problem is that central banks have no control over these decisions. They can only hope that the arduous and costly investment in plant, in fixed capital, training and employment *might* take place (but does not). Central banks had no grounds for *hope*, then, given Alan Greenspan (etc.) exaggerated the 'wealth effect' ('modest savers') and prevented regulation of derivatives, you name it (Blinder 2013; Pixley 2012).

Keynes spoke of this stupidity by saying liquidity is not an option for the whole society: he compared finance traders to the farmer who cannot sell the farm for a few days on a whim, put the proceeds into trading assets, and return to farming the next week. Known well to Keynes and Schumpeter readers, this illogic of liquidity runs the Fed, ECB and BoE: it is the reason that Orléan (2014) supports the Tobin tax to dampen asset trading.[6] The implications are clear: if everyone is a trader, no food, no services, no jobs, safety or shelter is produced. Trading must perforce be exclusive and, as inequality rises, pecuniary classes benefit from the benighted social landscape below.

Logical and ethical remedies reveal the extent of today's dangers too. At least, as Iwan Azis' and Andreas Nölke's chapters show, some remedies are already *successful* – not in most OECD. Thus, capital controls (or levies) and state-owned enterprises again show triumphs. Tom Palley proposes another measure to tame mobile capital, different from the Tobin measure and equally ignored in the OECD. He suggests that 'asset based reserve requirements' (ABRR) improve the monetary policy mix, particularly for the ECB. His discussion ties in neatly with Azis's debate on dangerous capital inflows to Southeast Asia from the Fed's QE, and Nölke's on limits. Palley agrees QE's impact of low, long-term interest rates has only increased stock prices and financial wealth, data shows. Also, banks gained huge reserves from QE, fostering dangers of 'inflationary private sector expansion ... a destabilizing asset price bubble', and exchange rate disruptions to the global economy (Palley 2014: 3–4).

The task for ABRR is broader to that of the US Fed's 1934 control over margin requirements gained in FD Roosevelt's bank reforms. Margin loans are bank advances to stock traders. They are foolish because when stocks collapse, banks call in margin loans first, and that leads, say on Wall St 1929, to a faster downhill spiral as stock traders sell frantically, *if they can sell*. But if the Fed raises 'margins' required *before* bank advances take off, that reduces a desperate sell-off: in the late 1930s and just postwar, the Fed basically stopped them, raising requirements to 90 and even 100 per cent.[7] Palley wants this monetary tool spread to 'a wide array of assets' and for other central banks. The authorities can adjust the reserve requirement

---

[6] Keynes's argument is clear in Caporaso & Levine 1992; See on Tobin: Introduction; Stafford 2017 'London's trading infrastructure' on High Frequency Trading: front running now called 'matching' and citing: 'Whilst German R&D goes into developing new industrial machinery and more advanced electronics (Siemens, e.g.), British R&D goes into how to beat others to a profitable trade in derivatives and securities.'
[7] See Pixley 2012: Fed Chair Greenspan refused to raise them above 50 per cent, for the 'modest' (sucker).

as needed (from zero to positive), and should apply it to banks *and* any financial institution that holds a specific asset (to avoid shifting evasion from banks). They are 'counter-cyclical', which means that reserve requirements discourage a spiral *up or down* (pro-cyclical). A typical spiral down is when central banks raise interest rates, giving severe employment consequences, and increasing costs for Treasury (at taxpayers' expense). Palley explains further effects of this add-itional policy approach:

The historic focus of bank regulation has been the prevention of bank runs and the traditional form of regulation has been reserves on liabilities (deposits). ABRR have a different focus which is avoiding excessively risky speculation, and they can also help shrink a bloated financial sector resulting from financialization (Palley 2014:5).

Thus, by regulating *specific asset bubbles* as needed, the scheme removes the 'collateral damage' that central bank rates have on entire economies. Rates are conventionally called 'a blunt tool' through to a blunderbuss. Instead, raising reserves on new mortgages can 'cool the market' (RBA); *also* requirements can drop quickly if one asset class founders. ABRR *could* increase the few tools available to member-state central banks in the Eurozone (Pixley in Chapter 3), preferably in tandem with the ECB against 'jurisdictional shopping'. Overall, the fact that new legislation is needed for ABRR everywhere is, as Palley says, not an argument against it.

Such proposed or proven capital controls, transaction taxes and margin requirements demonstrate, too, that lifting *financial repression* (a pathetic exaggeration) as in the data above, fostered large-scale unemployment and poverty. Freedom from controls with re-regulation to greater competition among business, financial sectors, regulatory havens and tax authorities since the 1970s have created extremes in inequality, precarious low paid work and cutbacks to 'red tape' and to support for those dependant on others. Privatization has played a large part in declining standards, more job losses and greater expenses for consumers. The rise in the 1 per cent started at the critical juncture of Nixon's dollar float 1971–3, Wall Street's consequent reincarnation, Fed Chair Arthur Burns' extensive attack on wage inflation in 1974–5, and Volcker's 1980 equally extensive attack on corporate price infla-tion. It stopped the US economy, and many authorities though not all, followed suit. Full employment ended.

Employment and Wage Relations

Politicians still seem to try patriotic preaching to salvage the collapsed electoral support from the landscapes of poverty they imposed. But expecting those who cannot be voted out to give up their towers of privilege and go quietly like the Soviet ruling class is probably a pipe-dream. Peak financiers and monopoly business managers, with their supporting lobbyists, right wing politicians, neoclassicals like Rogoff (not yet sufficiently shamed, it appears) demand further regressive tax cuts, more attacks on wages and increasing cuts to basic social services.

The United States's social services and wages have always been pitiful, compared to Sweden, France, Canada, others. In the 1970s wage-price spiral, Europe's D-bloc and Australia turned to consensus among employers and unions for dampening those inflations; other countries created heavy recessions instead. Central banks were then told to fight wage inflation, not all the other inflations; only the BoC and RBA refused to take such 'Inflation Targets' too seriously. They were not prepared to create (wilfully) the stagnation that spread across the world (Chapter 3).

The only country with a stimulus to counter the GFC effects, Australia also placed a progressive tax as a 'temporary' measure for the well-off to pay for implicit subsidies to banks. Like the United States, it also imposed controls on banks after the GFC. Later, a neoliberal Australian government removed the Australian Labor Government's 2008 legal requirement on banks to act 'in the best interests' of their clients. Washington DC threatens to remove that same part of Dodd–Frank, because it does such a neat trick. In one short phrase, it outlaws every bank's 'creative' options in ripping off clients. Victims like small business owners are subsequently reduced to living in garages from FIRE.

Most governments attacked unions successfully via monetary policy and legal restrictions on workers taking collective action. In 2017, a global literature shows that 'low wage growth' (a euphemism), 'may reflect a decline in workers' bargaining power'. Central bank talk is so timid this conclusion is buried (Bishop and Cassidy 2017), although the RBA is preaching for unions to demand wage rises. Central banks are worried that household debt and a property bubble might not be serviced while employers demand lower wages.

If one looks at the minimum wage story, one finds a varied picture. Shaun Wilson (2017) looks at Anglo American countries. The United Kingdom raised minimum wages to £7.50 per hour in April 2017.[8] The United States and Canada vary more than Australia, since states/provinces set minimum wages, idiosyncratically, and the United Kingdom and United States do not have unified union movements. The US does worst on minimum wages as a per cent of median full-time wages (at 37 per cent in 2014, to the top, New Zealand on 60 per cent) and in contrast, to the Continental and Irish EU states' average of 51 per cent of median wages, Southern and Eastern EU on 48. On the incidence of *low pay* full-time work in 2014, New Zealand had only 14 per cent on low pay, Australia 16; the United Kingdom 21, Canada one point more, and the United States *25 per cent* of the labour force. The OECD in 2014 estimated the real purchasing power of the Australian minimum wage was about highest in the world.

The head of the Australian Council of Trade Unions and feminist Sally McManus lodged an ambit claim with Australia's Fair Work Commission in April 2017. She sought a $45 per week increase to the minimum wage, criticizing how 'wage theft' is Australia's business model since 2013, and defends union rights to civil disobedience. The Prime Minister (a GS&Co former partner) supported a cut in weekend penalty rates. Minimum hourly pay hardly changed, at about $17. The latest UK rise to £7.50 is in AUD $12.33 per hour.[9]

Thus, progressive taxes (a la Piketty) are important (not if only for nuclear war finance). Higher wages take small amounts of the share from, and are thus indirectly a tax on, wealthy *rentiers* and corporate managers. Better wages moreover give direct sustenance and purchasing power to those who are physically part of their only property: to labour with skills and imagination; small business benefits overall. High central bank rates to control an asset bubble with a sledgehammer creates more jobless, also 'taxes' small business and household debtors. In the GFC modest savers also lost badly in the United States and elsewhere.

[8] O'Connor, S. et al. 2017: posed this wage rise against councils being squeezed by 'London' austerity.
[9] Comparative data: Wilson 2017: 256; Gordon M. 2017 'Hero or villain?' *SMH* April 1: 20 on McManus. Currency conversion on 2 April 2017

Shares of Capital

Here I move to discuss the relation between wages and labour–capital relations in fixed capital ventures, in comparison to the shares of mobile capital skewed to *rentiers* and the financial sector, not to modest savers. It is a thorny question except that it shows the dependencies of the powerful on the weaker: the forbidden, silenced problem. Although it's important to acknowledge these inequities via different theoretical approaches to be reviewed here briefly, the main aim is to show that whether one picks any of these approaches, few differ on the brute details of injustice, joblessness, underemployment, against airy assumptions of 40 years that poverty must grind down everyone except that 1 per cent. This thorny debate can point to the lack of democratic legitimacy of the rich and (in)famous that thwarts many political systems, but not fully explain this dubious legitimacy of the democracies. This is for others but not for them further to neglect money's relations and immense impacts.

After the GFC, when the collapse of indebted households removed excuses of decades of 'financialization' and 'democratization of credit', what was laid bare was that FIRE's defences were a sham. The argument was that money was merely handy, useful in exchange (as it is of course). It was alleged as only a 'veil' over the 'real' economy of goods and services, minor to *the fundamentals of material life*. The illogicality was money was not innocent; nor were the banks that created so much for the purchasing of commodities and property that do not bring lasting inclusive returns, and negatives when asset inflations crash. These advances relied on borrowers servicing loans from paid economic activity elsewhere, activity banks cared not to create.

That this has occurred so frequently in the past, makes one suspect financial sectors and their authorities were simply stupid. A further point is the policy mantra of austerity is not logical but tied to the way that mobile capital operates, or rather how this global sector reacts to the slightest change. The GFC exposed deeper problems, and on these, the Volume opens the varied debates. Was mobile capital more far reaching globally, than before? How 'mobile'? Were the many more people using banking and finance services the main 'suckers'? What of the further exploitation of workers? Was the only 'new' aspect the advent of full democratic rights and greater worker participation in the OECD by the 1970s the most crucial?

On the most difficult questions, I cannot delve into Marx's theory of money. Schumpeter took pot shots at Marx's reliance on Ricardo who clung to the idea of 'fictitious capital' (also Nitzan 1998), though praised Marx as a 'top-notch' economist. Weber criticized Marx and indirectly Schumpeter for not emphasizing that capitalist practice involves a 'continuous comparison of the profits on money loans with the profitability of enterprise' (Ingham explains 2004:201–5). We saw this (above) in the impact of QE, which failed to enhance job-creating enterprises. Therefore, money is no 'neutral veil' over the 'real' economy in which *real* goods are bartered and money a mere token. Marx saw through that orthodoxy, to the social relations of producing goods (and let us add services), and of exchange relations. According to Ingham, by arguing that labour produced 'use-value', a usefulness that 'should determine "value"', Marx remained close to the neoclassical conception of a 'real' material economy. The difference from orthodoxy is between REM's 'perfect information', and working-class interests. Veblen, we saw in the Introduction, politely showed that the neoclassical pursuit of 'the life history of objective values' and their 'laws' had nothing to say of the social relations of his day, or any other. Late nineteenth century robber barons, his 'financier-businessman', depended on 'the metaphysical stability of the money unit' since there is no 'objective value'. Thus, the *slightest* discrepancy Veblen said, was sufficient to create a depression or exaltation (1904: 232–38). He gave no room for 'laws' of declining profit rates either; arguments near Weber or Keynes.

Even if I accept that, why then the decades of attacks on jobs and wages, whether by central banks singling out *one inflation,* wages, and forgetting others in applying the NAIRU or Phillips curve, or by political and business lobbies' mass attacks on unions? One must leave Schumpeter here, since he excoriated FD Roosevelt's New Deal. Recall Schumpeter's great service in pointing to the deposited loan (not 'fictitious capital'). All deposits are used as money; a 'fraction' of saver deposits is enough to create a huge upside-down pyramid of bank advances. Bankers *deposit loans* and so 'manufacture money' *ex nihilo* (on future income streams of promises and contracts): the loans are spent and their proceeds are further deposited, and into other banks. This is how capitalist money expands, and it contracts in bank runs, when no one wants loans, or they pay back loans – the so-called *elastic* supplies of money. Ricardo's 'fictitious capital' is itself a fiction of what banks do. They create money that (only) might be invested into developing enterprises and jobs. Schumpeter warned of this downside in the 'business cycle' of dynamic capitalist enterprises but either, like Hayek felt governments should not 'disrupt' downsides (e.g. by a New Deal), or took a sociological conclusion that entrepreneurs as a class were now weak and socialism would take capitalism's place.[10]

Veblen did not see entrepreneurs in that light at all. Creativity is from 'workmanship', use of 'accumulated wisdom' and social knowledge: solidarity and cooperation can apply to a hospital or factory; whereas 'business' invests for profit; a claim on earnings, in other words on distribution. With the rise of absentee owners, the aim is to 'beat the average' (Nitzan 1998: 173; 176). Yet I suggest the metaphysical belief in money's stable value, if one includes anything possible that bolsters financier beliefs, can be linked to exploitation in the labour theory of value if this is a *social* value (as Bryan and Rafferty discuss). Financier belief gives an *anchor* for asset traders to run predictions. Or rather, since financiers prefer neoclassical worldviews of the 'real' economy in which exchange of goods and services is like barter which finds *real* values, the argument will be that *laws* of demand and supply (re jobs) are met if *labour* (human talent, cooperation and capacities) drops *its* price and stops its unpredictable demands. Labour's collective protests for their *social* value were criminalized in the United States in Veblen's time, whenever managers filled the pores of the working day, ran lock outs or went on capital strikes (legal).

Owners' profits are not about quality, productivity or efficiency but disruption and 'sabotage'. Ownership 'exacts obedience', can 'enforce unemployment'. The 'ability to produce' is not that which is capitalized, rather 'the power to appropriate'. This is how Nitzan (1998: 180–4) takes up Veblen's argument (also Schwartz's debate) although labour's social value (not *laws*) seems sidestepped.

To return to Weber or Keynes, for the absentee owner, a choice exists to seek profits in asset and money markets instead of enterprises. Marx in later pieces hoped that increased unions and voting rights in America were positive (which proved more so in Europe and elsewhere).

---

[10] Swedberg in Schumpeter 1991 'Introduction' (pp 3–98 for Schumpeter 1991, also see 'Social Classes' pp 230–283 too), explores his fascist leanings in the 1930s, yet rejection of Roosevelt's state intervention (p 27), and his *Capitalism, Socialism, Democracy*, and rise of trusts. Ingham 2004 calls him a 'fence sitter'.

After the Great Depression, social democratic states raised 'confidence' of business, up to a point: the mixed economy immeasurably improved economic activity and social justice. State-owned, non-profit enterprises like hospitals and schools fostered professional creativity and solidarity quite well, far better without absentee owners. Effective demand, that is, improved purchasing power at the lower income quintiles (social value), prompted more democratic needs of those excluded from the mainly white male workers enjoying this postwar life. Small businesses run by women and people of colour flourished given higher purchasing power. Wages and price rises of corporate conglomerates grew, to the point where *rentier shares* in dividends and profits dropped. The Kalecki moment, of employers wanting worker *discipline* of the sack, returned as Veblen said of owners. There had been no euthanasia of the *rentier*; the growing financial sector blasted full employment, the 'ungovernable' nature of democracy, and state-owned enterprises. (And funded war finance.) *Social* value was unpredictable (as Figure 9.1 shows).

If Keynes did not quite side with Schumpeter on the entrepreneurial dynamism from capitalist banking, even finally gave a role to *savers* preferences (such debates run to thousands of books), Keynes did aim for justice, the euthanasia of the *rentier* or absentee owner, and ideas that inevitable inflationary and deflationary tendencies needed state intervention. He did not invent the multiplier: some colonial governments like in Australia had practiced that for years. France or Germany also had thousands of state-owned firms. But quibbles apart, *preferences* of financial sectors (not savers *per se*) won in the conflicts of the 1970s to 1980s over the always shifting value of money. Wages (social value) were said to be the primary cause of money's inflation and not war debts, asset bubbles or oil cartels. Sensible controls over bank money's inflation were rebadged 'repression', and welfare spending, even consensus over wages, were taken as the enemy. The rest is history and austerity returned: not for logic's sake or efficiency, but for control.

Austerity

Still, debates hang on whether labour–capital divisions, the creative enterprise *versus* pecuniary business-financial interests, or debtor–creditor classes via the state are the more significant in the capitalist economy. These questions are bogged down in minute differences. All I can add is no decent social-economic theorist (or any contributor herein) insists that predictions can ever be made. Previously I tried to emphasize the role of uncertainty, and the powerful forces, economic, political and social that aim to secure the impossible. I remember an infamous occasion when Indigenous land titles were enacted in settler countries of invasion. One agribusiness owner screeched against it: 'We must have certainty'. The response to her is that everyone would like certainty, it's unattainable. But most rulers and their minions want that, against improvement, with honourable exceptions.

The struggle over who can eke out the barest modicum of fitful certainty (health care, union support) is relentless. The wealthy will never win this battle completely because, as I said, climate change denial and the nine nuclear-armed countries have set the world closer to doom than ever before. If the rich want to live on the moon, that would be great but entail losing pleasures of invidious distinctions. They refuse to be playboys and playgirls to give us amusing caricatures. A class and status driven society remains tenacious but can be and has been tempered.

At present, most restraint is lacking: traditional social but not biological invidious distinctions as is claimed – gender, ethnicity – are seemingly superimposed in modernity onto the two class divides (money and labour). The superior persona comprises the *rentier* owner, white male chauvinists that fictitiously turn biology into 'destiny'. Servants to this who allege a logic for more austerity, such as Rogoff (cf. Herndon et al. 2013) or Alesina (cf. Blyth 2013: 205–216), deploy data sets that knock off the restrained, cautious places or dare I say, the more egalitarian. They manipulate data to 'prove' their case. However, 'Austerity Kills' proclaim two doctors (Stuckner and Basu 2013) in a book which covers many cases of suicide and needless deaths, from Russia in 1990 to Britain today. Are sycophants to the rulers of labour and debt markets working for somewhat modified tyrants? Do we see robber barons or old patrimonial family oligarchical rulers?

Whatever one decides, the results are that wages must be quartered, but now against central bankers; the ill must die in private hospital car parks; yet the weakest must continue to be plundered. Anti-inflation policies produced stagnant economies; that fostered slides to deflation. As long as these *demanding people* from below are *put down* to

216

provide 'certainty', the top is secured, and more so if the majority
is illiterate and innumerate. The public sphere is thus impoverished.
The 'hungry mile' hour-jobs grow; wage theft sees only debtor and drug
prisons expand – at useless costs to the state. Governments subsidize
FIRE to preserve a capital mobility perhaps only apparent and dam-
aging to states. I only side for the extension of democracy not its
hollowing out, and the encouragement of *informed voters*. Everyone
understands that nuclear war is the end of everything, and often see that
impoverishment is morally wrong and logically counterproductive.
But on money, all remains a mystery to those who grow so rich out
of ravaging this double-sided coin.

As the Chapter's data show, inequality took off with liberalized
(re-regulated to competition) mobile capital. The 1970s perhaps
was a critical juncture but extended hindsight is better, except for
the evidence of a causal link in the decline of private and state investment with the growth of the one per cent. Disaffection and declining
legitimacy in the democracies grew, not only with the return of pernicious preaching about money as a thing. Actions to divorce electorates
from financial sectors that use populations, to *divide et emperor*, most
inauspicious for social cohesion, decent jobs or some security for all,
still plays quite a role.

References

Bibow, J. 2009. *Keynes on Monetary Policy, Finance and Uncertainty*
    London: Routledge
Bishop, J. & N. Cassidy 2017 'Insights into low wage growth' *RBA Bulletin*
    March Quarter: 13–20
Blyth, M. 2013 *Austerity* NYC: Oxford University Press
Caporaso, J. A., & D. P. Levine 1992, *Theories of Political Economy*
    Cambridge University Press
Economic Policy Institute 2012 'State of Working America: Income
    1913–2009' epi.org
Galbraith, J. K. 1986 *A view from the Stands* Boston: Houghton Mifflin Co
Herndon, T., Ash, M. & Pollin, R. 2013. 'Does high public debt consist-
    ently stifle economic growth? A critique of Reinhart and Rogoff'
    PERI Working Paper Series 322, April. University of Massachusetts
    Amherst
Ingham, G. 2004 *The Nature of Money* Cambridge: Polity
Martin, P., 2017 'Company tax' *SMH* 1 April.

Mills, C., 1953 'Introduction.' Pp. vi-xix in *The Theory of the Leisure Class: An Economic Study of Institutions*, Thorstein Veblen. New York: Mentor

Nitzan, Jonathan 1998 'Differential accumulation', *Review of International Political Economy* 5 (2): 169–216

O'Connor, S. et al. 2017 'National living wage rise heaps care costs pressure on councils' *FT* 1 April

Orléan, A. 2014 *The Empire of Value* Cambridge, MA: MIT Press Books

Palley, T. I. 2014. 'Monetary policy in the US and EU after quantitative easing: The case for asset based reserve requirements (ABRR)', *Real-World Economic Review*, Issue No. 68, 5–6 March

Palma, J. G. 2009. 'The revenge of the market on the rentiers', *Cambridge Journal of Economics* 33: 829–869

Piketty, T 2014 'Save capitalism from the capitalists by taxing wealth' *FT* March 28.

Pixley, J. F. 2012. *Emotions in Finance: Booms, Busts and Uncertainty*, 2nd edition. Cambridge University Press
    forthcoming *Central Banks, Democratic States and Financial Power*, Cambridge University Press

Ryan-Collins, J., Greenham, T. & Werner, R. 2011 *Where Does Money Come From? A Guide to the UK Monetary & Banking System* London: New Economics Foundation

Schumpeter, J. A. 1991. *The Economics and Sociology of Capitalism* R. Swedberg (ed.). Princeton University Press

Seccombe, M. 2016 'Reagan's "voodoo" at the budget's heart' *The Saturday Paper* May 7.

Stafford, P. 2017 'London's trading infrastructure' *FT* March 22

Stuckner D. & S. Basu 2013 *The Body Economic: Why Austerity Kills* London: Allen Lane Penguin

Veblen, T. 1904 *The Theory of Business Enterprise* New York: Charles Scribner & Sons

Wilson, S. A., 2017 'The politics of minimum wage welfare states: The changing significance of the minimum wage in the liberal welfare regimes', *Social Policy and Administration*, 51 (2): 244–264

10 | *Imagine*

Grassroots Against Financialization

HELENA FLAM

Imagine mass protests against risky new financial instruments or financialization. Too difficult? One would have to understand these terms first? Then imagine the Icelandic Revolution.

When in the midst of the international financial crisis of 2007–2008 foreign investors lost trust in three Icelandic banks that had rapidly expanded by relying on short-term financing, the Icelandic króna and the economy collapsed, while the ratio of debt to income surged to 240 for Icelandic homeowners. In the fall of 2008 at first tens and then thousands of people convened in front of the seat of the Icelandic parliament to demand that politicians step down. A phrase expressing the widely shared state of shock, disbelief and indignation quickly found its way onto placards. What eventually became known as the Kitchenware Revolution was very loud and definitely not dignified or peaceful. In fact it was punctuated by 3,000–6,000 large crowds throwing snowballs, paint, eggs, strained yogurt, fireworks, shoes, toilet paper, rocks and paving stones on the government buildings, even breaking windows and the police switching from supposedly more humane pepper gas to tear gas to calm these crowds down. These protests went on from October 2008 to April 2009 when a new government was elected. Unheard of: politicians and bankers responsible for negligence or corrupt deals were tried and sentenced to imprisonment, the Icelanders voted against the assumption of debt from the bailout in two referenda in 2011 and one-fourth of the population has been relieved of the loan burden, while the economy recovered (Fominaya 2014:151–154; Bernburg 2016: 1–7; Vogiatzoglu 2017; VC 2015; IFC 2008–2011, IFCP 2009).

A social movement expert recently asked whether the Icelandic mass protests were a precursor or an anomaly following a typical social movement research agenda: Did these protests pave the way for the subsequent Spanish, Greek or the US protests? Did occupying the central parliamentary plaza, relying on the social media to inform and mobilize and calling for inclusion in the democratic process fore-shadow the Arab Spring? In her view Iceland was a precursor because the protesters recognized that neoliberal politicians, who attributed the crisis to the uncontrollable global financial forces, were in fact themselves responsible for causing it (Fominaya 2014: 153–154). Yet it was also an anomaly because the international media took interest neither in multiple Icelandic tragedies nor in Iceland's unprecedented path to true recovery.

In my view Iceland was a great anomaly in several respects. The protesters correctly diagnosed the situation and, rather than to focus merely on the government or political elite, retained a double vision. They saw both those playing financial games, that is, bankers, and those who both facilitated and profited from these games – the politicians. However, what makes the Icelandic case unique is the decisiveness and consequence with which the protesters and the legal and political institutions went about demanding that the responsible persons be identified, heard or tried, and if found guilty, sentenced. In contrast, most protests – at least these that social movement literature addresses – focus on governments and their austerity politics. Even when repeatedly events make transparent the actual responsibility of the finance greedlords, and the institutions and financial instruments they developed (Flam 2012), these are not seized upon to press for investigations, hearings or trials and, if called for, punishment (see later in this chapter).

This text begins by presenting selected findings from "World Protests 2006–2013," an encompassing, press-based survey of protests. It shows two things. First, protests against the finance greedlords, institutions and practices compete with many other protest issues. This is largely due to the participatory method for generating demands for change which fail to produce systematic focus suitable for goal-oriented campaigning (cf Pianta and Gerbaudo 2012:5). Secondly, both "World Protests 2006–2013" and social movement literature seem to under-report on anti-finance protest. This is in part because they see financial capital as merely reinforcing existing crises and have no research program for studying credit-related struggles.

Zeroing in on anti-finance protest, I will take up Occupy Wall Street (OWS), a protest movement that began in Zuccotti Park in the Wall Street district in September 2011 and the Association for the Taxation and Financial Transactions for the Aid of Citizens (ATTAC), a French movement which emerged in 1998. Many public intellectuals and academics have argued either that OWS has no demands *or* that it is a major challenger to the financial sector. ATTAC's anti-finance platform has been underplayed. My argument is that ATTAC and OWS share in common that they challenge financial capital relying both on expertise and on popularizing discourses countering the self-glorification of financial capital. While presenting ATTAC I digress on anti-G20 protests in London in 2009, and Jubilee and Jubilee South transnational anti-government debt campaigns. This is to argue that, short of revolution, social movements have to combine *focused* anti-finance expertise, popular discourse and open protest to challenge the rule of financial capital.

Looking for Protests against Financialization

A multilingual – Arabic, English, French, German, Portuguese, Spanish, etc. - survey of protest events reported by a large number of press and independent sources is entitled "World Protests 2006–2013" (Ortiz et al. 2013: 9). Its authors analyzed 843 protests between January 2006 and July 2013 in 89 countries inhabited by 92 percent of the world population.

During this time, also regular middle-class citizens took to demonstrating. In, for example, 2012–2013 people in 119 countries saw their standard of living sink even further (Ortiz et al. 2013:15–17, 22). Only two of every five persons working age had employment and 900 million people were "working poor." Cuts in government expenditures entailed eliminating subsidies to food and fuel in 100 countries, wage-bill caps in ninety-eight countries as well as reducing public sector salaries and raising VAT. The largest number of protests occurred in higher income countries. In Europe hundreds of thousands of "indignant" citizens have occupied squares, especially in Greece, Spain, Portugal and Italy "to demand real democracy, decent jobs, and an end to the economic austerity and technocratic elites that benefit elites" (Ortiz et al. 2013: 8). In the Middle East and North Africa, great income disparities, high youth unemployment and a general lack of opportunities, compounded by deeply seated state and police corruption, have stood at the center of protests against mostly authoritarian regimes.

The financial and economic crisis of 2007–2008 had its own clear effects – demonstrations were accompanied by violent protests

(Ortiz et al. 2013: 12). A great majority of violent riots (48 percent) occurred in low-income countries, mostly in response to prohibitive food-price but also energy-price increases. A major increase in protests began in 2010, following the implementation of austerity measures meant to counter the global financial and economic crisis in all world regions.

Financialization and its consequences did not become a central target of mobilization in or after 2007–2008. The authors do not stop to ponder this, however. Instead they express the view widespread among social movement researchers: "[t]he financial and economic crisis of 2008 exacerbated pre-existing concerns about poverty, unemployment and rising inequality." (Ortiz et al. 2013: 8, see also the Introduction, Chapter 2, Chapter 5, Chapter 9 and Chapter 12 in this volume).

"Tax/fiscal justice" as an issue seems to address most directly the costs of the financial (and economic) crisis delegated to the citizens in its aftermath. In 133 protest events, it was posed as an issue – compared to a total of 2,257 issues raised in all surveyed protests (Ortiz et al. 2013: 15). But equally often (133) protesters saw "jobs, higher wages and labor conditions" as a grievance. Reform of public services was on their agendas 143 times. "Tax/fiscal justice" is a composite of many different grievances or sub-issues. Of these only "stop transfers to the financial and corporate sectors (e.g., Indonesia, Malaysia, Spain, United Kingdom, United States)" and "the strength of citizen movements to audit sovereign debts (e.g., Brazil, Ireland, Philippines, Spain)" (Ortiz et al. 2013:18) seem directly related to the aftermath of the financial crisis and/or wish to control better financial ebbs and flows. No count was provided.

The International Monetary Fund (IMF), European Central Bank (ECB) and International Financial Institutions (IFIs) were brought together to constitute another grievance category (Ortiz et al. 2013:15). Together they were named 164 times, so their share lies at 7 percent of all issues (2,257).

At the same time, the IMF was the *fourth* most important *main* target of protests after the governments, political and economic system, corporations and employers (Ortiz et al. 2013: 35, 40). In both high- and low-income countries it was targeted for promoting the "Washington Consensus" favoring corporations, wealthy investors and the financial sector. The protesters demanded that the IFIs close down and new ones be set up to promote development of all. Given the fact that the IMF has been imposing austerity policies on numerous governments every year for the past several decades, it is surprising that it scored lower than three other *main* targets.

As the *fourth main* protest target, the IMF was followed by the elites, the EU, the financial sector and, at a considerable distance from these, by the ECB. The survey does not say much about protests against the financial sector and the ECB: "[P]rotests against the financial sector ... and the ECB ... [concerned] ... their role in the economic crisis in the region" (Ortiz et al. 2013:35). G20 and the World Bank were, but seldom, the *main* targets of protests, whereby the low number of G20 summits explains the low number of G20-protests. G20 – a forum for meetings of finance ministers and central bankers which after 2007–2008 became a summit for the heads of state – was a *main* target of nine protests organized against nine summits held until 2013. Protesters saw G20 as a non-legitimate and non-democratic body that should not interfere with national policies (Ortiz et al. 2013:15, 41–42).

The key finding of the survey is that "[t]he most frequent target for protesters, by a wide margin, is their own national government – as the legitimate policy-making institution responsible for citizens ... [that should] take responsibility for economic, social and environmental policies" (Ortiz et al. 2013: 34, 40). This confirms the overall impression given by the survey that, with the exception of the IMF, financial institutions and their representatives did not become a main protest target across the globe between 2006 and 2013. In fact, most researchers see these protest waves targeting mainly governments and austerity measures (Della Porta et al. 2017; Bernburg 2016; Giugni and Grasso 2016; Ancelovici 2015; Fominaya 2014; Fominaya and Cox 2013; but see Pianta and Gerbaudo 2012:6–10). Many simply speak of anti-austerity protests.

It is a good question why financial institutions and their representatives receive so little attention. As the Icelandic case suggests, possibly the press only reluctantly reports on finance-caused tragedies, protests and citizen-oriented political responses. Since much research is based on the press reports, this generates an underestimation of protests focused on the banks, blocked access to savings, inability to pay mortgages, foreclosures, tax-financed bailouts, etc. Another possibility is that the journalists' vocabulary is not attuned to picking up new

protest agendas, limiting research. Most likely, protesters and researchers alike "remain stuck" in old thought categories. They see corporations, governments and external institutions imposing austerity
programs, resulting in rising prices, reduced benefits and subsidies,
dwindling life opportunities and curtailed democratic rights. They
see democratic institutions constrained by non-democratic forces. But
they have neither interest in how financial actors, institutions, practices
and products create crises nor concepts for tracing how they impose
constraints on democratic governments (for the interwar period, see
Kirchheimer 1969:133). Social movement research instead pursues its
set research agenda focused on the resources, political opportunity
structures, networks, issue framing and spaces conducive to anti-
austerity protests. It has not imported concepts for capturing the ebbs
and flows of mobile capital that is now capable of ruining entire
countries or regions within a split of a second nor for new financial
instruments that convert homes, water and crops in financial products
(see Chapters 2, 5 and 7, this volume). Outside the purview remain
inflation and deflation, blocked savings accounts, inability to pay
mortgages, foreclosures, devastation of entire social groups, neigh-
bourhoods, cities and regions (Flam 2012). Academic imaginaries are
still indebted to Marx, but not to Weber. Max Weber (1976:531–540)
in contrast to Marx argued that class struggles take place not just
between capitalists and workers, but also between creditors and
debtors. His, however, is a hardly acknowledged perspective (but see
Chapter 8, this volume). Let me now turn to OWS and ATTAC to
show how they deal with financial capital.

OWS

It has been a widespread belief that OWS has no demands (see, for
example, Pianta and Gerbaudo 2011:5). By the same token, OWS
has been celebrated for targeting the Wall Street. Its protests – seen
as the harbinger of the future – were greeted by a great outpouring of
enthusiasm. What can we learn from its Webpages?

OWS's menu, "InfoTent" (see WS IT in references) announces
protest marches at the top. Scrolling one gains the impression that
OWS is not primarily concerned with the financial sector or its victims,
although one finds such entries as Foreclosure Defense, Occupy Student Debt and NYC & Debt Assembly at the margins as well as

announcements of demonstrations against the corporate and financial
NYC district at the top. Its current Webpages testify to that its members
and sympathizers are absorbed by very many issues.

One has to scroll down to see Foundational Documentaries and
to discover the Declaration of the Occupation of NYC. The first two
lines of its Declaration of the Occupation of New York City, accepted
by the NYC General Assembly on September 29, 2011, indeed express
indignation about those who "have taken our houses through an
illegal foreclosure process, despite not having the original mortgage"
and those who "have taken bailout from taxpayers with impunity, and
continue to give Executives exorbitant bonuses" but the Declaration
has about twenty-three such lines, opposing, among others, discrimination and inequality, poisoned food, torture, labor rights loss, hostage-
taking skyrocketing student loans, outsourcing causing low pay
of healthcare workers, military and police intimidation of the press,
faulty products not recalled back, blocking alternative energy sources,
covering up oil spills, murdering prisoners, colonialism, torture and
murder of civilians overseas, weapons of mass destruction (OWS).
The Declaration thus suggests that OWS was not – not even in the
beginning – primarily a protest against the Wall Street. It confirms that
OWS activists find many issues urgent.

Perseverance is rewarded, however. Down on the left an entry called
NYC features thirteen sub-entries. One is called Alternative Banking.
Its first page invites one to join Alt.Banking OWS without offering any
explanation (Alt.B). Scrolling down reveals three long scathing texts
concerning banks and their CEO bonuses.

A text entitled "10 Worst things about Wall Street in 2013 (and
5 Silver Linings) #OWS" offers "a sample of the ways Wall Street
has manoeuvred, manipulated, defrauded and deceived us" during the
previous year. Titles such as "In Washington, It´s a Wash," "Still Too
Big to Jail," "Banks Manipulate Commodities, Fed OKs It," "Court
Evasion," "Never on Hold" or "Writing the Rules" are followed by
short texts criticizing various governmental institutions for kowtowing
to bank CEOs and the banks, while pinpointing specific instances
of bank CEOs avoiding responsibility for past criminal deeds or of
bank lobbyists trying to or in fact blocking or rolling back restrictions
imposed on the banking sector in the wake of the 2007–2008 financial
crisis. But Alt.Banking does not just focus on the Wall Street &
Washington nexus. It also takes up illegal and legal bank actions

deeply hurting homeowners, credit unions, and specific cities and their worker pension plans, while praising those who challenge the banking sector in their capacity as activists, journalists or politicians:

4. Zombie Foreclosures
The banks continued to exploit underwater homeowners. One of the worst abuses is called "zombie foreclosures" where the bank pretended to foreclose – evicting the owner – but then didn't file legal papers. This allowed the banks to continue to rack up interest, fees and penalties because the homeowners, reasonably, stopped making payments because they thought the homes were no longer theirs. To add insult to injury, when the banks sent out checks to homeowners in restitution for past misdeeds, they bounced.

5. Pillaging of Detroit
Detroit's largest creditors, UBS and Bank of America, made it clear .... they... go to collect on debts from highly-risky interest rate swap deals they made with Detroit's leaders before the 2008 financial collapse: they're coming for the art! ... held ... in public trust by the city. It ... remains to be seen whether the approximately $900 million... will ... pay off debts or ... pay ... city worker pensions.

6. Killing Credit Unions
According to MSN.com, credit unions offer low rates on loans, higher rates on savings, better credit cards deals, and lower fees. Perhaps because of these competitive benefits, the American Banking Association ran an ad campaign to revoke the tax exempt status for America's credit unions.

Five Silver Linings

1. **Occupy the SEC Gains Ground**
   Occupy the SEC's impact on the Volcker Rule (which originally aspired to banning proprietary trading and ownership of hedge funds by banks) could not be more evident. When the Volcker Rule was finalized in December, the hard work Occupy the SEC did writing a 325-page comment letter on paid off... In some cases, the final rule adopted their recommendations while in others the rule was modified in the direction of Occupy's suggestions.
2. **Radical Eminent Domain**
   Richmond, California Mayor Gayle McLaughlin ignited a fury on Wall St and in Washington by employing an eminent domain threat to force intransigent banks to renegotiate – and reduce

principal – for underwater homeowners. The move has sparked everything from lawsuits and threats of mortgage lenders leaving town to copycat actions in other underwater cities as far away as Irvington and Newark, New Jersey. Supporters of the promising tactic are calling it the Reverse Eminent Domain Movement and even Occupy 2.0... (SOURCE: Alt.B)

The Webpage of Alt.Banking has a black stripe running across its top. Clicking on Come to Alternative Banking Meetings! and an email from the contact person, cathy.oneil@gmail.com (received on 19.02.2017) reveal that The Alternative Banking Working Group of OWS has been meeting since 2011 every Sunday at Columbia University to discuss past and present financial institutions, their practices and their regulation based on a shared reading list. On its new Webpage and Events page Trump is focal, but finances are still important (Alt.B1, Alt.B2). "About us" shows a picture of mostly mature people and foregrounds their anti-finance activism:

"Welcome! ... We, the Alternative Banking group, are dedicated to making the financial system work for the 99% by pushing for better financial regulations, by evaluating and fostering ... alternative financial options, and by educating the public about the current dysfunction to inspire activism... We are financial professionals, accountants, technologists, economists, traders, engineers, housewives, househusbands, laborers, brokers, professors, students, activists and workers interested in reforming, revolutionizing and improving our financial system. We've been meeting since October 17th, 2011, soon after Zuccotti Park was occupied and since then ... We are extremely proud of the launch of our first book, Occupy Finance. ... We handed out hundreds of copies at Zuccotti Park on ... the 3rd Anniversary of the encampment... (see Alt.B3)... We also put out an educational and fun set of playing cards called the 52 Shades of Greed... (Alt.B3, Alt.B4)

Alt.Banking's first Silver Lining cited earlier gives a clue about another finance-focused OWS working group: Occupy the SEC. OSEC, as it is also called, was apparently founded in October 2011 as a working group of OWS. It has sought to influence financial regulators to work for the public interest (OSEC1, OSEC2). After initially meeting on a bench in Zuccotti Park, soon the group evolved into a bi-weekly "book club" at a diner near the park, and then started meeting weekly in the atrium of 60 Wall Street. It still welcomes newcomers from NYC at the same address, on Tuesdays at 7:30 (OSE3) and is also open to email members. Apart from regular citizens and activists, professional financial experts, employees or former employees of some of the largest financial firms, are among its members.

"SEC" in Occupy the SEC or OSEC for short refers to the US Securities and Exchange Commission (SEC) but OSEC has sought regulatory influence by addressing many other institutions apart from SEC. The group first gained attention after tackling a response to the proposed Volcker Rule, part of the Dodd-Frank Act of 2010, meant to limit proprietary trading at commercial banks, similarly to the Glass Steagall Act of 1933. OSEC submitted its 325-page rule-commenting letter to the SEC in February 2012. Its commentary explained why each rule is either useless or why and how it needs to be improved. Its commentary was apparently cited 284 times by the Federal Reserve Board when the regulations were ultimately put into effect in 2013. According to *The Economist* (2012), OSEC's "contributions to the debate on regulatory reform (including a tome on the Volcker Rule) have been well-received even by some leading regulators." Recently OSEC scored each member of the US House of Representatives on Financial Reform. It evolved into a major finance watchdog organization in the US. OSEC regularly calls legislators and responds to regulatory agencies. Its Webpage briefly summarizes some of its numerous interventions in specific finance-related issues. The interventions range from petitioning the Congress or appropriate government agencies to commenting specific legislative and regulatory proposals. Here is a sample of OSEC's actions (see OSEC1), showing, among others, that OSEC monitors the Dodd-Frank Act protective of ordinary consumers, investors and debtors to insure that it is fully implemented and, equally important, not weakened or repealed under the pressure of the bank sector lobbying efforts. The sample also shows that OSEC's expertise enables it to intervene in regulation plans concerning the so-called "new financial instruments" and their managers with the aim of diminishing domestic and international risks:

FOIA Request to SEC Requesting Lobbying Documents
December 16, 2016. Section 621 of Dodd Frank Act required the SEC to implement a rule prohibiting conflicts of interests in certain securitization transactions... over five years have passed and the SEC has still not finalized the rule... OSEC has issued a request to SEC... to bring ... lobbying efforts to light.

Petition to Congress in Opposition to the Repeal of the Dodd-Frank Act
June 8, 2016... organized a petition asking Congress to oppose the Financial
Choice Act ... That bill would effectively repeal the Dodd-Frank Act, which
currently contains many protections for ordinary investors, consumers
and debtors...

Comment Letter to CFTC Regarding Aggregation of Position Limits
November 13, 2015... submitted a comment letter to the Commodity
Futures Trading Commission ("CFTC") regarding that agency's notice of
re-proposed rulemaking regarding aggregation of position limits on certain
commodities contracts and derivatives. The proposed position limits regime
is already rife with numerous exemptions, such as broadly permissive provisions for hedging. The CFTC has now proposed an aggregation scheme that
would make it even easier for large commodities players to utilize subsidiar-
ies and shell companies to monopolize commodity markets...

Comment Letter to FSB/IOSCO on Systemic Risks in Asset Management
June 15, 2015... submitted a letter to the Financial Stability Board ("FSB")
and the International Organization of Securities Commissions ("IOSCO")
recommending that these international regulators address the systemic risks
posed by global asset managers... OSEC points to weaknesses in the
measures... proposed to designate asset managers or funds as Globally
Systemically Important Financial Institutions (G-SIFIs). OSEC also urges
the FSB/IOSCO to pursue industry-wide regulatory measures to address
systemic risks that asset managers pose.

Amicus Brief to U.S. Supreme Court in Bank of America v. Caulkett
March 23, 2015... submitted an amicus brief in [a court case] presently
pending before the U.S. Supreme Court... An unfavorable decision in the
case would hurt 2.1 million underwater borrowers who are at risk of ...
foreclosure ... (SOURCE: OSEC1)

To conclude: the first impression that financial capital is of marginal
importance for OWS becomes somewhat modified by the discovery of
two OWS groups: Alt.Banking and OSEC. Both were established in
2011. While OSEC located in the Wall Street pools finance and other
professionals, and has evolved in a finance-related watchdog that both
barks and bites, the Upper West Side's Alt.Banking is composed of
diverse professionals. It learned about the historical and institutional
factors leading up to the financial and economic crisis of 2007–2008,
its consequences and its continued reverberations. Both focus on the US.

While OSEC, composed of finance experts, has developed its expertise further to act the role of a watchdog, Alt.Banking had to acquire it first. Its book and the deck of cards are the outcome of a learning process. They are meant to counter mainstream discourses, especially about the crisis and the finance sector, in accessible everyday language.

Even knowing just a little about their history, composition and activities casts OWS in a different light. OWS has a very broad agenda, marked as it is by very many activists and supporters, but it does not "forget" to take on the financial sector. It attempts to challenge financialization in several ways: by organizing demonstrations and spreading the word about the debt-caused suffering, and about the collective ways in which foreclosure threats can be handled and foreclosures averted. In addition, it entails OSEC as a watchdog group and Alt. Banking as a group popularizing a discourse running counter to the neoliberal finance-glorifying creed. OWS's general broad agenda juxtaposed with these two OWS affiliates and their respective roles reminds of the ambitions of its European predecessor: ATTAC.

ATTAC

ATTAC was initiated in 1998 by a group of French intellectual activists who wanted to develop a discourse alternative to the mainstream neoliberal discourse (Pleyers 2010:115; ATTAC1). Ignacio Ramonet, the past chief editor of *Le Monde diplomatique*, wrote an editorial in which he argued, among others, that the Asian financial crisis was the proof of the deep harmfulness of the financial markets playing a hegemonic role in globalization processes (Ancelovici 2002:437; Muro 2003). He suggested creating Action for a Tobin Tax for the Aid of Citizens acting as a civic pressure group – a different version of which was at that time discussed by the EU parliament (cf., Introduction). Shortly thereafter thousands of support letters arrived, and several unions, civic organizations and newspapers held a constitutive meeting. They agreed on that credible alternatives to neo-liberalism, taxation of financial transactions and checking the damages caused by financial globalization were urgently called for. In 2001/2002 among its members one-third were teachers, intellectuals and students, and 556 unions, associations and organizations (Ancelovici 2002:439,444). Forty ATTAC organizations were set up in Europe, the Americas, Africa and Japan.

ATTAC's one aim was to spread easily digested knowledge about abstract and complex economic issues. A new discourse was to challenge neo-liberalism and to de-naturalize its vision of economy. This was in line with ATTAC's more general position that the states by embracing neo-liberalism opened up markets to global financial flows which in turn incorporate an increasing share of human activities and products in the market. ATTAC attributed to the states the power to reverse and counter these processes that endanger livelihoods, citizen rights and democracies. It attracted members with multiple memberships who built coalitions and mobilized numerous organizations. Its lobbying efforts were facilitated by the fact that over a hundred members of the French parliament joined ATTAC, while in the European Parliament it had its representation (Ancelovici 2002:441).

Following the crisis of 2007–2008, in 2009 ATTAC targeted G20 summit on such issues as de-deregulation, tax heavens and the under-representation of the governments from poor countries among its members. The protests were the first direct response to the financial and economic crises of 2007–2008. In London, they testified to the widespread outrage at the doings of the City (cf Pianta and Gerbaudo 2012:3). Over a number of days, various protests took place. On March 28 a 35,000 (wo)men strong demonstration initiated by Jubilee Debt Campaign, Trade Justice Movement, British Overseas NGOs for Development and the Trade Union Congress, demanded democratizing financial institutions to secure stable jobs, public services and green economy while ending global poverty and inequality (Wiki1). On April 1 about five thousand people joined the "G20 Meltdown" protest outside the Bank of England. G20 Meltdown was a radical, anti-capitalist and socialist organization conceived in Paris and formed in London in January 2009 (Wiki1). The aim was to "create a carnival outside the bank" and to "overthrow capitalism." Protesters referred to the day as "Financial Fools' Day." The protest started in the morning when four planned marches, each led by one of the "Four Horsemen of the Apocalypse" converged on the Bank: the red horse headed the march against war, the green horse against climate chaos, the silver horse against financial crimes, and the black horse against land enclosures and borders (Wiki1). Protest chants included "build a bonfire, put the bankers on the top," and some protesters shouted "jump" and "shame on you" at bankers watching from windows. Although the protest was peaceful, the police kettled it, employing batons and dogs, and depriving protesters of access to food, drink and lavatory facilities for seven hours (resulting in public criticism and court cases afterwards). Some protesters broke into a branch of Royal Bank of Scotland... During this summit, the leaders of the twenty biggest economies who convened to save the financial system agreed on a $ 1.1 trillion financial package. Of this $500 billion went to the IMF (Pianta and Gerbaudo 2012:3; Pleyers 2010:237–239).

G20 protests are instructive. They show that even when protesters take on financial capital, this issue competes with other urgent issues. Often protests are met by disproportionately high police numbers, violations of citizen rights to peaceful expression of opinion through pre-meditated crowd-control methods, such as kettling-in and unwarranted arrests, (civilian) police provocations to violence, and unprovoked frequent employment of violence. Still protests visibly opposing top-level political and financial decision-makers, along with financial watchdogs and anti-finance discourse-spinners, answer the question of what needs to be done, namely: a three-prong strategy has to be adopted to effectively confront financial capital (cf. Pleyers 2010:118–128).

Returning to ATTAC and its current Webpage, identical in English, French, German and Spanish, discloses that finances are still at its heart, even though national and regional ATTACs might put priorities differently. The 3rd sentence of its self-presentation states: "Specifically, we fight for the regulation of financial markets, the closure of tax havens, the introduction of global taxes to finance global public goods, the cancellation of the debt of developing countries, fair trade, and the implementation of limits to free trade and capital flows." (Attac1) ATTAC's demands list in contrast to OWS's Webpages makes very clear that it – at least on a programmatic level – is centrally concerned with finances (Attac2). Its homepage displays links to ATTAC in Africa, in the Americas, Asia and Europe.

ATTAC's Platform, reproduced today under About ATTAC (Attac3) defines it as an "International movement for democratic control of financial markets and their institutions." This definition heads the following statement adopted at the international meeting which took place in 1998, after the 1997 financial crisis:

"Financial globalization increases economic insecurity and social inequalities. It bypasses and undermines popular decision-making, democratic institutions, and sovereign states responsible for the general interest. In their place, it substitutes a purely speculative logic that expresses... the interests of multinational corporations and financial markets... Such a humiliating proof of impotence encourages the growth of anti-democratic parties. It is urgent to block this process by creating new instruments of regulation and control, at the national, European, and international levels... [this] requires a dramatic increase in civic activism. The total freedom of capital circulation, the existence of tax havens, and the explosion of the volume of speculative transactions have forced governments into a frantic race to win the favor of big investors. Every day, one hundred billion dollars pass through the currency markets in search of instant profits, with no relation to the state of production or to trade in goods and services. The consequences ... are the permanent increase of income on capital at the expense of labor, a pervasive economic insecurity, and the growth of poverty. The social consequences ... are even more severe for dependent countries that are directly affected by the financial crisis and ... subjected to... the IMF's adjustment plans... Interest rates much higher than in the countries of the North contribute to the destruction of national producers; uncontrolled privatization and denationalization develop in the search for the resources demanded by investors. Everywhere social rights are called into question..." (Attac3)

Although ATTAC no longer plays a dominant role, it developed counter-expertise in and related to the area of taxes and financial transactions and lobbying (Ancelovici 2002:443,444–445; Muro 2003:154–161). It apparently monitors decisions of the World Trade Organization (WTO), the Organisation for Economic Co-operation and Development (OECD) and the IMF (WikiAttac). One of its former members established the European Finance Watch in 2011 (see below).

So it would seem that ATTAC stands for another key example of mobilization against financial institutions, although it is not clear whether it can be equated with bottom-up or grassroots mobilization, given the fact that three-fourth of its founding members were institutions as originally intended (Ancelovici 2002:443). But for now, let me just note that ATTAC defines financial capital as the core international actor behind neo-liberalism, and compare it with OWS.

Despite all differences, ATTAC and OWS, or at least groups working under their names, share in common two ambitions: to advance and employ financial expertise to achieve legislative reforms checking the power of the financial sector and to put this expertise in relatively simple terms, countering the neoliberal discourse. The lesson that can be drawn from this comparison is perhaps that any long-term movement against financial capital has to feature one expert group and one expertise- digesting and popularizing group. It does not seem, however, like large activist majorities are interested or ready to take on the complexities of finance and financial legislation. They demand anti-austerity programs and blame their governments, thus letting mobile capital roam free.

What other lessons can be drawn from ATTAC? Compared to OWS, ATTAC is much more international. The IMF, the WTO, the World Bank, and the UN – mockingly called the Politburo of the Liberal International by the ATTAC's president Bernard Cassen because of their growing importance as key international institutional actors – were declared the major protest targets, in addition to the nation states (Ancelovici 2002:446, 453–454; Muro 2003). From its very beginning ATTAC has taken keen interest in the developing countries of the global South. It has harboured some issue-organizations, while others came out of it to constitute organizations in their own right. One such organization was Focus on the Global South (CARWD) (Pleyers 2011:115). It formed already in 1990 around Eric Toussaint, an activist-expert who accumulated enough resources to set up a five-person expert team focusing on the third world debt. CARWD has headquarters in Belgium but developed a network throughout Europe, Africa and Latin America. Toussaint co-founded ATTAC-International and in 2001 the World Social Forum (WSF). The issue of the third world debt remained on the agenda of ATTAC, and gained increasing importance within the WSF-Forums in part thanks to his activism and in part to the Jubilee South campaigns. Let us see what can be learned from the Jubilee and Jubilee South campaigns, both anti-government debt.

Jubilee and Jubilee South Anti-Government Debt Campaigns

The last quarter of the last century saw many governments in the developing (and then socialist countries) unable to service their debt (Moffitt 1983:93–132; Walton and Seddon 1994). As first came Mexico's announcement in 1982 that it could not service its debt. Peru and Jamaica went virtually bankrupt. The IMF imposed disciplining regimes on their governments to qualify for re-scheduling and new loans. Devaluation of their currencies, leading to higher prices, and austerity programs followed, shifting the debt burden to the population. National protests and campaigns in the indebted countries transmuted into transnational anti-government debt campaigns in the early 1980s. Protests confronted the IMF and the World Bank AGM in Berlin in 1988 and the G7 Summit in Paris in 1989 (Somers 2014:80). Transcontinental networking took place, followed by a shift to lobbying in the early 1990s.

In 1997 Jubilee 2000 was launched. The idea was, as in the Bible, that a Jubilee would restore, by reversing, right relations: debts would be cancelled, land redistributed, slaves would be freed. The central demand was that the poorest countries should have their un-payable debts cancelled by the year 2000. It brought massive transcontinental mobilizations. A Jubilee petition gathered 24 million signatures worldwide. 70,000 people came to the first major Jubilee demonstration against the G7 Birmingham Summit in 1998. 35,000 protested during the G7 Summit in Cologne in 1999 (Somers 2014:80).

Issue competition marked the Jubilee campaign, just like world protests 2006–2013 or OWS. Global North activists wanted the anti-debt campaign to end by 2000 to capitalize on the symbolism of the upcoming millennium, although it started in GB in 1997, in Africa in 1998, and in Latin America in 1999. Ending the campaign in 2000 would allow northern NGOs to follow their practice of switching to a new campaign issue every couple of years (Somers 2014:85). Global South activists argued that this was unrealistic even in terms of logistics (translations, networking, receiving northern funds, organizing events, etc.) but even more importantly that the campaign should stop first when it succeeds (Somers 2014:86).

The tensions over issue definition and asymmetries of power resulted in an open conflict when global North campaigners accepted the 1999 Cologne Debt Deal without discussing it with the attending global South activists. The Deal announced at the G7 Summit increased the level of debt cancellations, but did not modify austerity requirements, even though it asked for including civil society in the formulation of poverty reduction strategies (Somers 2014:88).

The Jubilee campaign illustrates that counter-summits and lobbying bring results. It also underlines the issue of power asymmetries among activists and the differences in how they define issues. Global North activists tend to frame debt as un-payable because of extraordinary, unacceptable human cost it implies. Their argument fits well into the predominant discourses of poverty reduction and development (Somers 2014:87–90). Global South campaigners, however, have been questioning the very legitimacy of "odious" debts incurred by dictators who never consulted the citizens that are now to carry the main burden of servicing and repaying them. They point to the colonial past creating sustained uneven development, unfair terms of trade and exploitative economic and financial systems. The Philippines Freedom from Debt Coalition proved that some loans were outright fraudulent. Jubilee South Africa renounced "apartheid debt" run up by the apartheid regime and that in the neighboring countries incurred to combat racism in and the aggression of South Africa. Even in some global North countries debt cancellation was achieved. In France *Platforme Dette et Développement* pinpointed that nearly 50 percent of debt resulted from "irresponsible, if not criminal" export guarantees by a French export guarantee agency to countries at war and well-known dictatorships.

The Lusaka Declaration of 1999 actually endorsed "the collective repudiation of illegitimate foreign debt payments" (Somers 2014:89), but even those global North campaigners who wished to abide by more radical terms agreed upon at the Rome conference in 2000, slipped into "debt relief" and "debt reduction" and spoke of "un-payable" debts more often than "odious" or "illegitimate" debts. As a result of all these tensions and splits, the movements went through a period of conflicts and fragmentation. Still, the campaign did not end. Jubilee South was launched in Johannesburg in 1999 at a south/south summit as an even more radical anti-debt movement based on dialogues embedded in regional networks and developments. It neutralized some north-south cleavages and initiated a successful Norwegian campaign to cancel Norwegian illegitimate debt claims. More: Norway gave funds to UNCTAD and the World Bank to do research on the concept of "odious" debt in international law, paving way for its legitimation. In 2007 G7 countries' campaigns put out reports documenting illegitimate debt cases in their respective countries (cf Enderlein et al. 2012 and Schumacher et al. 2015).

Not just public intellectuals but also many social movement researchers wait for protest to show the way. It is my argument that movements for "real" democracy and against austerity do not. There is so much emphasis on democracy and, consequently, issue competition, that even if one believes that the financial capital is a cause of all injustice and should constitute the main target of attack, democratic convictions stand in the way of pushing it as a single issue. As Jubilee shows, global North NGO's habit of switching to a new issue every two years exacerbates the democratic overkill, leading to a (wasteful) dispersion of protest energies.

Political Elites and Experts against Financial Capital

Although in Europe also some scientists, trade unions, NGOs, think-tanks and political parties have envisioned more or less drastic reductions in the power of financial capital and add demands for the regulation and taxation of financial capital and/or debt repudiation to their busy agenda (Pianta and Gerbaudo 2012:6; Ford and Philipponnat 2013:12), few focus on financial capital. The European Finance Watch differs in this respect. It was set up on the initiative of twenty-two European Parliamentarians, seconded by 200 other (Ford and Philipponnat 2013:12–17; FW1). One former ATTAC member headed the initiative in 2011: Sven Giegold, a German Green Parliamentarian, who still participates in the meetings of WSF, an offspring of ATTAC. Thierry Philipponnat, an investment banker and previously an executive board member of Amnesty International in France, was nominated as the first General Secretary. Its first executive board included Ieke van den Berg, also a former EU Parliamentarian, who specialized in economic and currency issues, and the representatives of the European Trade Union Congress, Transparency International EU Office and Friends of the Earth, among others. Among its staffers were professionals from finance. This "experts" NGO was kicked off by the EU funds but taps diverse other sources. Its (German language) mission statement says that it was set up in the realization that the financial crisis had showed that financial capital cannot control itself and that politicians do not possess instruments to fend off powerful financial lobbies. It defines itself as such instrument, intending to act in societal interest as an advocacy group which counteracts the powerful financial lobbies and makes sure that financial capital benefits productive economy (FW1). The cover of its first report shows a scale: on the one side are the people, on the other $, € and ¥ which weigh more. Even more pronouncedly than in the case of ATTAC, in this case finance-critical professionals and some politicians came together to develop and employ the necessary finance expertise as an instrument in (political, EU) lobbying for financial regulation. EU Finance Watch has worked out a number of research and policy proposals for the EU Parliamentarians and other groups (see Ford and Philipponnat 2013:12–17). It invests much energy in popularizing its findings.

That politicians can themselves form a movement to counter Western financial capital and its disciplining guardians, even though this is not a simple undertaking and takes much concerted effort, is a lesson one can learn from the leaders of emerging economies: when the IMF forced Indonesia's President Suharto to sign its draconic austerity measures document in 1998, the by now iconic image of the IMF's managing director, arms crossed, towering over the visibly cowed signing President caused much irritation, anger and massive protests (see Introduction and Chapter 2, this volume). Although the first attempts to stave off Western influence via the IMF and the World Bank by setting up a regional development bank failed twice, in the end the South-East Development Bank was set up by the like-minded political and financial elites. It buffers the region from the flows and ebbs of mobile capital.

Conclusion

Anti-austerity and real democracy – this is what protesters apparently demand and research on social movements investigates. However, inspecting two different OWS Working Groups as well as ATTAC and Jubilee anti-government debt campaigns showed that some well-known, but in this respect under-researched (but see Friesen 2012), movements instead focus on deconstructing financial capital. Importantly, they also formulate, and at times push through, their reform demands. Clearly, research should devote more attention to their activities.

In particular, very little is known about finance experts who had worked or are still working in the very financial sector which they, seemingly paradoxically, contest and wish to have monitored and controlled. Social research shows that *issue professionals* are very good at both networking and getting the issue on the institutional agenda, and some have an activist past (Lasse and Seabrooke 2015). In this case *issue professionals* posit a puzzle.

Secondly, a Weberian perspective on credit-market related class and status struggles should play a role. Struggles around credit – its availability as well as conditions for borrowing and paying back – have moved from the "periphery" to the "core" of the world. This is often acknowledged, but research on the action consequences is scarce. This research shows, however, that flat refusals to repay government debts preceded by strategic action to protect national assets, such as airplanes or ships, countered by property seizures, court cases, mounting international pressures and re-selling of the government debt to unscrupulous financial speculators as well as negotiations around debt-taking and –repayment involving very many different types of international actors mark this new world (see, ignoring the aggressive terminology, Schuhmacher et al. 2015 and Enderlein et al. 2012; see also Friesen 2012). Regional protection strategies, such as setting up of the South-East Asian Development Bank, against the actors deciding about the flows and ebbs of mobile capital, are also multiplying and deserve systematic research.

Not just the "rich" countries but also their "rich" citizens are affected by conflicts between creditors and debtors. It is important to work with research programs, literature and statistics that are cognizant of these facts. Rather than merely looking at unemployment, wage or poverty rates while trying to explain social mobilization, (social movement) research should look at a number of credit-market related factors. In countries where education, homeownership and a competitive standard of living is financed largely by credit, their patterns and the trends in their price developments over time should become focal just as inspecting stratified saving and credit-taking and – repayment chances. One should not forget to check monetary developments (inflation, deflation) and the punctuated impact national banks, government policies and transnational actors have on the ability to sustain one's life trajectory and a competitive standard of living, while taking and repaying debt. The felt threat of and the actual consumer debt bankruptcies and foreclosures have to be taken seriously, just like at present the fear of and the actual unemployment is. Equipped with this type of knowledge, researchers will have much better chances of understanding why and when (wo)men rebel. In particular, the struggles and negotiations around credit-taking and – repaying, generating a strong sense of injustice, will come into purview.

The main argument of the text is that social movements focused on financial capital (should) have a three – prong strategy to be effective. They (should) (i) acquire or develop financial expertise to successfully monitor and exercise finance-(de)constructing reform pressure; (ii) develop popular discourses and artifacts to awaken society to the importance of the struggle against financial capital, and, finally; (iii) focus protest on key financial actors and institutions, and political summits at which financial and/or political top-level decision-making takes place.

It is important to add that popular anti-finance discourses face a double burden. They have to counter not just the self-glorification of financial capital but also anti-Semitic, racist and anti-migrant populist discourses which blame Jews and migrants for the crises (Ellinas 2013). To help along public anti-finance and anti-summit protests, citizens, media and other actors must demand and protect democratic rights to organizing and the public expression of anti-finance stands, even if they are themselves indifferent to the issues these protests raise.

The understanding that all these forms of activism are necessary is not yet in place. Instead expertise-gaining and lobbying against financial capital is posited as less effective than large scale anti-summit protests and vice versa (see DK in references). Still, since precedents abound, (mutations of) the three-prong strategy, assisted by broad support for democratic rights, are likely to mushroom, and anti-finance movements are likely to make careers similar to those made by very many humanitarian and human rights organizations that started small and became big in the course of the last 40 years, such as, for example, Doctors with no Borders, Amnesty International or Human Rights Watch. Just like their predecessors, finance-deconstructing and finance-regulating groups are likely to form changing alliances and occasionally launch campaigns with sympathetic think-tanks, NGOs, finance ministers and/or politicians coming together to put some controls on or shield a country or a region from the ebbs and flows of mobile capital. In a rare of moment of optimism, I am willing to say: "It is only a matter of time."

Acknowledgements: Thank you to Tom Burns, Micha Fiedlschuster, Joc Pixley and Katarina Ristic for their comments. Thank you too to Jon Gunnar Bernburg for sending me his texts, Marcos Ancelovici for an up-date on his research and Sebastian Haunss for a useful reference. Hank Johnston assured me *Mobilization* did not cover material on the OWS finance groups. Thank you to Joc too for her English language edit.

References

Ancelovici, Marcos. 2015. *Crisis and Contention in Europe: A Political Process Account of Anti-Austerity Protests*. London. Palgrave Macmillan

2002. "Organizing against Globalization: The Case of ATTAC in France" *Politics & Society* 30, 3: 427–463

Bernburg, Jon Gunnar. 2016. *Economic Crisis and Mass Protest: The Pots and Pans Revolution in Iceland*. London. Routledge

Della Porta, Donatella, ANDRETTA, Massimiliano; FERNANDES, Tiago; ROMANOS, Eduardo; O'CONNOR, Francis; VOGIATZOGLOU, Markos. 2017. *Late Neoliberalism and its Discontents in the Economic Crisis*. Comparing Social Movements in the European Periphery. London. Palgrave MacMillan

The Economist. "Occupy Wall Street: Afterthoughts." September 22, 2012.

Ellinas A. Antonis. 2013. "The Rise of the Golden Dawn: The New Face of the Far Right in Greece" *South European Society and Politics* 18: 543–65

Enderlein, Henrik, Christoph Trebesch, Laura von Daniels. 2012. "Sovereign debt disputes: A database on government coerciveness during debt crises" *Journal of International Money and Finance* 21: 259–266

Flam, Helena. 2012. "Magic Thinking and Panic Buttons in the Callous Financial Transaction Chains" In *New Perspectives on Emotions in Finance*. Pp. 28–45, Edited by Jocelyn Pixley. London. Routledge,

Fominaya, Cristina Flesher. 2014. "Arab Spring, Indignados, Occupy: A Global Wave of Protest?" In *Social Movements & Globalization*. Pp. 148–197, NY. Palgrave MacMillan

Fominaya, Cristina Flesher and Laurence Cox. 2013. *Understanding European Movements: New Social Movements, Global Justice Struggles, Anti-Austerity Protest*. London. Routledge

Ford, Greg and Thierry Philipponnat. 2013. "The Role of Civil Society in Holding Financial Powers Accountable" *Journal of Civil Society* 9, 2: 178–195

Friesen, Elizabeth. 2012. *Challenging Global Finance*. London. Palgrave McMillan.

Giugni, Marco and Maria Grasso. 2016. *Austerity and Protest: Popular Contention in Times of Economic Crisis*. London. Routledge

Kirchheimer, Otto. 1969. *Politics, Law and Social Change*. New York. Columbia University Press

Lasse, Folke Henriksen and Leonard Seabrooke. 2015. "Transnational organizing: Issue professionals in environmental sustainability networks" *Organization* 23, 5: 1–25

Moffitt, Michael. 1983. *The World's Money*. New York. Simon and Schuster

Muro, Diego. 2003. "Campaigning for a 'Robin Hood Tax' for Foreign Exchange Markets" In *Globalizing Civic Engagement*. Pp. 150–163. Edited by John D. Clark, NY, NYC. Earthscan

Ortiz, Isabel, Sara Burke and Mohamed Berrada Hernán Cortés. 2013. "World Protests 2006-2013" Initiative for Policy-Dialogue and Friedrich-Ebert Stiftung New York Working Paper 2013, jointly published by Initiative for Policy Dialogue Columbia University, New York and Friedrich-Ebert Stiftung New York Office

Pianta, Mario and Gerbaudo, Paolo. 2012. "European Alternatives: Trajectories of Mobilisation responding to Europe's Crisis" Open Democracy, 30 March, www.opendemocracy.net/mario-pianta-paolo-gerbaudo/european-alternatives-trajectories-of-mobilisation-responding-to-europe%e2%80%99 (sighted on 02.03.2017)

Pleyers, Geoffrey. 2010. *Alter-Globalization: Becoming Actors in the Global Age*. Cambridge. Polity Press

Schumacher, Julian, Christoph Trebesch, Henrik Enderlein. 2015. "What Explains Sovereign Debt Litigation?" CESifo Working Paper No. 5319 (Center for Economic Studies and Ifo Institute)

Somers, Jean. 2014. "The dynamics of south/north relationship within transnational debt campaigning" *Interface* 6, 2: 76–102

Vogiatzoglu, Markos. 2017. "Iceland's Mobilization in the Financial Crisis" in Donatella Della Porta et al. *Late Neoliberalism and Its Discontents in the Economic Crisis. Comparing Social Movements in the European Periphery*. London. Palgrave MacMillan pp. 39–64

Weber, Max. 1976. "Machtverteilung Innerhalb der Gemeinschaft: Klassen, Stände, Parteien" In Wirtschaft und Gesellschaft, 5th revised edition, 2. Pp. 531–540. Part, edited by Johannes Winckelmann. Tübingen. J.C.B. Mohr (Paul Siebeck).

Walton, John K. and David Seddon. 1994. *Free Markets and Food Riots: The Politics of Global Adjustment*. London. Wiley-Blackwell

Online Sources

Alt.B, alternativebanking.nycga.net (sighted on 18.02.2017)

Alt.B1, http://altbanking.net/ (sighted on 19.02.2017)

Alt.B2, http://altbanking.net/speaker-series/events/ (sighted on 19.02.2017)

Alt.B3, www.inprnt.com/gallery/52shadesofgreed/ www.dropbox.com/s/jb3tvdcvysq7afp/Occupy%20Finance_secondprinting.pdf (sighted on 19.02.2017)

Alt.B4, http://altbanking.net/about/ (sighted on 19.02.2017)

Attac1, www.attac.org/en/overview or www.attac.org/de/%C3%BCbersicht
    (sighted on 19.02.2017)

Attac2, www.attac.org/en/we-fight (sighted on 19.02.2017)

Attac3, www.attac.org/en/whatisattac/international-platform (sighted on
    19.02.2017)

DK, Deutschlandradio Kultur, interview from 06.07.2009, online:
    www.deutschlandradiokultur.de/attac-g8-gipfel-ist-ein- auslaufmodell
    .954.de.html?dram:article_id=144389

FW1, Jahresbericht_2011_2012_Finance_Watch_Web-9.pdf – Adobe Reader

IFC, https://en.wikipedia.org/wiki/2008%E2%80%932011_Icelandic_finan
    cial_crisis (sighted on 13.02.2017)

IFCP, https://en.wikipedia.org/wiki/2009_Icelandic_financial_crisis_protests
    (sighted on 13.02.2017)

OSEC1, www.occupythesec.org/ (sighted on 19.02.2017)

OSEC2, https://en.wikipedia.org/wiki/Occupy_the_SEC (sighted on
    19.02.2017)

OSEC3, www.occupythesec.org/participate (sighted on 19.02.2017)

OT1, www.occupyto.org/ (sighted on 17.02.2017)

OT2, www.occupyto.org/contact-us/ (sighted on 17.02.2017)

OT3, www.occupyto.org/the-debt-resistors-operations-manual/ (sighted on
    17.02.2017)

NYC, Alternative Banking, http://alternativebanking.nycga.net (sighted:
    17.02.2017)

PBS, www.pbs.org.wgbh/frontline/film/money-power-wall-street/ (sighted:
    13.02.2017)

VC, www.venice.coe.int/webforms/documents/?pdf=CDL-PI(2015)020-e
    (sighted on 13.02.2017)

Wiki1, https://en.wikipedia.org/wiki/2009_G20_London_summit_protests
    (sighted on 22.02.2017)

Wiki2, https://en.wikipedia.org/wiki/2010_G20_Toronto_summit_protests
    (sighted on 22.02.2017)

WS, www.nycga.net/resources/documents/declaration (sighted on 13.02.2017)

WikiAttac, https://en.wikipedia.org/wiki/Association_for_the_Taxation_of_
    Financial_Transactions_and_for_Citizens%27_Action

WS IT, http://occupywallst.org/infotent/ (sighted on 13.02.2017 and
    17.02.2017)

11 | Money, State and Capital
The Long-Term Perspective

HELMUT KUZMICS

Among the many riddles that human beings may ask themselves, the problem of the wheel gauge of railway tracks is probably a minor one. The so-called Stephenson gauge of 1435 mm, starting in the 1830s in Britain, has apparently been successfully adopted nearly worldwide. Why? A popular, although probably wrong, hypothesis attributes this standard gauge less to Stephenson but to the width of Roman roads in Antiquity that depended on the size of a carriage and pair of Roman horses. What would we profit from such a long-term historical explanation? Apart from being true, it should be useful according to two further parameters: 1.) the regularity of a social pattern that we judge to be meaningful and important and 2.) the non-triviality of the explanation. If indeed the space required by two horses in a grey, distant past is still influential for the highly technicized present age, we are baffled. If we now deal with the peculiarities of the contemporary global web of inter- dependencies between 'states' and 'global mobile capital', the long-term perspective should satisfy both postulates too. But: How must the riddle to be solved look like? And: How far into the past should a processual view reach, to enable non-trivial findings?

The puzzle that meets the attention of economists, sociologists of finance and a critical public likewise consists of the coincidence of globally felt economic crises with massive changes in the distribution of income, wealth and jobs at the cost of the weaker throughout the marketized world. The former seem to be deeply rooted in the architecture of a global, but often uncoordinated system of finance, and the transformations it effects appear as uncontrolled or even uncontrollable like a disobedient nature rather than the work of humans. Quite apparently, these cannot be reduced to the 'endogenous' forces of the market alone, since states as political units are involved both in the causation of such crises and the attempts to cope with them. They control a territory and the legitimate means of physical violence of which they enjoy (or should enjoy) a monopoly. As such, states present a certain stage in the development of 'survival units' (Elias 2010a), as attack-and-defense units that control violence both within the confines of the state and, in form of armies, the means of violence against threats from outside, be it by states or non-state actors. This dimension must clearly be called 'non-economic', even if economic aims are pursued.

How far back into the past we should now direct our attention, to explain present, actual structures and processes in a non-trivial way, is not easy to tell. There is, for instance, a certain consensus between commentators of the great financial crisis since 2007/08 that we can trace back its origins to a sequence of events and measures starting at least in the United States of the early 1970s (Davies 2017). It was then that the limited gold standard of the US currency was abandoned and the system of fixed exchange rates replaced through markets and bond-traders. Both can be also seen as a consequence of the American war effort in Vietnam and the related increase of US national debt, that is, of mass-violence exerted by the state against another state. With this move, though, the state as survival unit lost control over money. The result meant also a shift in the function of money from being predominantly a means of exchange to money as credit; the process of money creation by credit was of course not new, but has changed its scale.

This change in money's role also signifies a transformation from its function mainly in the present, to another by linking past and present with an uncertain future. While earlier forms of money coined of gold or silver put strict limits to credit, state-guaranteed money or credit-created money allows for an enormous multiplication of the volume of money; between 1960 and 2010, the amount of money (US dollars) M1 in circulation has risen by the thirteen-fold; near-money even by the factor of 73 (Postberg 2013: 135). Part of this history and the pre-history of the global crisis of today was apparently (or allegedly) the failure of Western states to combat unemployment with fiscal means, by creating demand through state-indebtedness. The resulting 'stagflation' led to the new 'monetarist' philosophy according to which it became more important to fight inflation than unemployment, serving thus the interests of capital-owners rather than those of the non-propertied working classes. A period of absolutely high interest-rates (in the United States in March 1980, an interest-rate of 20 per cent

formed an all-time high),[1] was followed by the aim imposed on the
Federal Reserve Bank and other central banks to squeeze inflation to a
minimum in an apolitical, as neutral as possible way (Davies 2017: 19).
What followed was a credit crunch, a 'deliberately imposed monetary
famine' (Davies 2017: 20) that might have been as harmful to American
or British industry as the successful struggle of Thatcher and Reagan
against trade-unions and the outsourcing of manufacturing jobs to
the Third World.

Like a move in a chess-game that responds to the foregoing moves,
subsequent policy of the central banks that led to an enormous expansion of the volume of money cannot be understood without its previous history. What followed was the frenzy of the 1990s with its
corporate raiders, leveraged buyouts, 'merger mania' and speculative
bubbles (Blomert 2003) that became inseparable from the turn to an
unchecked share-holder capitalism. For this policy to become truly
global, the expansion of markets to the collapsing Eastern bloc and
the inferior Chinese state communism was fortunate. The hegemonial
struggle between the Soviet Union and the United States was but one
of many stages in the history of competition between rivalling survival
units (Elias 2010b). The actually, if rather unlikely 'peacefulness' of
the breakdown of the Soviet system (the empire crumbled away
without one single battle having taken place) belongs, thus, also to
the pre-history of the financial crisis 2007/08. Market penetration and
political integration to larger survival units did not coincide, though.
But within Western state-societies, dramatic changes occurred in
the power-balance between masses of salaried employees, and their
bosses who were now largely paid with shares instead of only fixed
earnings. Whereas in the mid-twentieth century the financial sector
generated profits that amounted to 10 per cent of all profits created by
American enterprises, their share rose to 40 per cent in the year 2012
(Nölke cited in Postberg 2013: 148).

The proximity to the process of money creation through the banking
system via credit seems to be responsible for this important shift in the
power-balance; a process that can be seen as largely unintentional in
its consequences and at least partly due to its autonomy relative to
the actions and intentions of those who depend on the whole process.
Elias (2012a) developed this idea in his multi-level 'game-models'

---

[1] www.tradingeconomics.com/united-states/interest-rate, accessed 4 April 2017.

and Postberg (2013) has elaborated this notion for an explanation of the present system of finance. A kind of neo-feudalism has emerged, with American CEOs' but also European bosses' earnings rising to unknown heights, and wages and salaries for most others declining. Two centuries of development towards more equality and 'functional democratization' (Elias 2012a) in the West seem to be reversed and replaced by what we might call 'functional de-democratization' (though not over the whole globe; people in some former colonial countries can become more powerful). Large groups of normal earners in traditional industrial societies have lost their bargaining-position and have become exchangeable; those profiting from mobility (notably from mobile capital) have gained.

In this unplanned dynamic, states and supra-state political units are not able to integrate and control as a supreme level of regulation the differentiating forces of the financial system that accompanied the new global division of labour in the real economy, although non-economic factors like wars and other hegemonial struggles between survival units created also new paths for the further development of markets. The acceleration and better timing of many economic processes enabled by the internet also led to new problems of control, as it is always the case when a non-linear dynamic poses challenges of a new qualitative kind.

But what do we now gain in addition to these insights by adopting a long-term perspective that transcends the last four, five or seven decades by extending the horizon to several centuries and that would help to explain the peculiar trend sketched above? Norbert Elias, who consequently advocated this view on the social by criticizing the 'Retreat of Sociologists into the Present' (Elias 1987) for its categorial mistakes thoroughly, has also formulated some methodological postulates. In his magnum opus *On the Process of Civilisation* (Elias 2012b), there are several: The emotional and bodily experience of human beings in civilizing processes cannot be separated, as 'psychogenesis' from their 'sociogenesis' in processes of state formation and division of labour, no more than two sides of a coin. Later stages build on earlier ones, although in this process, tradition might be combined with innovation. State and war are of no less importance than economy or knowledge. Many processes defy the intentions of those who originated them and produce unintended consequences that can found a new stable social order nevertheless. Even accidental events in their entanglement can create, thus, a so-called path-dependence (not Elias's term) of further social processes.

Social environments of a certain duration can shape relatively stable structures of personality that become visible from the outside as specific forms of 'social habitus'. The habitus of a warrior, courtier or merchant in its relative rigidity can become an explanatory determinant for the adaptability to faster social processes. The respective length and duration of long-term processes we have to assume, for explanatory purposes, always depend on the puzzle we want to solve and on the non-trivial contribution to existing explanations. In the *Process*-book, it was the discovery that a lot of the manners and mores still existing today can be better explained by pointing to their absolutist-courtly pre-history and less to their roots in the working bourgeoisie. The former's share in shaping the affective household of human beings living in present state-societies had been unduly neglected.

The historical argument implied here has two forms: explanation by indicating historical precursors or by finding historical parallels. Reconstructing the historical causal chain can, thus, shed sociological light on hidden social regularities that are erroneously taken for granted, by pointing to their origins in structures quite different from today. This applies, for instance, to the peacefulness experienced in the inside of modern state-societies comprising millions or hundreds of millions of human beings, compared with a more violent, anarchic past of the medieval feudal system with its dominant warrior-class. We take the absence of internal violence as a matter of course; only conditions in states torn by civil war and terror remind us of its non-triviality. The integrative and controlling force of states replacing smaller warring fiefdoms or tribes arose in a long, slow process with many setbacks.

The long-term history of the relationship between money, state and capital is now nearly as extensive as the history of modern society itself. Therefore, the following three examples only serve illustrative purposes for specific questions:

1. How can historical, processual analysis help better to understand uncertainty as it is generated by the contemporary global financial system – as un-rulability of the future via unlimited expansion of credit?

2. To what extent does the history of war and state formation provide a framework to complement our understanding of these seemingly purely economic problems?
3. Can the notion of a 'social (or national) habitus' related to the handling of money and financial capital, and resulting from historical differences in state formation be fruitful?

1.) Glancing over the history of money and credit, we see that uncertainty and fear of economic loss related to the institutional ways of handling money often surmounted that experienced in war and social unrest. This concerns all forms of money: 'Full money', metal money with gold or silver as guarantee for its value, was often threatened by inflation as a consequence of the permanent reduction of its silver or gold content. Massive inflation occurred, for instance, under the Roman Emperors Valerian and Gallienus during the crisis of the empire in the third century AD (cf. Omlor 2014: 13). In spite of the guarantees emperor and state tried to provide for the acceptance of money ('guaranteed money' replacing the reliance on the metal value of money), the resulting inflation became the central factor for the transformation of state demands from money to payment in kind or personal service (Millar 1966: 244). In the middle-ages, a counterfeiter's right hand used to be cut off (Borst, 1979: 383, who edited an original source from Pavia written in Latin 1027), according to regulations imposed and sanctioned by royal authority. But there were also always periods of general inflation of money for which princes themselves were responsible (Le Goff 1965: 285, who mentions Philip the Fair). Le Goff quotes Gilles le Muisit, the abbot of St. Martin in Tournai, who died in the year 1348:

Finances are dark and clear to no one
They rise and drop, one does not know what to do.
If one thinks to gain, the opposite is true. (My own translation, H.K.)

Not only were the poor massively hit, but also the landed warrior-nobility; their reactions to inflation led to revolts, pogrom-like persecution of Jews and the expropriation of bankers and rich religious orders (the Knights Templars). In a slow process, kings asserted their authority over feudal princes exactly because they could more and more rely on money revenues from urban merchants and craftsmen. As Elias (2012b) has shown, the centripetal process reversing feudal centrifugalism was based on money to finance superior armies; but for a long time to come, city-states, feudal princedoms and rising dynastic states coexisted without a clearly defined monopoly of the supply of money. Maximum insecurity was, of course, caused by war, not only for property, but for life and limb. Centuries later, during the Thirty-Years-War, armies were pre-financed privately before taxes could be levied 'by irrationally archaic methods and which never came in as they had been precalculated' (Mann 1978: 357; my own translation, H.K.). Credit not only helped to equip an army of 100,000 men, it also ruined the Dutch banker De Witte and drove him to commit suicide as he was incessantly persecuted by his terrified creditors. There is a striking contrast between the solidity of a baroque abbey from the seventeenth century, the feeling of security and silence that it generates, and the chaotic, frivolous character of a money business dealing with millions, even billions according to the value of these sums today. That wars are able to overstrain and even ruin state finances is nothing new. In this case, though, it was the private banker who was shipwrecked by a new kind of financial instrument related to an extremely risky attempt of taxation when even the imperial army to be raised was still not an army drafted by the state, but rather of mercenaries recruited by private entrepreneurship.

What we now call a 'state' was, then, only a state in germ. In a similar way, there exist now supra-national councils, federations, coordinating international bodies, even central banks (like in the so-called Euro-zone) and regular meetings of the G-7, G-20, 'troikas' and so forth, that transgress nation-state borders without disposing of the sanctions-potential of the nation-state. Behind the most efficient sanctions that really hurt are still only the most powerful states and if they do not want to control their own citizens, not much can be done.

2.) On first sight, the current institutions of the international financial system with their hedge-funds, too-big-to-fail banks, and highly specu-lative derivatives do not seem to be related to critical junctures of the past in which warlike state-competition played an important role. But there are significant differences between the financial cultures of former sea-powers, like Venice and other Italian city-states, Holland, England, or the United States after 1945, and the economic cultures of contin-ental powers based on the legacy of mercantilism or cameralism. The pooling of risks characteristic of maritime trade and a preference for

free trade in general, stand against the principles of state-interference
and guidance from above that were effective in the dynastic states of
the Ancien Régime in Europe. 'Rhenish capitalism' with its corporatist
elements, where 'Industriebanken' interested in long-term development
of the firm play a dominant role alongside a controlling state (Blomert
2003: 181–188), can be regarded as opposed to shareholder-value
cultures based on the absolute dominance of the stock-exchange.

   If there really is a political choice between both models, proponents for
the one or the other should be aware of their long-term historical path-
dependence from foregoing processes. Both the varieties-of-capitalism
approach (Hall/Soskice 2001) and the notion of different 'welfare
regimes' (Esping-Andersen 1990) refer to the various fates that states
suffered in wars against each other. The so-called 'Bismarckian' régime
can be set –of course, not in a too simplifying way – against an 'Anglo-
Saxon' economic culture. Historical sociology on this subject goes from
Sombart's war-time polemic *Händler und Helden* (1915), Schmitt's
Land und Meer (1942), to Perry Anderson's (1974) analysis of the
transition from feudalism to absolutism, and to Tilly's (1990) reflection
on a thousand years of complex relations between coercion, capital and
European statehood.

   Persuasion is easier to bear than coercion, and the latter's proximity
to authoritarian rule makes this model unattractive. But 'nations in
arms' with conscripted armies also felt the pressure to include and
integrate the lower working classes into a caring state that functioned
for them as a 'survival unit'. Dependence on their contribution to the
war effort might have been a further aspect of 'functional democratization' (Elias 2012a) as a shift in the societal power-balance. The
victory of the maritime, Atlantic powers (and Pacific allies) was not
complete in the year 1945. The thrust of globalization that came from
the United States during the Reagan-era might have profited substantially from the geopolitical defeat of the Soviet bloc. The bipolar
geopolitical order turned temporarily into a more or less mono-polar
system, which might have helped not only the US-economic model to
triumph, but also to reduce the attractiveness of the European welfare
state as an alternative.

3.) Social long-term processes produce relatively long-lasting institutions as well as rather stable forms of a social habitus, encompassing several generations. If it is the (nation-)state that provides the

corresponding mints to coin human affects and affect-controls with the means to direct them on a particular course, the result will be a 'national habitus'. We can, thus, still detect the traces of a 'gentlemanly code of behaviour' in forms of English national character today, mixed and alternating with a more market-oriented, middle-class canon of Puritanism (Kuzmics/Axtmann 2007). Elias, in his *Studies on the Germans* (2013), maintained that elements of a Dutch national character can still be deduced from the unique long period when groups of 'burghers' and not landed noblemen dominated in Dutch society. Their more peaceful, mercantile models of behaviour can be regarded as opposed to the more military codes of 'command and obey' of a Prussian-dominated Germany. Even if we should not underrate the welfare state-oriented counter-movement (Mennell 2007: 254–261) against the dominant state-hostile, capital- and risk-oriented elements in the American habitus, the outlines of something like an American national capitalism are certainly visible. China's capitalist success-story may also be partly related to ancient, pacifying codes that favour learning, diligence and the acquisition of wealth, as Max Weber earlier pointed out (Lee 1995).

But sometimes, it does not need such a long space of time to shape a lasting habitus. Coming finally back to the more actual processes discussed in the opening section of this contribution, also quite short-lived events can produce remarkable results. The German hyperinflation of the early 1920s has bred a collective trauma, as Taylor (2013) has shown in great detail. Until today, a German economic habitus places absolute priority on the stability of money, also after the financial crisis of 2007/08. German banks had taken part in the merry Casino-Banking of the 1990s and after, with no less zeal than their American counterparts, in fact not on the well-regulated home-market, but, for the time being, unpunished abroad. The following official German austerity policy – perceived as merciless in Greece – can be categorized either as rational precaution, or also as an unconscious reaction to the traumatizing experience of the hyperinflation nearly a hundred years ago. It caused the mass expropriation of the middle-classes and certainly contributed to the decivilizing thrust towards dictatorship, persecution and war. But today, no one really knows exactly enough whether this habitus of precaution is not, after all, perhaps quite rational, in the face of a galloping asset-inflation created by the unlimited expansion of the volume of money. But to decide this question will probably transgress the scope of an analysis as presented here.

References

Anderson, Perry (1974): *Lineages of the Absolutist State*, London: New Left Books

Blomert, Reinhard (2003): *Die Habgierigen. Firmenpiraten, Börsenmanipulation: Kapitalismus außer Kontrolle*, Munich: Verlag Antje Kunstmann

Borst, Arno (1979): *Lebensformen im Mittelalter*, Frankfurt/Berlin/Vienna: Ullstein

Davies, William (2017) 'The Big Mystique': Review of Ben Bernanke, The Courage to Act: A Memoir of a Crisis and Its Aftermath, 2015, and Mervyn King, The End of Alchemy: Money, Banking, and the Future of the Global Economy, 2016: *London Review of Books*, Vol. 39/3: 19–22

Elias, Norbert (1987): 'The Retreat of Sociologists into the Present', *Theory, Culture & Society*, Vol 4, Issue 2: 223–247

(2010a): *The Society of Individuals*, translated by Edmund Jephcott. German text edited by Michael Schröter; this volume ed. by Robert van Krieken [Collected Works vol. 10], Dublin: UCD Press

(2010b): *The Loneliness of the Dying and Humana Conditio*, ed. by Alan Scott and Brigitte Scott [Collected Works, vol. 6], Dublin: UCD Press

(2012a): *What Is Sociology?* translated by Grace Morrissey, Stephen Mennell and Edmund Jephcott; with a Foreword by Reinhard Bendix [Collected Works vol. 5], Dublin: UCD Press

(2012b): *On the Process of Civilisation*, ed. by Stephen Mennell, Johan Goudsblom and Eric Dunning [Collected Works vol. 3], Dublin: UCD Press

(2013): *Studies on the Germans*, German original edited by Michael Schröter; transl. by Eric Dunning and Stephen Mennell [Collected Works vol. 11], Dublin: UCD Press

Esping-Andersen, Gosta (1990): *The Three Worlds of Welfare Capitalism*, Oxford: Polity Press

Hall, Peter A. and David Soskice, (Eds.) (2001): *Varieties of Capitalism: The Institutional Foundations of Comparative Advantage*, Oxford: Oxford University Press

Kuzmics, Helmut, and Roland Axtmann (2007): *Authority, State and National Character: The Civilizing Process in Austria and England, 1700–1900*, Aldershot/Burlington: Ashgate

Lee, Eun-Jeung (1995): 'Max Weber und der "konfuzianische Kapitalismus"', in: *Leviathan*, Vol. 23, Issue 4: 517–529

Le Goff, Jacques (1965): *Das Hochmittelalter*. Fischer Weltgeschichte vol. 11, Frankfurt am Main: Fischer Taschenbuch Verlag

Mann, Golo (1978): *Wallenstein*. Special edition, Frankfurt am Main: S. Fischer

Mennell, Stephen (2007): *The American Civilizing Process*, Cambridge: Polity Press

Millar, Fergus (1966): Das Reich und die Krise des 3. Jahrhunderts, in: Millar, Fergus (ed.): *Das Römische Reich und seine Nachbarn. Die Mittelalterwelt im Altertum IV*, Fischer Weltgeschichte vol. 8, Frankfurt am Main: Fischer Taschenbuch Verlag, 241–250

Omlor, Sebastian (2014): *Geldprivatrecht: Entmaterialisierung, Europäisierung, Entwertung*, Tübingen: Mohr/Siebeck

Postberg, Christian (2013): *Macht und Geld. Über die gesellschaftliche Bedeutung monetärer Verfassungen*, Frankfurt/New York: Campus

Schmitt, Carl (1942): *Land und Meer. Eine weltgeschichtliche Betrachtung*, Leipzig: Philipp Reclam

Sombart, Werner (1915): *Händler und Helden: Patriotische Besinnungen*, Munich/Leipzig: Duncker & Humblot

Taylor, Frederick (2013): *The Downfall of Money. Germany's Hyperinflation and the Destruction of the Middle Class – A Cautionary History*, London: Bloomsbury Publishing

Tilly, Charles (1990): *Coercion, Capital, and European States, AD 990–1990*, Cambridge, Massachusetts/Oxford: Basil Blackwell

12 | Superdiversity, Exploitation and Migrant Workers

SHAUN WILSON

Introduction

World migration flows have reached record numbers (International Organization for Migration 2015), bringing with them many successful transitions and new beginnings. For many other displaced people, the experience of migration involves constant uncertainty, hardship and even tragedy. In the rich democracies, scholars have captured the changing patterns and complexities involved in migration and multiculturalism via the concept of *superdiversity*. These trends are rightly celebrated as a distinct accomplishment of a multicultural project of greater diversity and global openness. However, the experience of many migrants in the rich democracies is one of temporary work and limited visa rights (OECD 2016: 22–28, 33). Moreover, the same rich countries, most notably the United States, rely on undocumented workers (Fussell 2011). These developments therefore raise questions for social scientists about how transnational labour flows are implicated in emerging patterns of socio-economic inequality.[1]

I am grateful to Associate Professor Gaby Ramia of Sydney University and Professor Alan Morris of the University of Technology, Sydney. They introduced me to the concept of superdiversity, especially as it applies to international students and their housing. Those discussions have since encouraged me to offer this mostly conceptual contribution. I also benefited from papers presented at the Migrants@Work Research Group's Symposium on Migration and Work held at Sydney University on 6 February 2017.
[1] The International Labour Organization (ILO) estimates that there are around 150 million *international* migrant workers, with most migrating to high-income countries for employment (2015: xi–xiv). This ILO report also discusses relevant definitions of international migrant workers (2015: 25–34). Categories of *temporary* labour-based migration into OECD countries include working holidays, intra-company cross-national transfers, and seasonal work permits (OECD 2016: 22–28). In some countries, international students are also a large temporary migrant labour force (OECD 2016: 33). The ILO also points out that the size of the international undocumented migrant worker population is difficult to estimate (2015: 30).

Australia's situation illustrates my point. The last few years have witnessed a disturbing number of accounts of severe exploitation of migrant workers. Many of these workers were employed on the now-notorious temporary work visa scheme (called '457s'). The extent of these problems has caught a nation comfortable in its self-image as a tolerant land of the 'fair go' off-guard. Perhaps these discoveries represent something for Australians that the publics of other rich democracies have already come to tolerate. Indeed, migrants will risk exploitation at the bottom of the labour market in their struggle for resettlement and better lives.

This chapter considers the tension between the positive experiences of superdiversity and worrying signs of migrant exploitation coexisting with these developments. This problem remains largely out of sight for policymakers, and is not fully recognized in the migration literature. The first section deals with the concept of superdiversity. Despite its contribution, this concept is yet to encompass the range of experiences that can be brought under its umbrella. Here, I refer to evidence of the unequal treatment of migrant workers that can be traced to superdiverse environments. This evidence focuses on instances of severe exploitation of undocumented and temporary migrant workers. In the second section, I consider whether the frequently exploitative experiences of temporary migrant and undocumented workers involves anything distinct. After all, precarious *non-migrant* workers also experience exploitation. In addressing this question, the central task of the chapter becomes clear. It is to demonstrate how superdiverse environments help generate additional *mechanisms* through which migrant workers are exploited. In the third section, I draw on secondary literature from Australia, Singapore and the United States. The goal is to show how these mechanisms create conditions for 'super-exploitation'. These relate to how employers can 'leverage' visa arrangements, information asymmetries, financial dependence and transnational networks to exploit their workforces. The theme of this book is financial and capital mobility. My objective is to expand on this theme by highlighting *parallel* processes of mobility and inequality in the labour market.

Superdiversity, Hidden Inequalities and Migrant Workers

As a social science concept, superdiversity offers important potentials for sociological research (see Vertovec 2007). It does not merely account for the diversity found in the more multicultural societies of the rich democracies. It presents a new characterization of *radical diversity* that involves migrant populations achieving 'second-order' transformation in social interactions. This transformation is *multidimensional*, evident in hybrid identities, transnational networks spanning economies and cultures, and greater complexity in daily encounters (Meissner and Vertovec 2015: 545). Therefore, it is harder to characterize multicultural relations as involving 'linear' interactions between well-defined groups and long-established 'dominant' communities. Rather, interactions become multi-layered, and the challenge for social scientists is to represent adequately this newfound complexity.

Meissner and Vertovec are admirably committed to the critical development of their concept. They say: 'To be sure, like any sociological concept, superdiversity can and should always be critically interrogated, refined and extrapolated by way of fresh data' (2015: 542). However, the conceptual framing of superdiversity does not bring into concentrated focus one important feature of this deepening diversity. That feature is the *socio-economic inequality* that results from the stratification patterns unique to such environments. Highlighting this problem in no way denies the normative potential and real-world achievements of superdiverse communities. Instead, it draws the attention of scholars and policymakers to the unsurprising reality that growing complexity brings opportunities for highly unequal exchanges. One problem of superdiversity that has been already widely acknowledged is the absence of bridging social capital for migrants. This capital includes the vital resources of money, information, social support, social connections, and work opportunities. The scarcity of bridging capital is only one potential drawback of superdiverse complexity. Moreover, this problem is unavoidably bound up with the deeper problem of exploitation arising out of precarious work highlighted in this chapter.

Vertovec's (2007) original account of superdiversity offers clues to the *sources* and *generative mechanisms* of inequalities present in such environments. These include social stratification processes involved in differential migration statuses as well as migrant reliance on transnational networks. A more recent restatement of the superdiversity concept by Meissner and Vertovec makes *migration status* central to their conceptual work. They argue that: 'appreciating these channels and statuses is necessary for understanding the combined workings of multidimensional patterns on outcomes of socio-economic inequality' (2015: 547).

Here, we can add 'flesh to the bones' of this description. As we shall see, the *conditions* of migration (i.e. time, visas, rights) are implicated in severe forms of migrant inequality. These inequalities can be traced to coercive work contracts, curtailed mobility, surveillance from authorities and dependency on networks. Superdiverse environments are shaped by more than systems of law, communication, and finance. They are structured *socio-economically*, by employer strategies arising out of the availability and circumstances of migrant workers.[2] By identifying specific mechanisms used by employers to exploit migrants, we can appreciate how superdiversity contributes to inequality. Most examples highlighted here refer to exploitative practices derived from *temporary* migration status or *undocumented* status. However, clearly, these practices might apply more widely. International students, for example, are an important temporary migrant labour force in countries like Australia and others.

Exploitation, 'Superexploitation' and Migrant Workers

In what sense might the treatment of migrant workers in rich democracies be considered exploitative or even 'super-exploitative'? One response, drawing on many positive experiences of migrants, might rationalize 'instances' of exploitation as outliers or situations that migrants eventually overcome. However, such a response would miss important characteristics of superdiverse environments that promote exploitation, particularly in the workplace. Moreover, the experience of exploitation (in the broadest sense) is not confined to work. The disadvantage of some migrants leads to unequal treatment in other domains such as housing, and in relations with authorities.

The idea of exploitation in the social sciences is closely identified with Marxist analyses of capitalist labour markets. But it also features, as Erik Olin Wright suggests, as a 'shadow' in the labour market analyses offered by Max Weber in various places in his writings (Wright 2002: 839). The idea also resonates in liberal considerations of how illiberal 'injustices' emerge in these markets (see Little 2012; Freeman 2007: 114; Wilkinson n.d.). Moreover, the public invokes the idea of exploitation in clear instances where the strong take *unfair*

---

[2] Although chapter focuses exploitation of migrant workers *at work*, these workers also experience higher rates of unemployment.

advantage of the weak. Subsequent outrage provokes criticism, investigation, and demands for remedy.

The Marxist theme of exploitation, however, has distinct analytical advantages. It is a coherent explanation of how profits are realized by exploiting the labour power of wage-earners in capitalist enterprises. This coherence relates to the theory's identification of the *conditions*, *relations* and *mechanisms* that make exploitation possible (see Wright 2000: 10–16). The theory also insists that exploitation is *systemic* and, therefore, unavoidably central to employer strategy. In these respects, such a concept of exploitation overlaps with moral considerations about fairness and justice. Nevertheless, it applies more widely than exceptional instances – that is, to those isolated exploitative practices that invoke public outrage. The point here is that theory should acknowledge that exploitation is pervasive and structural. For liberals, this requires (at the very least) identifying the *wider* forces that tear away at 'just' social contracts.

In claiming that superdiverse environments contribute to worker exploitation, we cannot avoid an obvious question. Do vulnerable migrant workers experience anything different to other workers, especially disadvantaged ones? Two ways of responding to this question seem possible. The first proposes that migrant workers experience *more often and more intensively* the harsh features typical in low-wage work. Such experiences include informal or semi-formal employment, long hours, tyrannical employers, shorter contracts, and unpleasant jobs. Viewed this way, the exploitative experiences of migrant are not qualitatively different from those of other wage-earners. Rather, they are distributed unevenly to the disadvantage of migrant workers as a category.

The second response proposes that temporary migrant workers experience *qualitatively different* labour market experiences that amount to greater exploitation or even 'super-exploitation'. Broadly, the concept of super-exploitation captures those employer efforts to extract 'super' profits. These efforts might be aimed at either workers in low-status *social* locations or workers in the periphery – or both. Such efforts involve reducing wages and conditions to levels below those experienced by other workers, even below subsistence levels. Employers frequently seek out 'global opportunities' that involve socio-political and socio-technical conditions that produce super-profits. Instances include those low-paid and intensively employed workforces who live in developing countries. There, work can be unsafe and poorly regulated, unions non-existent, and police forces oppressive. Workers also may have fewer alternatives to the jobs available.

Even in rich countries, super-exploitation might involve situations where employers rely on *social* inequalities (even divisions) to extend profits. For example, feminists see patriarchal norms at work and in the family as enabling the super-exploitation of women. Theorists of racial inequality point to discriminatory practices at work that deny racial minorities of equal opportunity and pay. However, Wright sees some risk where these analyses become 'functionalist' explanations for why such social divisions arise more generally. Social inequalities are perpetuated by forces that operate *independently* of any advantage that the *economically* powerful might derive from them (see Kirby 2001: 10–11 [citing Wright]).

How might we capture, then, the role of employers in searching out super-profits? Clearly, employers are constantly seeking *opportunities* and *mechanisms* to generate profit – legal, technical, organizational, institutional, global, and extra-legal. Accordingly, employer strategy can be conceptualized as ranging from *opportunistic* through to *activist*. In the former, employers 'exploit' existing institutional, organizational and legal arrangements or even social inequalities to make profits. In the latter, employers actively pursue legal reforms or strategies like offshoring, and deunionization. And, in some instances, they consciously contribute to social tensions.

Given this characterization, we must therefore ask whether super-diverse environments provide *new* mechanisms in the chase for profit. In general terms, the prevalence of temporary migrant and undocumented work in rich countries provides grounds to suspect that opportunities for exploitation are changing. This possibility is not lost on researchers in the area of neo-dependency theory where super-exploitation is a recurrent theme. Valencia observes: '[super-exploitation] is no longer a tendency exclusive to the dependent economies, but one which, with the globalization of capital and the structural and superstructural processes that accompany it, will become generalized into ever less regulated labor markets and processes in the developed countries, affecting increasingly broad segments of the working class in those countries' (2014: 537).

The challenge for the rest of this chapter, then, becomes clear. The object is to identify those qualitatively *different* mechanisms for exploitation that can be realistically identified with superdiverse environments. This presentation only offers an initial encounter with the tasks associated with this challenge. A revised *heterodox* account of exploitation would require fuller integration of Marxist concepts with contributions from wider social science.

To reiterate – in many instances, the mechanisms of exploitation involved with migrant and non-migrant workforces are the *same*. It is now common to hear people describe as 'wage theft' those instances where employers deny workers their entitlements (see Fussell 2011). However, my focus here is on those *specific* mechanisms that superdiverse environments contribute to the analysis of exploitation. These include:

1. The threat of visa revocation or deportation for illegal residency;
2. Real (or perceived) employment immobility;
3. The reliance on 'networks of exploitation', to use Cranford's (2005) term and
4. The severe isolation from social networks that produces information and 'resources for contention' – i.e. voice and representation.

Some of the consequences of these mechanisms discussed here include:

1. The lowering of the 'reservation wages' of migrant workers;
2. The deunionization of existing workforces;
3. The creation of dependent sub-industries that rely on and reinforce exploitative temporary migration.

The remaining content develops an account of these mechanisms and their consequences. It does so by surveying the literature on migrant workers and their vulnerabilities at work. Examples drawn on here are from Australian, Singaporean and American (US) case studies, noting that these experiences frequently resemble those faced by workers elsewhere.

The Threat of Deportation

It is widely understood that labour contracts help define both the range and limits of 'acceptable' exploitation of workers. Short-term contracts, or onerous contract conditions, produce a range of responses from workers. These include greater effort to prove one's 'worth' to an employer to anxious efforts to 'survive' the job market. As I pointed out earlier, poor, poorly-skilled, or poorly-resourced migrant workers disproportionately encounter such standard conditions in labour contracts. One *additional* mechanism of exploitation is the power of employers to assert control over workers via the conditions of migration itself (i.e. visas, right to work).

A 2015 example from New South Wales featured by the Australian Broadcasting Corporation (ABC) highlights this problem. The news report detailed the plight of underpaid and poorly housed Filipino men. The workers, the report notes, are like many temporary migrants. They migrate for not only decent and stable employment, but also the promise of permanent resettlement. These migrants worked in wheat processing, but were 'sent home' after a dispute with the employer 'over their pay rate'. (Taranto 2015). As temporary workers, these workers were not entitled to the 'social wage' available to Australian workers (Medicare, etc.). However, their most serious problem was not the lack of access to health care. The journalist explains: 'they were promised $27 an hour, but after having thousands of dollars in "fees" unlawfully deducted from their wages, they're only receiving a little over $9 an hour' (Taranto 2015). She also notes that these workers 'were working 11-hour days, with only one day off a month', and 'until recently, 25 of them were living in a three-bedroom house; the queue for the shower started each morning at 4am' (Taranto 2015).

As observers of migrant situations are aware, these experiences are almost unremarkably common. However, what is important to recognize here is that this particular case of exploitation only became known because a trade union intervened. Their investigations traced the complex employment arrangements of these workers to a far-off Taiwanese labour hire firm (Taranto 2015). As the senior trade unionist involved told the ABC: '[this 457 visa] places workers in inherently vulnerable circumstances and means that often their tenure in the country is tied to their continued employment' (Taranto 2015). He added: '[this] gives employers enormous power and sadly we often see that power being exploited' (Taranto 2015).

The fact that residency status can depend on meeting the conditions of employment – as determined by employers – means that workers are well aware of the risks in exercising a voice. In turn, it makes sense that workers facing such circumstances lower (what economists call) their 'reservation wages' (see, for example, Falk et al. 2006) and tolerate greater exploitation. Fussell extensively documents these threats operate in her study of undocumented Latino day-labourers in New Orleans. She writes: 'Latino migrants typically chose to accept their wage losses when employers threatened them rather than try to make their case with the police' (Fussell 2011: 608). As we shall see later, toleration of exploitative conditions is made worse when workers also owe money to migration agents and labour hire companies.

Singapore is another high-income country whose wealth depends on an exploitative system of temporary labour migration. Authors Harrigan, Koh and Amirrudin (2017) note that low-wage migrant workers now make up an astonishing 27 per cent of the Singapore's workforce. They face conditions worse than in most rich democracies but that are better than in the Gulf States. Nonetheless, they identify the role of the *threat of deportation* as critical to Singapore's low-wage regime. The author state: 'Job insecurity and lack of bargaining power manifest amongst migrant workers in Singapore as a particular vulnerability to threats of deportation because the sponsorship system gives employers significant discretion over a worker's visa status' (Harrigan et al. 2017: 512).

The authors go on to investigate empirically the impact of the threat of deportation on the wellbeing of these workers. Such threats were commonly made *after* employees became involved in workplace conflicts with their Singapore-based employers over workplace injuries or low pay. The threat of deportation not only enforced work discipline. The authors found that such threats were contributors to poor mental health, *independent* of reports of injury and poor pay (Harrigan et al. 2017: 519).

Networks of Exploitation

Scholars focused on superdiversity stress the importance and benefits of *transnational* migrant networks (Vertovec 2007; Meissner and Vertovec 2015). Migrants do not merely *leave* their countries of origin but continue extensive interactions with their homelands. As we shall see, such interactions are not exclusively focused on travel or the flows of finance, goods and communication.

There is an understandable emphasis in the literature on the value of migrant networks in ameliorating transitions and mobility. However, the literature has increasingly recognized the potential for these networks to transmit harmful obligations and risk. Either way, these chains of interaction help demonstrate how migrant workers 'act' in embedded contexts. A focus on networks also adds to the ability of social scientists to explain new patterns of inequality.

In her account of undocumented Latino cleaners (janitors) in the city of Los Angeles, Cranford (2005) highlights challenges for conventional accounts of migrant social networks. To be sure, these networks are crucial for finding work, for preserving identity and connectedness, and for promoting social mobility. However, Cranford shows that these networks also serve as conduits for the exploitation of their memberships via both strong and weak ties. Drawing on empirical data, Cranford argues that migrant recruitment networks for LA cleaners were actually an efficient way of retaining a low-wage workforce. Networks were used to recruit workers, who were 'tried out' for a period of 'training' that was little more than unpaid work (Cranford 2005: 388). The same networks were used to recruit undocumented workers whose fragile migration status was threatened as a way to enforce work discipline (Cranford 2005: 388; see also Fussell 2011). In one instance, fear of deportation was a resource for an employer determined to replace a unionized workforce with a compliant one (Cranford 2005: 389).

Cranford also points out how the 'function' of migrant networks changes – depending on background circumstances. The implication here is that networks are mechanisms to channel the benefits and the *costs* of industrial change, particularly where employers seek to maintain profits when economic conditions worsen. When the cleaning industry hit rough times, the 'closure' of migrant networks did not protect against hardship. As Cranford observes: 'rather than producing upward mobility, exclusionary closure was part of a downgrading process' (2005: 393). However, the same networks enabled solidarity as well, where union organizing strategies were able to harness these pre-existing alliances (Cranford 2005: 393–395).

The Situation of Co-Ethnic Exploitation

Cranford's study also illustrates clear examples of what Velayutham (2013) and others call co-ethnic exploitation. By this, we mean exploitative strategies developed *within* the boundaries of an ethnic group that depend on *community-specific* resources available to entrepreneurs. Certainly, exploitative practices involving migrant workers go well beyond the boundaries of the pursuit of advantage within migrant communities. Nonetheless, a focus on co-ethnic exploitation further illustrates how vulnerabilities emerge from community networks. Velayutham's qualitative study of the range of experiences of temporary work migration by Indian nationals to Australia advances our understanding. He notes: 'the pattern of ... "co-ethnic exploitation" surrounding issues of agents, debt-bondage and workplace exploitation emerged very strongly. This typically involved an employer, manager and/or agent of co-ethnic background leading the exploitative practices' (2013: 356).

Velayutham describes how networks drive both information flows available to migrants as well as the set of expectations and obligations attached to employment. Clearly, migrant workers bring a set of hopes and expectations of succeeding in the host country. However, these are shaped by social ties that involve both information hierarchies and emotion-chains (Randall Collins's term) that can be exploited. For example, the author writes of the 'shame' of 'failing' in Australia for Indian nationals keen to 'make it' outside India (Velayutham 2013: 358). Co-ethnic employers can exploit 'information asymmetries' by setting pay and conditions to the standards of the country of *origin*. Community-level 'trust networks' (Velayutham's term) are also conduits for other kinds of control. These networks may transmit untruthful information (often inserted into labour contracts) that identify the deportation consequences of leaving a job (Velayutham 2013: 358). In sum: 'employers have the advantage of being fully aware of the background situation and vulnerability of these workers and therefore know where to exploit their trust and how far they can "push" the exploitation' (Velayutham 2013: 357).

The examples mentioned above give a clear sense of how transnational networks reach beyond mundane family and social ties. The economic agents that structure these networks – labour hire companies, migration agents and brokers, and transnational businesses – profit from migration. In many of the examples of migrant worker exploitation, agents and labour hire companies have an interest in the maintenance of exploitative activity. Workers report owing large sums of money to these intermediaries. In turn, these obligations shape how vulnerable migrants respond to difficult circumstances and remain trapped in them. Ruthless pressure to lower costs by employers is another factor in accounting for rent-seeking recruitment networks.

A report by US researchers on recruitment practices in the Gulf-country construction industry implicates cutthroat competition for ever-lower wage costs. This pressure pushes recruitment costs onto workers who rely on parasitic agents that are 'inflating fees at almost every step of the recruitment process' (Segall and Labowitz 2017: 30).

Conclusion

This chapter is primarily concerned with the 'mobile' migrant workforces that are reshaping experience and patterns of employment in rich democracies. Postindustrial societies with ageing populations need workforces in agriculture, care, retail and food services, IT and construction to directly service their needs. Moreover, employers and states are looking to keep costs contained. The result will be continued pressure to obtain labour flexibility through immigration as well as new patterns of inequality in the workplace. Therefore, it is increasingly difficult to refer to labour as an 'immobile' factor of production or to ignore the 'hidden' impoverishment of some migrant workers in the rich world.

My goals in this short contribution have been twofold. The first goal has been to take up in a limited way the challenge of expanding the *critical range* of the concept of superdiversity. The features of socio-economic inequality coincident with these developments must be brought into the picture. In aiming at this, my account does not start from the premise that superdiversity is inherently unstable or remotely undesirable. On the contrary, superdiversity as a reality and as a concept identifies the practical and normative potentials of greater migration and diversity.

The second goal has been to consider whether the exploitation of migrants represents anything *qualitatively* different from that experienced by other workers. My method for determining this has been identify 'mechanisms of exploitation' unique to the experience of migration, as described in the literature. Deportation threats, information and resource asymmetries, and networked relationships all contribute to migrant vulnerability to exploitation. Processes of exploitation and super-exploitation underline the need for a revitalized heterodox social science that can critically account for these developments.

The policy implications are clear: nation-states should devise genuine, specific and enforceable legal protections for migrant workers as well as stronger paths to permanent resettlement and citizenship.

266   *Shaun Wilson*

References

Cranford, Cynthia J. (2005) 'Networks of Exploitation: Immigrant Labor and the Restructuring of the Los Angeles Janitorial Industry', *Social Problems* 52(3):379–397.

Falk, Armin, Fehr, Ernst and Zehnder, Christian (2006) 'Fairness Perceptions and Reservation Wages: The Behavioral Effects of Minimum Wage Laws' *The Quarterly Journal of Economics*, 121(4): 1347–1381.

Freeman, Samuel (2007) *Rawls*, London: Routledge.

Fussell, Elizabeth (2011) 'The Deportation Threat Dynamic and Victimization of Latino Migrants: Wage Theft and Robbery', *The Sociological Quarterly* 52(4): 593–615.

Harrigan, Nicholas M., Koh, C.Y. and Amirrudin, A. (2017) 'Threat of Deportation as Proximal Social Determinant of Mental Health amongst Migrant Workers', *Journal of Immigrant and Minority Health* 19(3): 511–522.

International Labour Organization (2015) *ILO Global Estimates of Migrant Workers and Migrant Domestic Workers: Results and Methodology*, International Labour Office, Geneva.

International Organization for Migration (2015) '2015 Global Migration Trends Factsheet', Global Migration Data Analysis Centre. Online: http://publications.iom.int/system/files/global_migration_trends_2015_factsheet.pdf (accessed 19 April 2017).

Little, Daniel (2012), 'Rawls and Exploitation'. Online: http://understanding society.blogspot.com.au/2012/04/rawls-and-exploitation.html (accessed 18 April 2017).

Kirby, Mark and Wright, Erik.O. (2001) 'An interview with Erik Olin Wright'. Online: www.ssc.wisc.edu/~wright/kirby_wright.pdf (accessed 18 April 2017).

Meissner, Fran and Vertovec, Steven (2015) 'Comparing Super-Diversity', *Ethnic and Racial Studies* 38(4): 541–555.

OECD (2016) *International Labour Migration 2016*, OECD Publishing, Paris. Online: http//:dx.doi.org/10.1787/migr_outlook-2016-en (accessed 18 April 2017).

Segall, David and Labowitz, Sarah (2017) *Making Workers Pay: Recruitment of the Migrant Labor Force in the Gulf Construction Industry*, New York University Stern Center for Business and Human Rights. Online: http://bhr.stern.nyu.edu/factsheet-contruction/ (accessed 18 April 2017).

Taranto, Claudia (2015) 'Workers Without Borders: The Rise of Temporary Migrant Labour'. Available at: www.abc.net.au/radionational/programs/earshot/the-rise-of-temporary-migrant-labour/6472368 (accessed 10 April 2017).

Valencia, Adrián Sotelo (2014) 'Latin America: Dependency and Super-Exploitation', *Critical Sociology* 40(4): 539–549.

Velayutham, Selvaraj (2013). Precarious Experiences of Indians in Australia on 457 Temporary Work Visas. *The Economic and Labour Relations Review* 24(3): 340–361.

Vertovec, Steven (2007) 'Super-Diversity and Its Implications', *Ethnic and Racial Studies* 30(6): 1024–1054.

Wilkinson, Will (n.d.) 'Occupy Wall Street and the Deradicalized Rawls', Big Think Website. Online: http://bigthink.com/the-moral-sciences-club/occupy-wall-street-and-the-deradicalized-rawls (accessed 18 April 2017).

Wright, Erik O. (2000) *Class Counts*, student edition, Cambridge University Press.

(2002) 'The Shadow of Exploitation in Weber's Class Analysis', *American Sociological Review* 67(6): 832–853.

(2015) *Understanding Class*, New York: Verso.

13 | The Bitcoin or the Reality of a Waking Dream

MASSIMO AMATO

Bitcoin is a fact and a symbol. Better, it is a blend of hyper-concrete technological facts and of abstract and self-referential visions. In this respect, it is a mirror of our times, and of the deeper meaning of the 'capital mobility' that characterizes them. I will try to describe the project in its constituent elements, so that its symbolism appears with the utmost clarity.

It all begins with an announcement, coming from no-where, and uttered by no-body: a pseudonymous author proposes an anonymous currency. The only thing we know is the date: in 2008, in the thick of the financial crisis, Satoshi Nakamoto (whoever this is) posts on the Internet an article titled *Bitcoin: A Peer-to-Peer Electronic Cash System.*

Indeed, the title itself says it all: Bitcoin is a system and method for issuing a *digital cash*, the bitcoin, which is 'anonymous as a bank-note, but safe and efficient as an electronic currency' (Amato and Fantacci 2016, 3). The 'payment system' designed by Nakamoto allows transfers that are as anonymous as immediate for any amount, from micro to large payments. 'Immediate' does not just mean that transfers are instantaneous, but also that *they are not mediated* by any third party. Nakamoto insists on this point, and advisedly, since it is the keystone of his 'vision': the system can allow 'any two parties willing to transact directly with each other without the need for a trusted third party' (Nakamoto 2008).

The explicit aim of the system proposed by Nakamoto is therefore the disintermediation of the banking system through the provision of an alternative accounting system capable of preventing the risk of double spending. Whereas the formal system of payments assigns this control function to central operators keeping on their books the accounts of all the actors, thus ensuring the uniqueness of the payment as well as the (potential) solvency of the payer, Nakamoto concocts a social network of exchangers in the form of a peer-to-peer network.

What makes possible this social network is a technical network that 'timestamps transactions by hashing them into an ongoing chain of hash-based proof-of-work, forming a record that cannot be changed without redoing the proof-of-work' (Nakamoto 2008). There is no centralised ledger anymore, because the system allows access to a *universal ledger*, which is distributed and open to all. These two combined characteristics mean that the 'truth content' of this ledger is not ensured by the reliability of an *identified* central third party, but by an anonymous process of validation of the payment blocks. The validations are obtained by competitive tendering, through competing operators called to solve complex computational problems. The competition is structured so that no attacker can control the system ('Central Processing Unit'), by thus falsifying payments: 'As long as a Majority of CPU power is controlled by nodes that are not cooperating to attack the network, they'll generate the longest chain and outpace attackers' (Nakamoto 2008). This non-cooperative but competitive *proof-of-work* is such that it makes payments recorded on the ledger definitive and non-modifiable: it forms 'a record that cannot be changed without redoing the proof-of-work'.

An algorithm run by the competition between computing operators replaces the third party. These same operators, with their computing activities, generate the money that will be used for payments – a process called 'mining'. The *bitcoin as a money* is, in fact, the currency in which the operators are remunerated for their validation work of *Bitcoin as a payment system*. The Bitcoin system allows payments *in only one currency*, the bitcoin, which is generated by the operation of the Bitcoin system itself.

Enthusiastic supporters of Nakamoto claim this conspicuous self-referentiality to be the achievement of a higher degree of freedom, that is, as a liberation from the control of a third party, which, by its monopolistic position, is always prone to arbitrariness. In particular, precisely because it has to prevent double spending, a banking third party is paradoxically put in a position to control the creation of money itself, thus triggering a process of monetary multiplication based on debt relations.

The mining activity of the computing operators cuts off this risk at the root. The semantic analogy between bitcoin mining and gold mining is not at all fortuitous. The extraction work (i.e. bitcoin mining) makes possible a currency that, even more than gold, cannot be duplicated through the fractional reserve banking system. As this duplication/multiplication work undermines in an inflationary way the monetary standard, Bitcoin is intended to provide an 'untouchable' (electronic-algorithmic gold)-standard.

The analogy with gold does not concern only the extraction, but also what is extracted, i.e., the fact that the bitcoin, like gold, is given in a finite amount, and cannot be made available indefinitely. The hyper-liberalist mistrust of fiat money receives here a high-tech answer. The bitcoin is programmed to be extracted in a given and unchangeable amount of 21 million bitcoins, which are divisible by 10^8 (the 'satoshi' represents the 'cent' in the Bitcoin system).

To sum up: what we are dealing with here is the junction of a potentially disruptive technology with an actually conservative monetary conception, linked to one another in such a way that it is difficult to imagine them separately.

Undoubtedly, this separation is what many people (including banks) are trying to obtain: the greater part of the investments that are currently being made in this field bet on the improvement of the blockchain technology *as such*, regardless of the currency. However, the fact remains that, (1) in order to keep in function the system of distributed ledgers that allows the peer-to-peer transactions, the proof-of-work needs to be remunerated with *an internal money* and (2) in order to function without third parties and *human decision-makers*, the system itself requires a finite amount of money – a feature which raises the question of how the 'proofworkers' will be paid once all bitcoins have been extracted.

This is not the place for forecasts on the bitcoin ability to establish itself as a new monetary standard. The immediate objection is, in fact, that we are still (too much) at the beginning. However, its factual marginality compared to the financial system as a whole (in April 2014, its capitalization was less than one thousandth the amount of money available in Euros, and in 2015 it was equal to 0.02% of the capitalization of Wall Street) cannot be used to argue the insignificance of the phenomenon. Which is essentially *a symbolic one*.

What we must look at attentively, is at what the bitcoin *wants* to be. To put it in a formula: the bitcoin aims at being the *final form of capital*, i.e. of the capital *uniquely defined* by its mobility, understood in turn as a uniform ubiquity, irrespective of any possible dynamics of the real economy and of social life.

The key idea is that with the bitcoin, *the debt is no longer* the source of money issuance. This is the case with central banks, but also with chartered banks and, finally, with 'shadow banks': entities that use 'large quantities of short-term debt to fund a portfolio of financial assets and that [are] not a chartered bank deposit' (Ricks 2016, 2).

However, it is the obsession, inherited from Hayek, against debt-money, and the even more Hayekian will to conceive money as that commodity which is endowed with the highest level of moneyness, that force Nakamoto to fix from the beginning the quantity of money without any possibility of variation. The only way to make bitcoin a *valuable thing* is to *establish* its scarcity in such a way that no third entity could ever alter it. This is what allows the peers using it to consider it as the object of their exclusive and unconditional property.

However, this very characteristic of the bitcoin, certainly much attractive until one simply wants to *hold* it, i.e. *not* to use it, makes the bitcoin extremely dangerous as soon as it comes into contact with the real economy, and has therefore to be used in real exchanges, i.e. *ceded*. A currency given in a fixed amount is, in fact, just like gold in limited supply, a structurally deflationary currency, in the sense that its value tends to increase with the amount of exchanges made in that very currency. Yet, this structural upward trend determines in its possessor, as a rational strategy, the decision *to postpone its use*, and therefore not to use it for real exchanges, and to *hoard* it.

It is a well-known fact: as the most rational strategy with the bitcoin is to hoard it in view of its increase in value (e.g. in terms of dollars or euros), the bitcoin is structurally affected by high volatility. So, one of the main characteristics of money, i.e. the stability of its purchasing power, is structurally undermined.

As a currency, bitcoin does not seem to be particularly well suited to serve the widespread and permanent network of exchanges that characterizes every real economy. One could argue, however, that its greater solidity as a hoardable asset makes it particularly suitable to serve not so much the present exchange (spending money to get consumption goods), but the *intertemporal exchange*, to finance real investments. Even here, however, we can make the same objection, based on the deflationary character of bitcoin. In fact, bitcoin is a currency that is systematically favourable to creditors, for reasons that are opposite to those for which inflation is a phenomenon that favours debtors. The fact however remains, that real investors are *debtors*, who, indebted for a *nominal* amount of bitcoin, run the risk of having to return this nominal amount, which however in the meantime has become much more expensive for them to obtain *in real terms*. The bitcoin unbalances and undermines a relationship that is already in itself very unstable and risky: the relationship between borrower and lender. Moreover, it unbalances it in favour of who is waiting to be paid in nominal terms, the creditor, and not of who actually makes the real investment, the debtor.

Not particularly useful for the instantaneous exchange of consumer goods, very dangerous in the field of capital goods, the bitcoin proves to be an ill-conceived currency, precisely because it is built as a pre-defined quantity. This structural feature of bitcoin has prompted the Bank of England to issue a very clear opinion, which is, indeed, a quite shareable one: 'In most existing digital currency schemes, the future path of supply is pre-determined and governed by a protocol that ensures that the eventual total supply will be fixed. This has the effect of removing any discretion from the determination of the money supply. This would pose a number of problems for the macroeconomy: for example, it could contribute to deflation in the prices of goods and services (and wages). Importantly, the inability of the money supply to vary in response to demand would cause likely welfare-destroying volatility in prices and real activity' (Bank of England 2014b, 6).

However, maybe bitcoin simply *is not* what it claims to be, i.e. *it is not a currency*; and Bitcoin based on the blockchain, which is undoubtedly an ingenious and effective system for transmitting encrypted information, *is*, properly speaking, *not a payment system*. Especially if 'to pay' means 'to repay a debt', namely 'to make peace' between creditor and debtor, thanks to a money capable of representing them *both*.

What is bitcoin if it is not a money? It is still the Bank of England which makes the point: 'beyond a general increase in public willingness to use and trust computing technology, interest in and the adoption of digital currencies appears to be driven by three key factors: ideology, financial return and the pursuit of lower transaction fees' (Bank of England 2014, 6).

If we exclude the transaction motive (since it is very likely that, once all bitcoins are mined, the reward of validators must rely on fees that, in regard to how the system works, would not be less expensive than the fees of a centralised payment institution), what remains is: *financial return* and *ideology*.

Now, this is a very interesting feature for the collective research that this book promotes, as the main characteristic of the bitcoin is *to merge the two motives*, without there being any way to distinguish one from the other. We may therefore put the following thesis: bitcoin is the quintessential mobile capital, and precisely because it *operationally* embodies its *ideological* claims, i.e. the claim of 'capital', as a social relation and way of thinking, to impose a univocal and uniform interpretation of the economic space.

The 'bitcoinian' obsession against the third party is a first way to see all that: the meaning conveyed by the term 'third party', in fact, is not simply the empirical meaning of 'manager of a centralised ledger', always on the brink of abusing his position ('quis custodiet custodes?'). It is a *symbolic* one: namely, it is the symbol of *a position of thirdness*. 'Thirdness' is a term introduced in English language by Charles Sanders Peirce. But we can use it to translate the French word 'Tiers', that by Alexandre Kojève indicates the crucial phenomenon for understanding the sense of law, namely the impartiality of the judging function, or the word 'ternarité' in Pierre Legendre. In Saussurian terms, we can express its sense as follows: thirdness is the element that *binds stably*, and gives meaning to, the relationship between a signifier and a signified, so that a chain of signifiers can develop. This Saussurian sense of thirdness is precisely what we find in Keynes when he speaks of the institutional nature of money, at the very beginning of his *Treatise on Money*. Given that money is at the same time money and money of account, what matters for monetary architecture is the relationship *established* between the two functions of unit of account and means of payment. This establishment is made by what Keynes calls 'the State'.

The criticism of the current third parties is empirically quite understandable, if we consider the fact that our present payment system is a public good (better, *a common*), and that at present the private banking system holds it hostage. However, Nakamoto's rejection of the third party is not only empirical. It is a *transcendental* one, because what is rejected is both the likelihood and the likeability of a shared rule of law in trade. Yet, we have to consider the consequences of this rejection. Indeed, the thirdness of the third *party* means that, in order to be really 'third', this *party* is deemed to be im-*partial*. If it is not, it is its position as a responsible third that allows the parties to a claim for a 'redde rationem villicationis tuae' (give an account of your management, Luke 16, 2).

An empirical abolition, like the disintermediation of banks made possible by Bitcoin cannot however be deemed a transcendental refutation. Who, or what, plays then the role of the impartial third in Bitcoin? What happens with Bitcoin is that, having abolished the banking third parties, their place becomes vacant, *and the algorithm takes the place*.

On pseudo-anarchist discourse about the algorithm as an instrument of liberation from power, we cannot go here into too much detail. But there is one thing that we need to see with some precision: in the anarcho-capitalist project of Bitcoin, the arbitrariness of the arbiter (which is always possible, but always correctable in principle) is replaced by the mechanical operation of the algorithm, not only for payments, but, in general, for the fulfilment of all the various obligations that enliven our social and economic relationships. 'Smart contracts' are in truth everything except contracts, because they shirk from the instance of negotiation and therefore of interpretation, in the name of automatic execution. The question now is: what kind of movement is regulated by the algorithm?

The discourse of Bitcoin is not only an extreme ideological position, but, as we said, a position that is fully consequent to the way in which the bitcoin is called to work, not as money *but as capital*. The volatility of Bitcoin is certainly a serious obstacle for considering it as a currency, and still a good argument for not giving up on third parties (see for example Haldane's alternative proposal to use the blockchain for electronic money issuance by a central bank[1]). But its *mobility* is instead a good reason to consider it as a particularly *pure* form of *capital*.

To understand how to understand this 'pureness', we can get help from Keynes. In Chapter 16 of his *General Theory* ('Sundry observations on the nature of capital'), we can read: 'It is much preferable to speak of capital as having a yield over the course of its life in excess of its original cost, than as being productive. For the only reason why an asset offers a prospect of yielding during its life services having an aggregate value greater than its initial supply price is because it is *scarce*' (Keynes 1973). In the real world of the real economy, what is productive is labour, assisted by instruments that, if there is no financial hindrance in their production, are produced to cover their cost.

---

[1] See Haldane and Qvigstad (2014)

In the capitalist world, instead, capital is identified with its (homogenous) yield. And the 'freedom of movement' is not the freedom of operators, who are simple functionaries of the capital, but of the capital itself. Behind Hayek, and his notion of money as the object of absolute property, that no debt-based inflationism should ever put in danger, we must learn to see Marx and his determination of money (Geld) in terms of *absolute value*. The capitalist wealth is money, and commodities are nothing but money. What we must see behind Nakamoto's obsessive search for a fully decentralised system of 'payments', is not the will to enforce the competitive freedom of exchangers in a real economy. What is at stake is *the freedom of capital*, which consists essentially in its freedom to be homogeneous to itself, i.e. to search without any hindrance its maximum yield, and therefore to tend asymptotically, thanks to competition, to a uniform rate of return.

Here lies the symbolic value of bitcoin. On this point, I would like to conclude by tying even more explicitly my conclusions to the research that animates this book.

Weber was right in arguing that, if there were to be a global 'empire', capitalism might not survive. What the logic of capital requires is not the 'universal homogeneous State' that Kojève was deducing from his Hegelian idea of law, but *a state of global homogeneity*. In this sense, capitalism's proper state is 'globalization' as an *indefinite* process, namely as process not hindered by any thirdness arrogating to itself the right *to set the end* of the process. Moreover, already by Hegel the *Aufhebung* of the State as the 'local' embodiment of reason, is not the Super-State, is not the community of states, but the *Weltgeschichte*, namely the 'global history', which is the history of the expansion of a *Weltmarkt* designed, says Marx, for the only commodity that really matters, i.e. for *money as capital*.

The bitcoin is a currency fully disembedded from social relations. In this sense, the concept of freedom embedded in the Bitcoin is not at all democratic. And indeed, from a symbolic point of view, the bitcoin says very clearly to what extent there is incompatibility between the need of capital for a totally homogeneous space of movement, and the need of 'citizens' to have a 'city'.

Dematerialized from a technological point of view, the bitcoin is notwithstanding a very 'heavy' currency, and for this reason a dangerous one from a political point of view. Being the money of the creditor, bitcoin is *perfectly antisocial*, precisely because it has no capacity to *lighten* that social relationship which is crucial to any economy, i.e. the relationship between debtors and creditors. To this end, the only adequate money is a money that is so *light* that it can *disappear* from the hands of both creditors and debtors. A money that, with its disappearance, can assure *thirdness*: the impartiality of that, which *mediates*.

But, as Keynes said in 1923, 'it is not easy, it seems, for men to apprehend that their money is a mere intermediary, without significance in itself, which flows from one hand to another, is received and is dispensed, and disappears when its work is done from the sum of a nation's wealth'. (Keynes 1971, 124)

References

Amato M, Fantacci L (2016), *Per un pugno di bitcoin*, Bocconi University Press

Bank of England (2014) 'Innovations in payment technologies and the emergence of digital currencies', *Quarterly Bulletin*, Q3, www.bankofengland.co.uk/publications/Documents/quarterlybulletin/2014/qb14q3digitalcurrenciesbitcoin1.pdf

(2014b) 'The economics of digital currencies', *Quarterly Bulletin*, Q3, www.bankofengland.co.uk/publications/Documents/quarterlybulletin/2014/qb14q3digitalcurrenciesbitcoin2.pdf

Haldane A, Qvigstad J (2014), 'The evolution of central banks: a practitioner's perspective', www.norges-bank.no/pages/100044/14_2_Haldane_and_Qvigstad_28_June_2014.pdf

Keynes, J M (1971), A Tract on Monetary Reform (1923), in *Collected Writings of John Maynard Keynes*, Vol. IV, London: Macmillan

(1973) *The General Theory of Employment, Money and Interest (1936)*, in *The Collected Writings of John Maynard Keynes*, Vol. 7, Macmillan, London

Nakamoto S (2008) 'Bitcoin: A Peer-to-Peer Electronic Cash System', https://bitcoin.org/bitcoin.pdf

Ricks M (2016), *The Money Problem: Rethinking Financial Regulation*, University of Chicago Press

14 Capital Mobility and the Fragmentation of Monetary Sovereignty

DAVID WOODRUFF

This brief essay discusses the way capital mobility – in particular, the tidal flows of capital into and out of emerging markets – may undermine an important aspect of monetary sovereignty: *legal* sovereignty over money.[1] Contemporary states virtually universally claim, and often achieve, a monopoly on the legal definition of acceptable means of payment on their territory. As a means of payment, money is what is needed to clear a legally specified obligation, such as a tax obligation or a formally contracted debt. Knapp's famous assertion that money is "a creature of law" encapsulated a deep insight into this significance of the weaving of money into the integument of legally defined transactions constitutive of modern capitalism. A state unable to maintain the capacity to insist that what it defines as money plays these legal roles has lost monetary sovereignty.

In order to understand the circumstances in which a state can lose monetary sovereignty, a simple incentive-based analysis of the circumstances in which legal orders successfully structure behaviour in voluntary transactions is helpful. As I have argued elsewhere, one can usefully distinguish two incentive patterns that prompt individuals to conform to rules. In one pattern, incentives are very general, applying with identical effect to large numbers of individuals. Such incentive patterns arise from what game theorists term a "co-ordination game," in which what makes sense for each individual to do depends on what other individuals are doing. Common examples are choices of language or driving on a particular side of the roadway. Individuals match their choices to the prevailing ones because there are unavoidable costs to doing otherwise – in these examples, frustrated communication

---

[1] For a longer and more general discussion, and for references on empirical matters mentioned below, see Woodruff (2013).

or roadway accidents. Such incentive patterns can be referred to as "broadcast orders" because they affect large populations identically.

The prevalent use of money is often analysed in this vein. Someone who sells goods or services for a buyer's money relies on being able to spend that money in her turn for something she needs, or will eventually need. She is relying on the fact that others will similarly rely on money. Money's value to the individual results from a prediction that others will find it valuable, a prediction that is accurate just to the extent that others are making parallel predictions. Money's value emerges as a joint, self-fulfilling prophesy, much like the expectation that drivers will all stay on the same side of the road or that a particular language is most likely to be understood in a particular place. In standard definitions of money's functions, money serves as a medium of exchange when someone uses it as an intermediate step facilitating the conversion of something she has to sell into something she wishes to buy, and a store of value when it is held in anticipation of a more distant transaction. The difference in time horizons notwithstanding, in both of these cases, money's value is general to some community that shares the expectation that it will be valuable.

However, conformity to rules – including, as we shall see, conformity to rules specifying the means of payment for legal obligations – may also derive from incentives of a radically different pattern. Some rules create incentives that impinge on different individuals in different ways, or differ across different circumstances. For instance, consider rules against theft. In addition to different individual moral assessments on theft, there are a vast variety of circumstances in which the costs and benefits of theft differ. Walking the streets of London early in the morning one can find boxes of vegetables lying unguarded on the pavement outside restaurants, awaiting the arrival of staff. Deliveries of diamond rings to jewellers, however, never take this form. The incentives facing potential thieves are obviously quite different across these cases. These cases illustrate one reason for this, namely, the extent to which potential victims of theft feel the need to guard against it. An additional factor is the prospect of punishment for violation of the rules against theft, but this prospect, too, will differ enormously depending on circumstances. If it is the case that rules against theft are generally observed, this is the result of the calculations of potential thieves applied to these widely variegated individual circumstances in light of different incentives and prospects for successful enforcement.

In this light, it is entirely unsurprising that even in states held to have a strong "rule of law," there are areas in which theft is rampant (wage theft from low income or informal workers, for instance) and others in which it is all but unknown (early morning vegetable deliveries). It seems appropriate, therefore, to speak of "cellular order" in such cases to emphasise the local character, or potentially local character, of the relevant incentives and decisions.

In ordinary times in contemporary capitalist countries, the idea of a challenge to the legal sovereignty of a nation-state over the definition of money seems fanciful. Officially issued money is in general and effectively exclusive use as a means of payment (i.e., as a means of clearing legally specified obligations). Nonetheless, this general conformity to the rules defining means of payment reflects the patterns of incentives characteristic of cellular order, rather than broadcast order. Someone who uses money to pay a legally specified obligation, such as a tax or a debt, is doing so not based on an expectation that some broad community shares a prediction about money's value, but because she expects that delivery of the money will clear the obligation and forestall any coercion designed to enforce it. If there were another way to clear the obligation, the costs and benefits of employing it could be considered. In particular, creditors may be more or less capable of insisting on payment, the court system may be more or less capable of enforcing debts, and the tax authorities may be more or less capable of demanding payment in official money.

Let us consider an example, drawn from Argentina during the waning days of its peso-dollar peg in the late 1990s and early 200s. During this period, when the country was suffering from recession and deflation, a number of Argentina's provincial governments found they had insufficient revenues to pay the salaries of state workers. They reacted by paying salaries in *bonos* – locally issued bonds with a face value denominated in pesos. Importantly, these were not IOUs, a promise to pay workers pesos at a later date. Instead, provincial governments encouraged their use in grocery stores, in part by promising to accept them in payment of local taxes. The provincial governments sought to clear their legal obligation to pay salaries by offering an alternative means of payment; workers protested, but had little bargaining power to enforce payment in the official peso. Challenging central authorities' monopoly on issue of the means of payment, provincial governments ascribed that status to their own *bonos* for local tax payments.

The motivation behind the use of *bonos* can appear somewhat mysterious. Since all involved understood that those receiving *bonos* would rather have had pesos, and on secondary markets they traded at a discount against pesos, one might assume that it would have been simpler just to cut salaries but continue to use pesos as a means of payment. However, such outright reductions in salaries, and in particular in salary arrears, were difficult to achieve for legal reasons. The *bonos* allowed debts of a particular nominal peso value to be cleared with *bonos* of lower value. In general, monetary surrogates such as *bonos* arise when debtors and creditors bargain their way to a *de facto* debt write-off that is difficult to achieve *de jure* due to complications in reducing the nominal value of debts. The widespread use of monetary surrogates represents a loss of monetary sovereignty understood as a monopoly on the definition of the means of payment. Note that the spread of monetary surrogates does not represent a "flight from money" driven by doubt about its future value; pesos were more highly valued than the *bonos* substituting for them. It also bears emphasis that circulation of the peso, and its use to retire obligations, did not cease. *Bonos* emerged in particular circumstances, replacing the peso as means of payment in some "cells," but without challenging the broadcast order underpinning the peso's use as medium of exchange.

The origin of monetary surrogates in debts sheds light on the connection of this loss of monetary sovereignty to mobile capital, a connection that was particularly stark in the Argentine episode under discussion. Monetary surrogates are used when the nominal values at which debts were initially contracted become unsustainable in light of changed circumstances for one or both parties to the debt. In Argentina, the design of the currency board implementing the peso-dollar peg ensured that when dollars flowed out of the country, the supply of pesos would shrink in at least rough correspondence, putting downward pressure on prices and raising interest rates. The results were, of course, recessionary. The outflow of capital from emerging markets in the aftermath of the crises of 1997–1998 (see Chapter 2 in this volume) thus had devastating effects on the Argentine economy. For some debtors, this represented a change in circumstances radical enough to make a repayment of their debts in the official means of payment impractical; their creditors had to acquiesce.

In a broader frame, *bonos* and similar monetary surrogates (as well as local currencies such as the Sardex described in Chapter 15 in this volume) can be viewed as illustrations of Karl Polanyi's great insight that efforts to resist arbitrary economic destructiveness are all but inevitable (Woodruff 1999). It was just such destructiveness that dismantling productive organisations or local government capacities in response to capital outflows would have represented; the rapid recovery of the Argentine economy after the end of the currency board demonstrates how short-sighted implementing such "hard budget constraints" would have been. The cellular character of the order underlying money's means-of-payment function enables makeshift reconstructions of monetary institutions and the fragmentation of legal sovereignty, creating imperfect bulwarks against the calamitous effects of capital outflows.

References

Woodruff, David M., *Money Unmade: Barter and the Fate of Russian Capitalism* (Ithaca, NY: Cornell University Press, 1999), 110–145.

"Monetary Surrogates and Money's Dual Nature," in *Financial Crises and the Nature of Capitalist Money: Mutual Developments from the Work of Geoffrey Ingham*, Jocelyn Pixley and G. C. Harcourt, eds., 101–123. Houndmills: Palgrave Macmillan, 2013.

15 | Complementary Currencies as Weapons in Times of Financial Instability

LAURA SARTORI

At the beginning of the twentieth century, Max Weber dramatically posed money as a weapon in the economic struggle between producers and consumers. Creditors and debtors continuously confront each other with opposing interests, the (fleeting) outcomes of which are reflected and quantified in the final price of goods and services. This is a neat departure from the classical and neoclassical economic idea of money as 'naturally' arising from the *real* economy and serving the purposes of a complex system of economic exchange, which allegedly exceeds the mechanism of barter. In this perspective, prices are just a neutral veil that covers, but does not hinder, the efficient functioning of the market. In between these opposing views, Karl Marx and Georg Simmel faced the problem of money and its nature, adding relevant sociological issues, but without substantially questioning the core of economic theory of money. Marx suggested that money, and thus prices, represents not only a veil, but has double layer that covers and masks the functioning of capitalism. Money expresses the dominant economic forces in a given mode of production that, in turn, masks a specific set of conflicting social relations. With a different angle, Simmel – whose contribution about money has been generally welcomed and mainly publicized as strongly connected to the concept of modernity – draws attention to the often forgotten link of creditors and debtors to the community, which recognizes mutual obligation and allows for its liquidity.

Years later, Geoffrey Ingham (2004) conceptualizes money as a social relation of credit and debt, sociologically questioning the nature of money and its production. If the latter comes out of opposed interests, there is a need for authority – such as the state – to balance and settle conflicting power relations between creditors and debtors through the act of naming rights over money, that is the definition of money of account. With a scent of sarcasm, we can think of money as

282

a fiction. It covers conflicting interests that inform and sustain continuous economic and social struggles, while at a theoretical level, it is often dismissed as a neutral tool that facilitates economic exchange. Usually money is used as a singular noun, while in practice it is represented through 'monies', acquiring multiple guises and meanings, as Viviana Zelizer wittily underlined (1994).

Money is a fiction insofar as its narrative unfolds around key words such as stability, uniqueness, objectivity and standardization. As a result, main actors (economists, banks and monetary policies) are traditionally represented as autonomous and detached from conflicts and disorders and, with a high degree of conformity, are perfectly aligned toward a common goal of covering and masking what Dodd (2014) calls the 'social life of money'. One major point is that money is a social and political construction where social and institutional arrangements contribute to its nature and uses.

Money is a fiction whose plot suddenly explodes, asking for new characters and formats. In normal times, money is not a debated subject. Instead it gains public recognition in times of economic crises when – as John Maynard Keynes suggested – its failures and straws are made evident. Also, Simmel noted that thinking of stable money is conceivable only in an ideal society.

When money walks to the centre of the stage, it becomes clear that it has social and political connotations bearing concrete consequences, unequally distributed among the characters of the living reality. Again, Simmel and Keynes agree that there is a differentiated array of implications of money on society, depending on the economic and cultural capitals of existing social groups.

Diversity and inequality bring us back to Weber's intuition that money is a weapon to conduct, address and regulate struggles and conflicts. Can complementary currencies (CCs) act as a modern weapon in the economic struggle of the twenty-first century?

Sardex among a Variety of CCs

CCs are monetary networks using a specific medium of exchange to complement, not substitute, the national currency. CCs can involve only businesses (B-to-B, like Sardex or the Swiss cooperative bank WIR); or businesses and consumers (B-to-B, like Fidelity Frequent Flier programs, LETS,[1] Bitcoin), only consumers (C-to-C, Time Banks, LETS) or businesses and their employees (B-to-B, when employees accept part of their salary in C-to-C). Many typologies, which differ for the issuance model and the operational level (local, regional, national), have been proposed (as cited in Sartori and Dini 2016), without achieving, though, a formal universal agreement on CCs' definition.

Sardex (Sardinian Exchange Network) is an Italian complementary currency operating at the regional level through a mutual credit system. The way in which transactions are conceived and designed, the absence of an interest rate, as well as its legality in parallel with the national system are distinctive characteristics (Sartori and Dini 2016, Littera et al. 2017). As a currency, Sardex is nominally equal to 1 Euro but it is not convertible into Euros or any other currency. The Euro is the unit of account whereas Sardex is the medium of exchange. It can only be 'spent' and 'earned' through economic participation in the network, and it is electronic. In Sardex, transactions involve a positive entry in the centralized electronic ledger – in the seller's account – that balances an equal and opposite negative entry – in the buyer's account – according to the double-entry book-keeping method.[2] This reinforces the perception of money as a social relation of credit and debt (Ingham 2004; Amato and Fantacci 2012), and de-emphasizes its perception as a commodity, which can be traded as any other good as orthodox economic theory assumes.[3] By design, positive and negative balances

[1] Local Exchange and Trading System (LETS) and Time Banks are local or 'community' networks. LETS was invented by Michael Linton in 1980, on Vancouver Island, during an economic downturn. The main purpose was to provide a medium of exchange to support economic transactions because regions with a negative trade balance tend to be chronically short of cash, but not of the ability to trade locally. LETS is a mutual credit system, but it is focused on individuals, with some participation by local businesses, rather than the other way around. Time banks credit the time someone works for someone else on a person-hour basis. The credit can be redeemed by accepting the same person's or someone else's work, for the same amount of time.

[2] Whereas in the creation of bank 'credit money' the two entries of the double-entry systems identify the creditor and the debtor, and therefore the social relation between them of liabilities and assets, respectively, in the case of mutual credit systems both the credit and the debt are towards the circuit rather than between the transacting parties. Therefore, this system amplifies the perception that (bilateral) economic action is embedded in (multilateral) social structure.

[3] Similar systems have been used in many historical periods and cultural contexts, and even at larger economic and geographical scales as, for example Keynes's *Bancor* as the unit of account used for the European Payments Union (1950–58).

do not accrue interest, which motivates the holders of positive balances
to spend them with the positive outcome of fostering the local economy. Moreover, CCs register a velocity of circulation that is far higher
than traditional currencies (Gelleri 2009), as confirmed by Sardex: it
is exchanged approximately ten times faster than Euros. The absence
of interest on negative balances also implies that there is no penalty
during negative cash-flow fluctuations, i.e. when the buying party is in
need of credit. This is particularly relevant to the fact that, like the
Swiss WIR, the core of the membership is constituted by SMEs.

Along with technical and economic features, what characterizes
Sardex is its coherent link to the community. It uses a diverse idea
of economic exchange, to build and anchor local firms into solid
networks of trust relations, helping integrate smaller, sparse firms
into a community that is not only economic but bears social values.
In the few years since it was established, Sardex became a building
block for the local territory and its economy. The social dimension –
embedded in, and installed as its operating system – is key to understanding how it was possible. Sardex resembles a 'Zelizer circuit' since
it created a specialized network that employs a distinctive medium
for economic exchange with finite and clear boundaries separating
members from non-members and exerting control over exchanges.
Circuits also develop a specific mode of sociality based upon shared
meanings, which in this case rely on a strong Sardinian cultural identity. Even more important for a community where economic and social
benefits meet, is the potential recognition of other commercial partners
within the circuit, which becomes 'mutual awareness'. It builds on the
community's shared meanings, being fundamental for a CC growth.
Mutual awareness does not emulate or imply trust, but an understanding that it is possible to go beyond the local (town and market)
perspective thanks to a newly-defined broader community. This is
a strong incentive to scale up and to think differently about one's
personal business and the local economy. As in other circuits, Sardex
emerges at the intersections of capitalist market and pressing problems
(Zelizer 2005), such as modest firms' social capital, limited and local
inward-looking markets, clusters in traditional economic sectors, economic depression, money shortage.

See Amato and Fantacci (2012) for more details and examples, and in Fantacci
and Gobbi's Chapter 4 herein, also see Pixley's Introduction.

The reasons for establishing and for adhering to CCs vary consistently across time and space depending on selected social, economic and political outcomes. They might differ in what they want to achieve, as in stimulating the economy of a territory, supporting local shops in a neighbourhood, or building alternatives to capitalism. As an example, in cases such as LETS or Time Bank systems, motivations to join are usually related to ideals about a society where people and their social relations are prioritized in comparison to globalized markets (Pacione 1997; Tibbett 1997). In contrast, in Sardex, motivations appear to be – at least initially – merely economic (such as finding new shares of a market or additional lines of credit).

Yet, at some point after adhering to the circuit, different forms of social benefit become evident to most of the participants: it is a social motivation that keeps them renovating their membership. For example, they develop specific attitudes (a trust between trading parties who do not know each other, or a sense of shared meaning within a broader community) that were previously absent that become as important as the economic incentive. This is why in Sardex economic benefits alone are not a guarantee of success because participation needs to be supported by social values (which is the main reason why local currencies are created when the national system fails to meet local demands). As a matter of fact, a sustainable CC cannot rely on a fluctuating availability of participation based solely on ideological commitment, like in some LETS.

Overall, Sardex has proven to be successful in reconciling economic actors in a local territory, mobilizing untapped economic and social resources. Although the main motivation to participate in the network is, among a large majority, economic, members recognize social benefits as they interact within a growing community.

Sardex as a Weapon?

As monetary systems, CCs like Sardex, with their specific features by design, such as being B-to-B and bearing no interest rate, can take on the role of a new actor in the narrative of the fiction about money. Sardex represents indeed a different way of organizing money within a community and all the relations of credit and debt it entails. It resembles a 'Zelizer circuit' with defined boundaries, and the use of a specific medium of exchange by a community that shares meanings and grows out of mutual awareness, trying to counterbalance local pressing problems.

Sardex cannot be dismissed just as an alternative easier credit line to the credit crunch that (especially poor performing) SMEs experience in time of economic crises, as many economists and financial experts suggest. It is not a direct response to global banks and their detachment from small businesses needs and interests. It is more complex and nuanced than that, because economic transactions within the circuit do not bear a mere economic value, but they embed social values and relations, helping the overall performance of the CC.

Nonetheless, mutual credit systems like Sardex (and its Swiss predecessor WIR founded in 1934) substantially are the offspring of severe economic crises where the fictional money does not work, calling for a new narrative. Sardex distances itself also from traditional LETS or Time Bank systems (the more widespread and well-known form of CC) by design and motivation, since it was born out of a cultural and political project firmly rooted in the local economy that encompasses and addresses not only credit issues (Sartori and Dini 2016).

Through a peculiar blend of economic and social benefits, CCs like Sardex could really serve as a weapon to survive the economic struggle between opposed factions of interests. It opens up a complementary market where consolidated unbalanced structures of power relations (e.g. banks and SMEs) can be challenged. One path that contributes in that direction is a new thinking and acknowledgement of the social relations tightly related to the production of money where, as Ingham suggested, monetary discourses and social meanings are directly connected to the social and political struggles underneath. Sardex unmasks some critical working mechanisms of the traditional monetary system, whose consequences Sardex tries to overcome through a combination of economic and social benefits. In other words, it uplifts the veils underlined by Marx and Simmel, offering a tool for leveraging unbalanced power relations. In contrast with traditional economic policies directed to solve normal 'pressing problems' in times of crisis, there is no claim for a new or more perfect form of money that enhances the stability of the system. Rather, there is a concrete chance that this complementary currency behaves in a non-neutral fashion, but interacts with, and 'disturbs' the community's social structures where it circulates. In this sense, Sardex can modify and enrich the mainstream narrative about money, taking up the role of a new character/actor and addressing unmet needs of local societies (SMEs like in Sardex or consumers in some LETS). In this fiction, understanding the script of money, along with its ownership and control, is a topic that acquires more and more importance. As suggested by Mellor (2010), far from being a private matter, money should be used to serve social purposes and understood as a public good, subject to democratic control. Sardex offers its own vision, enriching the plot we have been sketching out in this chapter.

References

Amato, M., Fantacci, L. (2012), *The End of Finance*, Cambridge: Polity.

Dodd, N (2014), *The Social Life of Money*, Princeton University Press, Princeton.

Gelleri, C. (2009), Chiemgauer Regiomoney: Theory and Practice of a Local Currency, in *International Journal of Community Currency Research*, 13, pp. 61–75.

Ingham, G. (2004), *The Nature of Money*, Cambridge: Polity.

Littera, G., Sartori, L., Dini, P. and Antoniadis, P. (2017) From an Idea to a Scalable Working Model: Merging Economic Benefits with Social Values in Sardex, in *International Journal of Community Currency Research* 21 (Winter), pp. 6–21 ISSN 1325–9547. DOI http://dx.doi.org/10.15133/j.ijccr.2017.002

Marx, K. (1867/1954), *Capital*, Vol. 1, Lawrence and Wishart, London.

Mellor, M. (2010), *The Future of Money*, Pluto Press, London.

Pacione, M. (1997), Local Exchange Trading Systems as a Response to the Globalisation of Capitalism, in *Urban Studies*, 34, pp. 1179–1199.

Tibbett, R. (1997), Alternative Currencies: A Challenge to Globalisation?, in *New Political Economy*, 2, pp. 127–135.

Simmel, G. (1900/2011), *The Philosophy of Money*, Routledge, Oxford.

Sartori, L. and Dini, P. (2016), From complementary currency to institution: A micro-macro study of the Sardex mutual credit system in *Stato & Mercato*, 2, pp. 273–304.

Weber, M. (1922/1968), *Economy and Society*, Berkeley-Los Angeles CA: University of California Press.

Zelizer, V. (1994), *The Social Meaning of Money: Pin Money, Paychecks, Poor Relief and Other Currencies*, Princeton NJ: Princeton University Press.

(2005), Circuits in Economic Life, Working Paper, University of Milan, http://www.socpol.unimi.it/papers/2009-06-26_Viviana%20Zelizer%20.pdf.

Index

absentee 'owners'. *See* shareowner
    value
American Recovery and Reinvestment
    Act (2009) 148
arbitrage on assets 203–204
    see also banks; mobile capital
Argentinian peso-dollar peg disaster
    279–280
    see also money; states; surrogate
    currencies
ASEAN 55
Asian Development Bank (ADB) 53,
    237
Asian Financial Crisis (AFC) 22, 26, 52,
    165
    how began 52, 54, 68, 162–163, 207,
    280
    see also crises in general
Asset Backed Securities (ABS) 124
asset based reserve requirements
    (ABRR) 207–208
    see also margin loans; supervision;
    Tobin tax
ATTAC Association for Taxation of
    Financial Transactions for the
    Aid of Citizens 30, 229–231
    Platform of 231–233
    see also Tobin Tax
austerity. *See* inequality; bond markets;
    states
Australia
    stimulus (2008) 20
    temporary migrant workers 261,
    264
    see also mobile labour markets

bailouts of banks 74;or 'bail-in' EU 80;
    or Australia 85
    French banks 74
    impact on states 122

on the Rialto 193
    private 146
Banco del Giro 194
    see also central banks
Bancor. See ICU; Keynes;
    complementary currencies
Bank for International Settlements (BIS)
    14, 41
Bank of Canada (BoC) 81, 87, 209
Bank of England (BoE) 3, 15, 143
    bailouts of 146
    on bitcoin 272
    on money creation 22, 145, 202
        banknotes re war 103, 197
    no full employment remit 27
    note issue 145
    not copied (save in USA) 82, 193
    and regional inequality 83
    reliance on Fed 149
    renewed charter re war 105
bankruptcy. *See* debt
banks 9–12, 16
    balance sheets 146, 190
    creation of money of 17, 145
    deposit loans (via fractional reserve)
        206, 212–213, 270
    evade rules 147
    'foreclosuregate' 17
    history of money of 144–145, 189
    hold payment system hostage
        273
    lending purposes of 10, 38, 142,
        173
        limits on foreign in EM 165
    levy on 61–62
    licenses of, 9, 19
    mentality of executives of, 10–12
    merchants of debt 71
    no longer 'boring' 156
    so-called 'culture' of 12, 16, 200

289

banks (cont.)
  to orthodoxy 145
  subsidiary in Venetian Republic
    186–187, 195
  unstable collective practices of 133,
    145–146, 150
  use of QE 99; 207
    no productive lending from 206
  vested interests of 101, 164–165
    see also money (creation of), MBS;
      bailouts; supervision, deposited
      loans
Barclays Bank 12, 81
Barings Bank 146
Basel Committee for Banking
    Supervision (BCBS) 41–42, 44,
    146–147
  Basel III, 43
Bergsten, Fred 135
Bernanke, Ben 13, 59
Bibow, Jörg 75, 78, 205
Bitcoin 32, 268
  algorithm as anti-social libertarian
    mechanism 273–274
  consists in profit and ideology
    272–273
  disruptive and conservative idea
    270
  'heavy' and dangerous 275
  reliability of anonymous ledger 269
Bismarck, Otto von 78
bond markets
  in euro bets 74
  plebiscites or 'vigilantes' 75–76
  resistance to 56
  see also debt; money
bonos as provincial state monopoly of
    means of payment 279
  see also Argentinian peso; deflation;
    money; surrogate currencies
Blyth, Mark 31
Braudel, Fernand 184–185
  on rise of mobile capital 196
  'school' of 185
Bretton Woods 20–21, 27, 38, 138, 161
  benefit to the IRC of 137
  end of 165
  like gold standard 97–98, 103
  role in war finance 93
  see also dollar float; ICU; Keynes;
    Triffin

Brexit 82–83, 116
  nationalism of 177
British Financial Services Authority,
    FSA 40
Brown, Gordon (PM of UK) 14
Brüning "Hunger Chancellor" 75
Bundesbank 71
  raised interest rates 72
  as 'model' 75–76
Burns, Arthur 208

Camdessus, Michel 26, 237
Canadian Parliament 19
capital controls
  in China and India 158, 173–174
  and haute finance 102–103
  as a levy 59–60
  motives for, today 116, 164–165
  at national level 63, 170
  policy discretion for 62, 96
  in South Korea 26, 60–61, 174
  see also banks; Bretton Woods
capital liberalisation
  account 52–53
  with austerity 100–103
  in Central Eastern Europe (CEE),
    158
  dangers of 63, 105
  for emerging markets 162
  failures of 53–54, 59–60
  or financial deregulation (1979 on),
    202–203
  Greenspan loved 206
  negative on production of goods,
    services 203
  to peace 108–109
  resistance to, *see* CMIM; China and
    India
  and US war finance 93, 100
  see also banks; mobile capital;
    Mitterrand
capital goods (Department I) 88
capitalists
  disruptive 9, 11, 213
  mercantile 186
  inefficient 200
  insecure 102
  social relation in securitising 126–127
Central and Eastern Europe economies
    (Czech Republic, Slovakia,
    Poland, Hungary) 166–167